D0953600

THE VISUAL ARTS, PICTORIALISM,

AND THE NOVEL

MARIANNA TORGOVNICK

The Visual Arts, Pictorialism,

and the Novel

JAMES, LAWRENCE,

AND WOOLF

PRINCETON UNIVERSITY PRESS

PRINCETON, NEW JERSEY

Library of Congress Cataloging in Publication Data will be
found on the last printed page of this book

ISBN 0-691-04031-1

Publication of this book has been aided by
The Henry A. Laughlin Fund of Princeton University Press

This book has been composed in Linotron Granjon

Clothbound editions of Princeton University Press books
are printed on acid-free paper, and binding materials
are chosen for strength and durability

Printed in the United States of America
by Princeton University Press
Princeton, New Jersey

To
Stuart, Kate, and
Elizabeth

CONTENTS

PLATES

ACKNOWLEDGMENTS

A generous grant from the John Simon Guggenheim Foundation supported the writing of this book, providing a productive year of leave from Duke University; this grant was perhaps the single factor most responsible for the prompt completion of this study and is most gratefully acknowledged. Funds awarded by the Duke University Research Council made possible several research trips and supported more mundane expenses like photocopying and typing. An ample Summer Research Fellowship from Duke allowed me the free time to extensively revise and in some parts rewrite the book. The various forms of financial aid from Duke, as well as a year's leave of absence during my tenure as a Guggenheim Fellow, are also gratefully acknowledged.

Less material but equally real debts are due to my students at Williams College and Duke University, and also to colleagues at both institutions. Karl Kroeber of Columbia University gallantly read two versions of the manuscript and provided suggestions; those followed no doubt improved the book. George H. Ford of the University of Rochester provided many sources and references and general comments that testify to his expertise in most matters concerning fiction. Avrom Fleishman of The Johns Hopkins University made some very able and admirably specific suggestions which greatly aided revision. Viola Hopkins Winner of the University of Virginia also made helpful suggestions. An anonymous reader gave me some hints toward completing the manuscript.

Brief portions of the Introduction have appeared previously in *Novel*; an early version of Chapter Six appeared in *Contemporary Literature*. I thank the editors of both journals for permission to reprint. The quotations from Vanessa Bell's letters in Chapter Three are used by courtesy of the Henry W. and

Albert A. Berg Collection, The New York Public Library, Astor, Lenox, and Tilden Foundations, and of Professor Quentin Bell.

Reproduction of paintings and illustrations was made possible by the generosity of Princeton University Press, which supported publication of the book with a grant from the Henry A. Laughlin Fund. My editor at Princeton, Jerry Sherwood, and her assistant, Robert Brown, were frank and helpful in all matters, at all stages. Miriam Brokaw copyedited the manuscript quickly and efficiently.

David Page of Duke University photographed nineteenth-century illustrations for inclusion in this volume. Taos Photographic Labs provided photographs of D. H. Lawrence's art. Deborah Gilliland and Dorothy King typed the manuscript.

I acknowledge with appreciation permission to reproduce paintings granted by the following individuals or institutions: the Trustees of The Wallace Collection, London; The Nelson-Atkins Museum of Art, Kansas City; The Walker Art Gallery, Liverpool; Saki Karavas, Esq., Taos; The Tate Gallery, London; Anthony d'Offay, London; Mrs. Angelica Garnett; a private collection, courtesy of Davis and Langdale, New York; Ben Uri Gallery, London; Mr. Luke Gertler, London; and The Museum of Modern Art. Most of those named provided photographs at minimal cost. In all but two cases—it seems churlish to be more specific—fees for reproduction were generously waived.

Finally, I thank my family for providing so much to make life rich and interesting when I was not writing and thank my younger daughter for arriving, thoughtfully, after my first draft had been written. Over a period of several years, Marie Maddox, Wanda Glover, Barbara Davis, Susan Maxson, and Libby Washburn provided the kind of superb child care that made the writing of this book a pleasant and educational experience for everyone involved.

THE VISUAL ARTS, PICTORIALISM,

AND THE NOVEL

INTRODUCTION

Theorists and critics of literature recognize that the visual arts often play a profound role in the verbal arts; artists in both disciplines also frequently assert such connections. Examples are easy to find, especially in the Modern period with which I will deal. Indeed, many movements in the visual arts during this period had a close relationship with literature. In some cases, like those of Futurism and Surrealism, manifestoes were as important as paintings in the promulgation of the movement, and its manifestations appeared in both media. In others, like Cubism, leading artists associated closely with prominent writers—as Picasso did with Gertrude Stein. And the writers and painters often understood or emulated, both theoretically and practically, what their cohorts were undertaking.

Even when relations were informal or based upon a misunderstanding of the sister art, cross-references occur frequently. Emile Zola was, for example, an early supporter of the Impressionists, seeing in their choice of subjects a painterly analogy to his own choice of everyday subjects for the novel—a misreading of the Impressionists, but one consistent in Zola's art criticism. In fact, alliances like that between Zola and the Impressionists form the basis for some views of the avant-garde in the nineteenth and twentieth centuries, and also the basis for some views of Impressionism as a new and elegant expansion of realism.[1] As early as 1879, the French aesthete and novelist Huysmans articulated a broad similarity between Modernist experimentation in painting and in the novel: "I have often thought with surprise of the opening which the Impressionists as well as Flaubert, de Goncourt, and Zola have created in art. . . . Art has been turned upside-down, enfranchised from the bondage of artificial institutions."[2] Other French writers and artists also interacted: one thinks, for example, of Degas' affinities to and rivalries with the Naturalists, of Odilon Rédon's unwelcome attempts to illustrate Flaubert's *La Tentation de Saint Antoine*, of Proust's interest in art and his uses of it in his novels and of his special liking for Turner and Monet.[3]

Both in France and in England, moreover, leading artists on occasion did book illustrations: Turner, Burne-Jones, Hunt, Beardsley, Delacroix, Manet, and Bonnard, to name some of the more prominent. Major painters also drew subject matter from novels by authors like Sir Walter Scott, with quoted material from novels a commonplace in the catalogues accompanying many major exhibitions, like those of the Royal Academy. It is thus not surprising that connections between painting and the novel were frequently asserted by leading artists and writers. Reading Balzac, James thought of painting, commenting, in "The Lesson of Balzac," that "To the art of the brush the novel must return." Reading Balzac, Cézanne also thought of painting, recording that the task he initially set himself as a painter was the rendering, in paint, of a literary metaphor, Balzac's metaphor of napkins as white mountaintops in *La Peau de chagrin*.[4] Also on the side of the dialogue emanating from visual artists, Picasso in a letter to Françoise Gilot couched aspects of his art in terms of a literary metaphor: "Painting is poetry and always written in verse with plastic rhymes, never in prose."[5]

Roger Fry, leading exponent of Modern art in England and a close associate of Virginia Woolf, had (as Woolf herself described it) a long-standing though incomplete "theory of the influence of the Post-Impressionists upon literature," and attempted to establish a broadsheet "in which the two arts should work out their theories side by side." Like Fry, Woolf recognized that "many of his theories held good for both the arts. Design, rhythm, texture—there they were again—in Flaubert as in Cézanne."[6] In another essay, on the painter Walter Sickert, Woolf maintained that "though they must part in the end, painting and writing have much to tell each other: they have much in common. The novelist, after all, wants to make us see."[7] Her remark is echoed in those of other Modern novelists, including Henry James and Joseph Conrad.[8]

Some of the above quotations, like those from Woolf, give rise to uneasiness: are not "design, rhythm, and texture" inter-disciplinary metaphors, after all? And at what point must paint-ing and literature "part in the end"? Yet again, to what extent is "seeing" a metaphor for "knowing"? Do we, moreover, really "see" things in literature as we "see" objects of art? And (if not) how might novelists exploit the difference? But these insistent cross-disciplinary metaphors and inspirations cannot be merely perverse. They confirm, I believe, the soundness of the impulse to explore further relations between the arts, an enterprise fraught with perils, but still necessary and worthwhile. Worth-while because, as Wendy Steiner maintains in *The Colors of Rhetoric*, the ways that different periods (and, we may add, different genres and different writers) interpret and use the interart analogy reveals much of what is essential to the period's, genre's, or writer's overall aesthetics[9] and also their connection to conceived realities both philosophical and historical. Worth-while, because major novelists—among them, James, Lawrence, and Woolf—thought about the novel in terms of the visual arts, and did so fruitfully.

II

Two common approaches have been taken to fulfilling the prom-ise of interdisciplinary studies. The first explores connections between art and literature, and often other forms of intellectual activity as well, within a given period. Typically, and danger-ously—for the approach has proven imperialistic—the critic ex-plores a number of periods, even the entire sweep of Western culture. Once, the approach expressly relied on the general prin-ciple of *Zeitgeist*, the positing of a universal world-spirit guiding all the activities in a given age. Though the term *Zeitgeist* has rarely been used in recent criticism, analogous, secularized con-cepts frequently emerge. Thus, Mario Praz calls the shaping principle of each age the "ductus" or handwriting of the age, and proposes a basic element of style that links the arts within each synchronic unit. The last sentences of Praz' *Mnemosyne: the Parallel between Literature and the Visual Arts* exemplify some basic problems with the approach. After completing a survey of the centuries, identifying a "ductus" for each, Praz arrives at the Modern period and concludes:

> Parallels between the visual arts and literature ... seem to be almost obvious in past ages, [but] they are not so obvious in modern art. ... I feel, however, that there is a close relationship between the development of art and literature also in the modern period, one may even say chiefly in the modern period, when creation goes hand in hand with an overdeveloped critical activity debating critical problems which are common to all the arts.[10]

Slightly before this concluding section, Praz gives some examples of what he means, including this one: "The technique of stream of consciousness, though having different origins ... is related to impressionism in painting" (p. 189).

Both these statements raise, without answering, multiple questions: What forms do relationships between the arts take? Does critical debate foster analogies between the arts, as the first quotation implies, and is such fostering desirable if critical debate is "overdeveloped"? What are the "different origins" of stream of consciousness and impressionism and how do they lead to the same result? What exactly is meant by "impressionism" in fiction? For that matter, what exactly is meant by "stream of consciousness"? The quotations' sense of interart affinity rests, moreover, essentially on the way the critic "feels," with the relationship between the arts described, paradoxically, as "stronger" because the critic cannot articulate its nature. Ultimately, of course, the statements depend on the idea of *Zeitgeist* or similar conceptions—conceptions grand but often vague and that frequently require stripping a period of all the counter-tendencies and quirks that make it interesting. As Alistair Fowler notes when writing of "Periodization and Interart Analogies," a critic like Praz "will be unlucky not to make plausible observations ... but he will be lucky if his examples and comparisons are not arbitrarily selective, or if he is not faced with an overwhelming army of exceptions."[11]

Studies of relationships between art and literature that rely on *Zeitgeist* or similar principles are most often successful for periods like the seventeenth and eighteenth centuries, when the *ut pictura poesis* doctrine ("like painting, poetry") was widely current and sometimes emulated by practitioners in both the visual and verbal arts.[12] When critics have turned to periods skeptical of or indifferent to *ut pictura poesis*, comparisons sometimes degenerate into vagueness or a level of selectivity in the representation of "period" that makes an informed reader uncomfortable. Studies of relationships between Modern art and literature—like Wylie Sypher's *Rococo to Cubism in Art and Literature*—have been peculiarly vulnerable to embarrassing cultural generalizations, like this one: "cubism is an art that expresses the condition of modern man, who has been forced to live in a world where there are, as Whitehead puts it, no longer any simple locations, where all relations are plural."[13] The myth of "simple" earlier ages had, one would have thought, previously been laid to rest.

Working a vein similar to Sypher's, but with more subtlety and sense of theoretical complexity, Wendy Steiner proposes, in *The Colors of Rhetoric*, the term "cubist" as apt to describe the major line of development in art, literature, and epistemology in the twentieth century, as well as the overall development of the interartistic comparison itself. Although she does not explicitly make the claim, hers is implicitly a cubist methodology, insofar as the book consists of three more or less separate analyses, each examining the interartistic comparison from a different perspective: twentieth-century criticism, especially semiotics and post-structuralism, and the interart comparison; the implications and rise of nonsense in the two arts; the history and usefulness of the term "cubist" as a designation of literary period.

Because Steiner focuses on a restricted chronological unit and chooses exemplary works and figures with documentable connections to the visual arts, she escapes the excesses of Sypher. And she provides a useful theoretical framework based on a distinction between interartistic comparisons before the twentieth century—which asserted the common mimetic properties of art and literature—and the interartistic comparison in the twentieth century, which she sees as asserting the common semiotic properties of art and literature, with productions in both media as "signs of reality and things in their own right" (p. xii). Both views creatively distort the dialogue, balance, or dialectic between the materiality and the semiotic quality of art that Steiner believes necessary for effective art.

As Steiner herself realizes, the term "cubist" to designate the essential aesthetic of the twentieth century responds better to some works of art than to others. Certainly, it is less inclusive than the more current terms Modernist and Post-Modernist—both a merit and a fault. Steiner argues that period concepts ought to be in a constant state of reformulation, entering into a cubistic dialogue with the works they subsume but which simultaneously modify them. Based on René Wellek's earlier argument, Steiner's position has a point and is in many ways appealing.[14] Her conception of periodization accepts the period label as a heuristic device, enabling and not proscribing future discourse, or as a kaleidoscopic play. But whether period conceptions, once accepted by the academy, retain their heuristic, kaleidoscopic properties seems doubtful.

Thus, the very positing of the term "cubist" implies a hierarchy of characteristics in Modern art in which tendencies counter to the cubist must inevitably struggle for legitimacy. To use an example relevant to my study, the twentieth-century novel obviously has tendencies cubist and non-cubist; among the latter are the important (though certainly not invariable) emphasis upon the moral function of fiction and the idea of organic unity (perhaps subsumable under the inclusive rubric of "things in themselves," but perhaps not). My feelings about the term "cubist" are also, no doubt, guided by my own selection of exemplary Modernists. Neither James nor Lawrence nor Woolf makes Steiner's list of cubist writers, though each is surely central to the development of the novel in the period of which Steiner writes. Each, moreover, *might* be fitted into the cubist framework, though I see little to be gained by that maneuver. Still, like the term "baroque," the term cubist may prove useful in providing an occasion for the re-examination of period concepts and may point toward ways of redefining how we label twentieth-century art as a whole. And *The Colors of Rhetoric* suggests that interdisciplinary criticism is in the process of defining new and more satisfactory paths than those previously taken.

A frequent by-product of the approach through period (in Steiner and other critics) is the noting of broad analogies between literary technique and technique in the visual arts. Thus, both art and literature in the first half of the twentieth century may be shown to have experimented with multiple points of view: Cubism in the visual arts, for example, and the technique of multiple narrators in novels like William Faulkner's *The Sound and the Fury*. Again, many painters and novelists delighted in shocking the conventional bourgeois audience and in evolving the concept of elitist versus popular art. Certain works of art as well as certain works of literature affiliated themselves with programs political or personal for the restructuring of society— Futurist art and the novels of D. H. Lawrence, for example. Yet again, the shuffling of time and place and the use of startling juxtaposition informed both some art and some literature. In art, for example, one thinks of the prominence of collage or the startling compositions of paintings like *Les Demoiselles d'Avignon* or, more generally, of the Surrealists. In literature, analogous effects include the complex manipulation of time in the first two sections of *To the Lighthouse* and the more radical disorientations implicit in the work of writers like Gertrude Stein.[15] When focussed on specific authors and joined to a documentary approach, such speculations on analogous techniques often succeed quite well, and I will occasionally make such comparisons in the chapters to follow. Too often, however, such speculations remain very vague and general, as in the studies by Praz and Sypher mentioned earlier, in part because they "almost never make explicit the basis of a given comparison—why perspective is parallel to point of view, for example,"[16] but instead rely on an often unexamined critical consensus that the comparisons are valid.

The second major approach commonly taken to fulfilling the promise of interdisciplinary studies of the novel might be called documentary: the critic notes all references explicit and implicit to works of art in literature and then traces their historical sources in the visual arts. Critics working on a particular literary figure, for example, carefully trace the author's exposure to the visual arts and tastes therein, using, especially, publications, journals, and letters. They frequently identify works of art referred to in the fiction and often also make some analogies between the author's interests in the visual arts and what we find in his writing. Several very good studies following the documentary approach exist for the authors with whom I will work: Jeffrey Meyers' *Painting and the Novel* (which contains fine chapters on James and Lawrence), Viola Hopkins Winner's *Henry James and the Visual Arts*, Charles Anderson's *Person, Place, and Thing in the Novels of Henry James*, and Keith Alldritt's *The Visual Imagination of D. H. Lawrence* all deserve mention.[17] No book of this kind currently exists for Virginia Woolf, although a detailed history of the painters with whom she most closely associated— her sister, Vanessa Bell, and Duncan Grant—does exist in Richard Shone's *Bloomsbury Portraits*.[18] From such sources we can learn, for example, that the Venetian portrait Milly Theale beholds in *The Wings of the Dove* is probably Bronzino's *Lucrezia Panciatichi*, a painting James knew and one linked via the pearls worn by its subject and by Milly to "the dominant themes of the book: . . . the morbid ambiguity of aristocratic wealth."[19] Thus too, we can learn that Fra Angelico's *The Last Judgment*— mentioned in *The Rainbow* as one of Will Brangwen's favorite paintings—inspires much of Lawrence's imagery in the novel (imagery of angels, light, ascension, archways, and doorways), and shapes, in part, Ursula's development.[20] Or we can find that the factory frieze described by Loerke in *Women in Love* has a real-life model in *The Merry Go Round* by Lawrence's friend, the painter Mark Gertler, and we can learn the history and details of that relationship, helpful in sorting out Lawrence's attitudes toward Loerke in the novel.[21] This is useful stuff, and I will frequently rely on documentary sources in the chapters that follow. And yet it is very far from giving us a full sense of how the visual arts are used in the novels of James, Lawrence, and Woolf, very far from accounting for the strong affinities between the two arts felt and articulated by so many artists and critics. Very far, in part because—as this book will show—the influence of particular works of art is often less significant than the role of the theories of artistic movements or, more precisely, than how novelists conceived of and used those theories.

III

My own approach will be both more modest and more audacious than these common approaches, studying the interdisciplinary model as it develops in a single (and relatively new) genre, the novel. To minimize the scope and range of the study and thereby minimize the danger of overly general cultural assertions, however, I will focus on a single period of literary and art history— what in literary studies is called "Modernism," extending roughly from 1880 to 1940. Within the Modern period, moreover, I will study just three authors—Henry James, D. H. Lawrence, and Virginia Woolf—all authors involved quite directly with the visual arts as artists, critics, or both. I will thus heed Jean Seznec's "Art and Literature: A Plea for Humility" by grounding my work in the factual connections between writers and the visual arts.[22] Focussing-in still further, I will illustrate my discussions with just a handful of fictions by each author, rather than attempting to account for the entire canon or complete development of each. This limitation of scope will have two purposes: first, since not all the fiction by each author uses the visual arts in rich and complex ways, a complete account of all the fiction by each author is not necessary for my purposes, although a sense of the shape of the career does inform my readings; second, the finest novels by each author (written, generally, in their middle to late careers) use the visual arts in the greatest variety of ways and, I would maintain, are the most "successful" novels in part *because* of their relationship to the visual arts. For Henry James, the novels that concern me most will be *The Portrait of a Lady, The Ambassadors*, and *The Golden Bowl*; for D. H. Lawrence, *The Rainbow* and *Women in Love*; and for Woolf, *To the Lighthouse* and *The Waves*. The handful of novels and novelists with which I will work serves as a controlled sample for interdisciplinary experiments, a sample that will allow me to move carefully and selectively beyond the Modern period to discuss more general relationships between the visual arts and the novel as a genre.

The limitation in period will allow me to follow some of the more successful studies of literature and the visual arts. If we compare, for example, two recent studies—*Encounters: Essays on Literature and the Visual Arts* and *Images of Romanticism: Visual and Verbal Affinities*—it becomes clear that the second volume's focus on a single literary movement, unfolding within a limited number of years, and with a limited number of major artists, allows for a more satisfactory discussion and a more persuasive documentation of affinities between visual and verbal art than does the broader scope of *Encounters*, with essays covering the whole span of English literature.[23] The limitation of temporal scope will also have a very real practical advantage for a literary critic with some training in art (though obviously much less than in literature), working in the interdisciplinary mode.

The focus will be further sharpened since most discussion will be grounded in each author's demonstrated interests in the visual arts. For Woolf, the relevant movements are Impressionism, Post-Impressionism, and abstract art, especially as viewed and interpreted by artists associated with Bloomsbury. For D. H.

Lawrence, the relevant sources are his idiosyncratic preferences and dislikes as charted in his history of the visual arts (to be summarized later), Cézanne, and the Futurists (Cézanne was, incidentally, a key figure for Woolf's associates also). For James, no single movement except Impressionism is crucial, although various artists admired by James (like Tintoretto) are important. As a literary critic, let me frankly say what will become apparent in the pages that follow: I make no claim to usurp the role of the art historian and expect that art historians specializing in these areas could say more about the movements in and of themselves than I possibly could. My study, however, is primarily intended to illuminate literature, though I hope that some of what I say will be interesting and provocative to those with primary interests in the visual arts.

What I will attempt to provide and illustrate below is a vocabulary—a vocabulary that suggests several methodologies—for discussing ways in which Modern novels use the visual arts.[24] The vocabulary refers not only to ways in which authors can use the visual arts but also to degrees of involvement with them: from small ways and often superficial involvement, to large and diffuse ways influencing large portions of the novel and assuming great importance in the meanings and interpretation of the text. I will allot each term discrete chapters in the pages that follow and will attempt to discuss them separately; but I acknowledge freely considerable overlapping. Indeed, rather than using the visual metaphor of the pigeonhole for my terminology, I suggest the visual metaphor of a continuum. The continuum begins with *decorative* uses of the visual arts and continues through *biographical, ideological,* and *interpretive* uses (the last subdivided into *perceptual* and *hermeneutic* uses). While it is possible to imagine additional terms, the continuum accommodates all of what I have found significant and much of what other critics might find significant in the novel's uses of the visual arts and of pictorialism through the Modern period—the richest period, as this study will show, in the novel's relationship to the visual arts through 1940. Both the terms within and the boundaries of the continuum might be somewhat altered if this book used different exemplary texts, especially if it used recent novels (like those by Latin American novelists) that refer to newer visual arts, like photography, film, and television. But the possibility of different findings based on different exemplary texts or periods is always with us in literary studies; and the implications and effects of uses of the newer visual arts seem to me significantly different from those involved in uses of the traditional visual arts, and hence properly excluded from the scope of this study.

As the image of the continuum implies, a use of the visual arts that falls into a given segment usually includes aspects of all the segments that precede it. I should also note that any given use of the visual arts can stop at any point along the continuum, even the first, with the lesser degree of involvement with the visual arts implying no dishonor. If, however, an author's uses of the visual arts habitually involve only the first stage or two, we can safely say that his involvement with the visual arts is less complex, less intense, less significant for his work than for some other authors. Thus, the continuum provides a rhetoric of ways that novels can use the visual arts and pictorialism in which uses small in scale can be seen as contributing to uses large in scale. Most important, it provides a way to distinguish and compare uses typical of certain novelists or certain periods in the history of the novel with those of other novelists or other periods.

IV

The first segment of the continuum of ways that novels use elements drawn from the visual arts may be called *decorative*. Passages of description frequently stand out as influenced by the visual arts and suggest a particular movement or an actual work. Sometimes the historical work or artist is actually named. Many examples of descriptions originating in historical movements or works of art exist in the novels of James, Lawrence, and Woolf. One example has already been mentioned—the description of a painting in *The Wings of the Dove* easily recognized as a Bronzino portrait. Less circumscribed but still definite examples abound in Virginia Woolf's writing. One of Woolf's best-known dictums, for example, pays tribute to the importance of the 1910 exhibition of Impressionist and Post-Impressionist art organized by Roger Fry in London. Mixing considerable ingenuousness with an accurate sense of how influential the painter's art was to be in the evolving Modernist idiom, Woolf announced (tongue vaguely in cheek) that "in or about December, 1910, human character changed."²⁵ Congruently, in the descriptive prologues that introduce sections of *The Years*, descriptions for years *after* 1910 show Impressionist and Post-Impressionist models absent in the generally realistic descriptions that introduce earlier years. "1911" begins, for example, with the following:

> The sun was rising. Very slowly it came up over the horizon shaking out light. But the sky was so vast, so cloudless, that to fill it with light took time. Very gradually the clouds turned blue; leaves on forest trees sparkled; down below a flower shone; eyes of beasts—tigers, monkeys, birds—sparkled. Slowly the world emerged from darkness. The sea became like the skin of an innumerable scaled fish, glittering gold. Here in the south of France the furrowed vineyards caught the light; the little vines turned purple and yellow; and the sun coming through the slats of the blinds striped the yellow walls.²⁶

In a discussion of the metaphors we use to describe novels, Reuben A. Brower cautions that the value of such metaphors "depends, as James frequently implies in his remarks on the novel as drama, on keeping alert to points where the analogy does *not* fit."²⁷ Finding this a worthwhile caution, let me note two things before discussing the passage just quoted. First, although the description reads like a transcription, in words, of an Impressionist painting, it is not, in fact, the description of a painting, but more generally "pictorial" or "capable of translation into painting or some other visual art."²⁸ For reasons that I will explain shortly, I do not believe that the distinction between historical works of art or art objects "created" within the text and pictorial elements ultimately matters much, so long as the term "pictorial" is used strictly. But I note the difference here and will return to the question of pictorialism later. Second, certain elements in the description would be extremely difficult to render in paint—especially its sense of temporality and grad- ualness. But, bathed in light, the whole strongly suggests the Impressionists and their emphasis on the effects of light through windows and light on landscapes. And surely the Impressionist style would come closest of any painterly style to giving Woolf's words the visual embodiment in the reader's imagination that they seem to demand.

As the art historian Arnason puts it, the centerpiece of the Impressionist credo, the foundation of their expansion of realism was the recognition that "reality rested not so much in the simple objective nature of the natural phenomena—in mountains or trees, or human beings or pots of flowers—as in the eye of the spectator. Landscape and its sea, sky, trees, and mountains in actuality could never be static and fixed. It was a continuously changing panorama of light and shadow, of moving clouds and reflections on the water" (pp. 21-22). Indeed, the Impressionists' fondness for *series* of paintings revealing the effect of light on objects is very close in spirit to the sequence of unfolding light that Woolf records here and uses so masterfully in the prologues of *The Waves*. Also like the Impressionists (and even more like the Post-Impressionists), are certain details that violate norms of realistic art from the Renaissance to mid-nineteenth century. Those sparkling eyes of "tigers, monkeys, birds" are out of place in the South of France landscape ostensibly described, but com- mon in the exotic subjects and dreamscapes of some Post-Impres- sionists. The passage also juxtaposes sky, flower, sea, and field so that while the sea arguably dominates, conventional laws of perspective have been altered to give the subordinate elements a prominence and, perhaps, a spatial displacement common in Post-Impressionist art and easier for a reader familiar with this art to imagine than for a reader simply familiar with more traditional art. Most like the Impressionists, however, is the single metaphor in this passage: "The sea became like the skin of an innumerable scaled fish, glittering gold." When one tries to visualize the sea as "an innumerable scaled fish," realistic detail breaks down: "an innumerable scaled fish" is far less literal than the "leaves ... spotted red and yellow" or the "veil lifted above a woman's head" found in the earlier prologues from *The Years*. In the visualization of the description (and does it not demand visualization?) the work of the Impressionists helps. For there, indeed, the sea often appears as "the skin of an innumerable scaled fish, glittering gold."

When small and isolatable units of the novel—like allusion, description, or metaphor—show a definite, definable use of the visual arts, I will call this a *decorative* use. I will also use the term decorative when characters in novels are painters or sculptors but their vocation has virtually no consequence or felt influence in the novel. Some readers may be surprised at this use, but will, I hope, on reflection find it valid. In *Sons and Lovers*, for example, Paul Morel's artistic vocation seems to me a decorative rather than a more substantial use of the visual arts. Being an artist, in fact, simply suggests Paul's sensitivity, his solitude—most of all his passion for flowers. In a Victorian and early Modernist setting, having his hero be a Darwinian botanist (like Charles in John Fowles' *The French Lieutenant's Woman*) would perhaps serve most of Lawrence's purposes. If, on the other hand, Paul's preoccupations as an artist reflected elements of the novel's themes or form, or figured prominently in Paul's fate as a character, the use of the artist figure would probably not be just decorative but would fall further on in the continuum.

Both quantitatively and in terms of significance, the decorative use of the visual arts constitutes the smallest degree of involvement I will discuss. It sends us to another discipline, but not for long. It asks us to think about the visual arts, but not too hard. Although it is a use of and, in some sense, a tribute to the visual arts, it has no real implications beyond itself. We can usually say that a particular decorative element appears because of a biographical reason—James knew Bronzino's work or Woolf admired Impressionist and Post-Impressionist art. But we do not learn very much about the psyche of the author or its effects on the work from decorative uses of the visual arts, hence their difference from instances in the next segment on the continuum—*biographically motivated* uses.

Discussions of biographically motivated uses of the visual arts in the novel include, of course, work in the documentary mode described earlier, but that is not really the goal of this study. The interest here is rather in putting the facts *to work* in explaining the author's psyche or in showing how a given involvement with the visual arts shaped that psyche so as to influence aspects of the author's fictions. Given my factually grounded approach and decision to avoid suggestive but unsubstantiated analogies between the arts, all the subsequent segments in the continuum are somewhat biographical as well. What determines that some uses of the visual arts in novels be described as biographical and others as falling later in the continuum is that the primary implications of biographical uses send us back to the author's *life* and not more deeply into the author's *work*. At the beginning of the book, a chapter will summarize the most pertinent facts for James's, Lawrence's, and Woolf's involvement with the visual arts as necessary background for the remainder of the book, especially for readers unfamiliar with this aspect of their careers. A detailed essay on Virginia Woolf's relationship to her sister, especially as it influences the use of the visual arts in *To the Lighthouse*, will provide, however, my best example of a biographically motivated use of the visual arts in the novel.

Descriptive terms imply methodologies for the discussion of art and literature, and this is true in an especially clear way for the biographical. For investigating the influence of the author's life on his use of the visual arts is a method as well as a way of describing how authors use the visual arts in novels. John Russell's essay "D. H. Lawrence and Painting" may serve as an example of the methodology as it has previously been used. It recounts the facts about Lawrence's "career" as a painter and then draws conclusions that primarily explain patterns in Lawrence's psyche but also suggest how Lawrence's involvement with the visual arts helped to shape his career as a novelist.

Russell notes that Lawrence tended to see painters and painting as extensions and mirrors of his own motivations as a creative writer. Lawrence thus cast painters he favored, like Cézanne (alone, incidentally, among the Moderns to please Lawrence) as D. H. Lawrence figures, seeing in Cézanne, for example, a "lifelong struggle to reinvent the language of art" parallel to his own attempt to reinvent the language of sexuality and the language of fiction.[29] Of the 1929 London exhibition of Lawrence's paintings, an exhibition disrupted when the police seized the art as immoral, Russell notes that Lawrence used his paintings to "set up a definitive confrontation, on a new ground of his own choosing, with the authorities who had treated him as a common criminal" (p. 241). Russell's conclusions make the kind of vital connection between the visual arts, the biographical facts, and the shape of the career or work too often lacking in the documentary mode. He makes good the claim to demonstrate why "it is worthwhile to think about D. H. Lawrence in the context of painting, and to think about painting in the context of D. H. Lawrence" (p. 243).

For an author like Lawrence, the biographical frequently blends into the next segment—the ideological use of the visual arts. An ideological use of the visual arts embodies major themes of the fiction—especially its views of politics, history, society or, more generally, of "reality"—in descriptions, objects, metaphors, artist figures, or scenes based upon the historical visual arts or in the same aspects of fiction conceived and experienced pictorially. As we shall see, especially for Virginia Woolf, an ideological use of the visual arts can also involve the derivation of a theory of fiction from theories in the visual arts.

Jack Lindsay gets at an aspect of Lawrence's use of the visual arts initially biographical, but ultimately ideological, when he describes the novelist's relationship to the Futurists in an essay called "The Impact of Modernism on Lawrence." Lindsay correctly notes that the Futurists' work helped to clarify for Law-

rence, "the contemporary human condition, which helped Lawrence to bring his general repudiation of the system and his
personal experience of the dehumanizing forces into a coherent
and dynamic system, at once moral and artistic."[30] As Lindsay
puts it—quite well—the Futurists gave Lawrence the clue to
"the precise phase of alienation which he felt had now come
upon men" (p. 47). Lawrence's fascination with the Futurists
and his dislike of their art (biographical facts) influenced his
fiction in the portraits of Gudrun and Loerke in *Women in Love*
and also, more generally, in his evolving ideas of characterization, use of mechanical imagery, and his views of historical
development and the path of contemporary society. More will
be said about much of this later in the book. But Lawrence's
extension of his personal tastes into socio-historical theory and
artistic method will allow a distinction here between solely biographical and more complexly ideological uses of the visual
arts. Had Lawrence used his dislike of the Futurists' personalities
and art to create artist figures like Loerke, whose work resembles
that of the movement, merely to satisfy his personal animosity,
we would be dealing with a biographically motivated use of the
visual arts: the biographical facts would influence the fiction
significantly but would serve almost entirely to gratify the author's personal idiosyncracies. Because, however, Lawrence used
his encounters with the Futurists to evolve a larger ideology
concerning Modern society, and because he used situations, images, and artist figures based on his experience of the Futurists
to elucidate these larger, less personal issues, I would describe
Lawrence's use of the Futurists in his novels as one that *might*
be biographically motivated but *ends* as ideological.

The goal of an ideological use of the visual arts is quite often
didactic. And here something odd happens: even small units of
the novel (which seem at first decorative) often assume an ideological content that they did not have in their original source
in the visual arts. A simple example occurs in Lawrence's *Sons
and Lovers*, a work with relatively little relationship to the visual
arts, despite its hero's vocation. One of the few descriptions in

the novel influenced by the visual arts—specifically by Lawrence's knowledge of Cézanne—comes in the opening description of the miners' homes: "The Bottoms consisted of six blocks of miners' dwellings, two rows of three, like the dots on a blank-six domino, and twelve houses in a block."[31]

The mathematics in this description is, at first, confusing, but the visual impression it communicates is not, especially if one has seen the paintings of Cézanne, in which houses often appear as generalized rows of dominoes. But although it seems likely that Lawrence would not have used this image unless he had known Cézanne, the ideological contents of Cézanne's visual image and Lawrence's pictorial one emerge as quite different. Part of the difference is in coloration: Cézanne's houses are usually light orange or yellow, while Lawrence's are black with coal dust. But more important is what Lawrence's metaphor implies. Cézanne paints houses in a generalized domino pattern because his interest is in things other than particular houses and residents. Lawrence means to suggest, however, not just a quality of form, but also the pejorative sense that the houses are depressingly anonymous.

A special variation of the ideological, one almost deserving of a special place on the continuum for itself, is the iconographical use of the visual arts. If, indeed, images in novels were perceived as images in paintings often are—as primarily related to other *paintings* rather than to ideas about the world, experience, or the nature of art—iconographical uses might belong on the continuum somewhere between decorative uses and more sustained ideological ones. But, in fact, images in novels tend to be given a symbolic value by the reader or critic—expressed in abstract words—rather than coolly perceived iconographically (in the manner of many art historians) as an object with antecedents in other painted or sculpted objects, but without immediate accompanying verbal equivalents or abstract symbolic qualities.[32]

In the authors I will study, several motifs common in the visual arts recur in the fictions. In Lawrence, for example, one thinks of the juxtaposition of mechanical objects (especially trains) and animals (especially rabbits and horses). Turner loved this juxtaposition, and used it in paintings like *Rain, Steam, and Speed* (1844). Lawrence loved it too, using it repeatedly in his fictions, from the opening paragraph of the early "Odour of Chrysanthemums" to the complex, later instances in *Women in Love*. For Woolf, motifs common in paintings, like light on the sea, the landscape, and through windows (motifs used often by her artist-sister Vanessa Bell)[33] are common too in the prologues that introduce sections of *The Waves* and *The Years*. The window and the still life, once again motifs popular with artists like Vanessa Bell, also assume a special value in novels like *To the Lighthouse*, though, as I have said, the reader's and critic's tendency is to connect such visual motifs with abstract ideas rather than with a historical series of visual images found in earlier art. The window, for example, is commonly interpreted as the interface between inner and outer worlds, as the boundary across which Mrs. Ramsay negotiates with her "old enemy" life; the still life (like the bowl of fruit arranged by Rose) is commonly seen as representing the unifying potential and yet fragility of art. Such uniform and immediate verbal "translation" is more common for literary images than for the painter's images, however.

The final segment on my continuum of the ways that novels can use the visual arts is *interpretive* uses, a segment I will subdivide into two. The first division is *perceptual* or *psychological* uses and refers to the ways in which *characters* experience art objects or pictorial objects and scenes in a way that provokes their conscious or unconscious minds. Instances of this kind abound in all three novelists, and several will be examined in some detail in later chapters. How often in James, for example, "reading" a scene—especially in retrospect—as one "reads" a painting becomes crucial for the character's understanding of reality, with the following questions—all equally applicable to realistic paintings—of interpretive importance: How do the figures stand or sit in relation to each other? To the background? What significant gestures (frozen in the analyzing mind rather than dynamic as in the dramatic metaphor James so often used for his work) count for interpretation? What does this collection of visual cues mean? How does it compare to other visual cues received, and will the comparison yield their meaning? Many of James's grandest scenes depend on questions of this kind and on what I am calling perceptual or psychological uses of the visual arts and pictorial elements: Isabel evaluating her visual impression of Mme. Merle and Osmond; Strether by the river; Maggie observing Charlotte and the Prince after their visit to Gloucester, for example.

More self-consciously than James, Woolf developed during the 1920's a theory of perception and memory as originating in visual images that finds rich expression in novels like *To the Lighthouse* and *The Waves*. I have never come across a critical discussion of this aspect of Woolf's thinking, but find it inescapable and significant.[34] In *The Waves*, Bernard notes that "Visual impressions often communicate ... briefly statements we shall in time come to uncover and coax into words."[35] In Part III of *To the Lighthouse*, Lily "coaxes into meaning" moments vividly remembered as pictures and even partly rendered in paint (like Mrs. Ramsay sitting with James on the step). She also glosses visually imagined scenes held in the consciousness for many years (like the "picture" of Mrs. Ramsay being helped from a boat by Mr. Ramsay at the moment of their betrothal). Similar and even more complex processes exist in the work of D. H. Lawrence, as when Birkin meditates on the South Pacific and African statues.

The second subdivision of the interpretive segment is *hermeneutic* uses, referring to the ways in which references to the visual arts or objects and scenes experienced pictorially stimulate the interpretive processes of the *reader's* mind and cause him to arrive at an understanding of the novel's methods and meanings. In connection with both perceptual and hermeneutic uses, but especially hermeneutic uses, I will suggest two terms to describe the functions in interpretation of the repetition of visual elements: insinuation (in which covert or subversive ideas are introduced into the fiction encoded in art works or pictorial moments) and visual rhyme (in which art objects or pictorial moments accrue meaning in a way similar to that of iconographic elements in painting). Both devices render meaning dynamic and relatively unstable, insofar as the perceiver's mind constantly reinterprets visual stimuli and the visual stimuli constantly regroup to provide further interpretive data, some of which resist the translation into words commonly meant by literary meaning.

The emphasis here on the *perceiver* of the work satisfies instincts implicit in much recent interdisciplinary work, including that by art historian Rudolf Arnheim and literary critic Ernest Gilman. It also responds to the call in a special art and literature issue of *New Literary History* for more emphasis on the role of the audience in interdisciplinary studies.[36] Because this is perhaps the most complex idea that I will be developing in this book, I would like to reserve further discussion of it until later in the study, and to evaluate it in part by comparing modern and nineteenth-century fiction.

All along the continuum, but especially near its end, a variety of interesting theoretical questions allied with, though not identical to, those considered in this study will suggest themselves. The extent to which all descriptions (and not just those derived in one way or another from the visual arts) call upon the visualizing capacity, for example, might lead into a consideration of the theory of literary description, an area of inquiry of renewed interest, because it so pressingly involves the nature of mimesis and representation.[37] The sense in which all figurative language and images call to some degree upon visualization might lead into investigating the nature and effect of figurative language, and into the question of how the mind receives and interprets metaphors.[38] The persistence of the vocabulary of the visual in Western philosophy, both philosophies of perception and epistemology, might lead my investigation toward the consideration of very large and diffuse philosophical questions, a consideration that might almost constitute a mini-history of Western philosophy.[39] Understood more literally, investigation of visualizing impulses similar to those involved in pictorialism might lead to questions about the psychology, phenomenology, and even the physiology of perception, perhaps even to quasi-scientific experiments on whether readers "see" the same kinds of imaginary pictures when presented with the same literary passage. Other adjacent areas of inquiry come to mind: semiotics and media like film, for example, or the traditions of the emblem and hieroglyph, in which "sensual signifiers turn into the scattered elements of an ethics."[40]

You can perhaps "see" the difficulty. Pursuit of questions like these would add further disciplines to an already interdisciplinary study. And investigating some of them would obscure my interest in how *novels* present the nature of visual perception rather than the true nature of perception as it occurs in actual eyes or actual brains, or even as it has been conceived in philosophy, physiology, semiotics, psychology, or some other scholarly discipline. Moreover, in the case of questions like the nature of figurative language, the pursuit would properly lead outside the novel as a genre and into a consideration of poetry, drama, all writing, and even ordinary experience.

It has, therefore, seemed wise once again to heed the plea for humility in interdisciplinary studies and to resist the imperialistic urge that so often asserts itself. The questions raised by uses of the visual arts in novels and the nature and effect of pictorialism based upon movements in or works of art have seemed sufficiently numerous and complex to prohibit the addition of broad and equally complex questions that are similar or adjacent, but not identical. I have, therefore, not addressed these similar and adjacent questions at every point that they might arise, though I do, in local instances, make distinctions concerning or cite sources that address these questions, when the coincidence of ideas seems irresistible. As a result, this study may raise as many issues of a general nature about the ways in which the visual enters narrative literature as it answers about ways that novels use the visual arts and pictorialism. But that is as it should be. For the implications of the questions that cluster around the visual in literature and visual perception are sufficiently diverse and sufficiently resonant to deserve full study in other books and essays, rather than an incidental consideration in this one.

V

I would like now to turn to the second element of this study announced in its title and alluded to several times above—pictorialism in the novel. The idea of pictorial elements in the novel is vital to my argument; I cannot really do without it, nor can interdisciplinary criticism in general, if it is to move very far beyond the documentary mode. And yet this aspect of my study will doubtless be more controversial than most others because it inevitably involves a somewhat subjective sense of what constitutes a "pictorial element." Less certainty exists here than will exist in those chapters grounded in the author's biography or in art objects and artists having definable historical sources.

The problem with the term "pictorialism" (sometimes called "literary pictorialism" though I have dropped the "literary" as fully inherent) has not been so much in actual definitions as in applications. The definitions are, in fact, reasonably uniform and reasonably clear. In *Henry James and the Visual Arts*, Viola Winner's definition is similar to that quoted earlier from Jean Hagstrum's *The Sister Arts*: pictorialism in literature is "the practice of describing people, places, scenes, or parts of scenes as if they were paintings or subjects for a painting, and the use of art objects for thematic projection and overtone" (p. 70). Hagstrum's definition, the best-known and most influential, is worth repeating in full: "In order to be called 'pictorial' a description or an image must be, in its essentials, capable of translation into painting or some other visual art" (p. xx). By "in its essentials" Hagstrum means that descriptions or images need not exclude non-pictorial elements; all that his definition requires (and this seems sensible since he deals, after all, with literature) is that the "leading details" be pictorial and that no explicit, verbally didactic elements dominate. Hagstrum feels, moreover, that such pictorial descriptions or images "need not resemble a particular painting or even a school of art," though, in fact, the pictorial elements that interest me do resemble particular schools of painting and, on occasion, particular works of art.

My difference here from Hagstrum indicates one problem with the term "pictorialism" as it is often used. As E. H. Gombrich demonstrates in *Art and Illusion*, it is extremely difficult to "see" what our culture's artistic conceptions and conventions have not enabled us to see and render. Younger art scholars now challenge Gombrich's hegemony in perceptual theory in important and interesting ways: by pointing out, for example, that his views support a mimetic criterion for art which devalues certain forms of artistic expression, and that even the culturally relative view cited above assumes the existence of a prior reality that measures the worth of each new perception and rendering.[41] His general idea that perception is culturally conditioned, however, seems fully persuasive and accepted even when his larger premises are not; and that idea raises a significant problem with the term "pictorialism" as it is generally used. For if even visual artists have difficulty in perceiving and rendering what they have not been taught to see, how much harder it would be for a reader to "translate" verbal elements into "pictures" that speak an artistic idiom unknown to him. Thus, for a reader utterly innocent of the Impressionists, the passages quoted earlier from Woolf's *The Years* probably would not seem especially pictorial; they might even seem bafflingly unpictorial. A reader familiar with the Impressionists would, on the other hand, be easily "capable of translating" Woolf's words into an imaginary picture. One problem, then, with Hagstrum's definition (and one he does not address despite his excellence as a critic) is that individual readers' visual capacities will vary according to both natural abilities in visual imagination and according to prior exposure to the visual arts. I will maintain awareness of this principle, and believe that basing my studies on art movements known to the novelists will minimize the problem.

Although available definitions of "pictorialism" are fairly clear, both Winner and Hagstrum, but especially Hagstrum, range in their discussions through elements only arguably pictorial. Indeed, it sometimes seems that Hagstrum gives his definition only as a convenience, since many of the matters he discusses do not appear to have a very strong connection to pictorialism. Since the definitions in themselves are fairly clear, I hope to do better, in part by making sure that each unit of the novel deemed pictorial is *either* directly based on the historical visual arts *or* capable of being imagined as a painting or sculpture like those in movements known to the author. Several additional safeguards will assure that the term "pictorial" will be used with precision. First, I will be most comfortable with discussions grounded in a historical work or movement of art or a work of art "created" in the text (like Lily's painting in *To the Lighthouse*). I will, however, feel almost as comfortable when my discussion is grounded in a scene or object described as being vividly "seen" or "framed" (terms common in James) or as "like a work of art" (a favorite of Woolf's), or when words within a description or scene allude to the visual arts and hint that the scene or object is to be experienced pictorially. Woolf, for example, usually alludes to the visual arts in descriptions I find pictorial, as in the following instances from *The Waves*, which portray light in a starring role as it bathes and submerges objects in a room, and are based on the same Impressionist style discussed previously for *The Years*: "A deep *varnish was laid like a lacquer* over the fields"; "The evening sun, whose heat had gone out of it and whose burning spot of intensity had been diffused, made chairs and tables mellower and inlaid them with lozenges of brown and yellow. Lined with shadows their weight seemed more ponderous *as if colour, tilted, had run to one side.... Rimmed in a gold circle* the looking-glass held the scene immobile as if everlasting in its eye"; "*The precise brush stroke* was swollen and lopsided; cupboards and chairs melted their brown masses into one huge obscurity" (pp. 183, 208, 236, my emphasis). Similarly, but with less certainty and with more hesitation unless other pictorial indicators are present, an insistence on form and color, especially if the colors "skinned my eyes, for me" (like those beheld in Manet by Gilly Jimson, hero of Joyce Cary's *The Horse's Mouth*) will indicate a degree of pictorialism.[42]

Although somewhat less certain than the above indicators of pictorialism, two others will tempt use of the term "pictorial" and successfully tempt if, after imagining the reactions of the skeptical reader, the term still seems appropriate. In a review of Alan Spiegel's *Fiction and the Camera Eye: Visual Consciousness in Film and the Modern Novel*, Richard Pearce observes that "novelists, painters, photographers, and film makers share a similar set of attitudes and values, a similar way of dealing with time, space, being, and relation. Flaubert [like his Modernist heirs] not only visualizes the world of his novel, moment by moment, he establishes a point of view. As in film, we see not only a character, object, or action; we are aware that we are seeing it, and we see it from a particular perspective."[43] For the authors in this study, we may discount all the art forms mentioned by Pearce, except for the novel and painting: they either did not know very much about films or were indifferent to the artistic potential of both the cinema and photography. The comparison between novel and painting in terms of a carefully controlled and elaborately rendered visual perspective on things beheld remains, however, tantalizing. When, accordingly, a passage strongly suggests a narrator's arranging objects for the reader's visual imagination as the artist arranges them in a painting, or when a character's eye controls the perspective and presents objects or actions for the reader's visual apprehension much as the mirror does in the quotation above from *The Waves*, this book will apply the term "pictorialism," using it most comfortably, however, in the presence also of one of the other indicators of pictorialism described above.

A final notation about the term pictorialism should be made and will apply throughout the study. Since literature is a medium in words, no literary passage can be one hundred percent pictorial; we will do well to remember Hagstrum's requirement that only "leading elements" be pictorial and that a pictorial passage contain no dominant, verbal, didactic elements. Similarly, writing can be pictorial in many ways or unpictorial in many ways. For example, most of Jane Austen's writing and some of D. H. Lawrence's may be described as "unpictorial," but very different aspects of style and narrative form justify the designations. It is interesting, however, that each may have a comparable motivation in eschewing the pictorial in wishing to articulate a hierarchy between the grossly physical (that which can be seen and visually described) and the moral or spiritual.[44]

In an essay on Joseph Conrad, Edward Said nicely indicates the relationship between words and pictures that often pertains: "Writing cannot represent the visible, but it can desire and, in a manner of speaking, move towards the visible without actually achieving the unambiguous directness of an object seen before one's eyes."[45] An observation made by Foucault apropos of Velasquez' *Las Meninas* is also pertinent: "the relation of language to painting is an infinite relation. It is not that words are imperfect, or that, when confronted by the visible, they prove insufferably inadequate. Neither can be reduced to the other's terms: it is in vain that we say what we see; what we see never resides in what we say." And yet "through the medium of ... language, the painting may, little by little release its illuminations."[46] In the analyses below, I hope to make clearer the varieties of ways in which novels promote or retard pictorialism. But, once again, it should be borne in mind that pictorialism, as *words imaginable as a painting or sculpture*, is never a complete or unequivocal phenomenon.

VI

Some of the strategies in this study, especially as it approaches pictorialism in large units of the novel and interpretive uses of the visual arts, will involve challenging traditional dichotomies between the visual and the verbal, even while acknowledging that such dichotomies have a certain validity and that one art never totally replicates another. The best-known caution against mixing things visual and things verbal is that of Gottfried Lessing in *Laocoön: An Essay on the Limits of Painting and Poetry*.[47] Lessing makes a famous distinction between the visual arts as essentially spatial and the verbal arts as essentially temporal. That is, the visual arts are holistically perceived, whereas literature is perceived as a sequence of words, unfolding in time. Lessing's distinction usefully warns us that analogies between painting and literature should not be pressed too far and that analogies are never identities. But, without wishing to revive the weary notion of *ut pictura poesis*, we should not let his admonition—found, after all, in a historically conditioned polemic *against* the *ut pictura poesis* doctrine—utterly deter us from investigating the uses of the visual arts in literature and the nature and effect of pictorial elements in novels. Indeed, Lessing's prohibition never really applied to either, though it might have to the second, if the novel had been a dominant form when he wrote. Lessing's distinction has been challenged, moreover, along suggestive lines: by experimenters in cognitive psychology, by analysts of the act of interpreting paintings, by literary critics working in the reader-response mode, and by those who feel that *ut pictura poesis* conveys truths more figurative than literal.

Using scientific methods and instruments, cognitive psychologists have unsettled widely accepted ideas that reading pictures and reading printed pages radically differ. They have shown that the eye does not really perceive paintings holistically, nor really perceive words sequentially. Their physiological findings may not have definitive consequences for aesthetic and literary theory; such claims seem, at the least, premature. But they provide a new and scientific basis for critics working in interdisciplinary areas and suggest unexpected similarities between the biological acts of viewing paintings and reading texts. In charting the eye movements of subjects when regarding both paintings and printed pages, for example, Paul Kolers has concluded that "in reading and looking, people use many different inspection strategies, have many different options available, to achieve ap-

proximately the same end—an interpretation or comprehension
of the object being examined."[48] In viewing a painting, the eye
fixes at a number of points, the points varying with the observer
and his skill as a reader of paintings. Similarly, a page is read
with patterns of eye fixations that vary widely, not at all in
accord with the traditional idea (based, one may note, on an
ethnocentric view of language) that we read simply from left to
right, word by word, line after line. In two diagrams of eye
movements discerned, the first for paintings, the second for a
printed text (pp. 157-58 in Kolers), the patterns are closer than
we might have expected, given Lessing's dictum, although the
patterns for reading texts tend to be both fewer and more rigidly
governed by clockwise motion.

On the basis of such evidence, some cognitive psychologists
have suggested that we discard traditional dichotomies between
the visual and verbal and use instead a distinction more firmly
rooted in the *medium* of the art being experienced. In *Languages
of Art*, Nelson Goodman, for example, proposes that we use the
terms "pictorial" and "linguistic" instead of the terms "visual"
and "verbal."[49] Goodman's suggestion seems useful, but it introduces a certain confusion for literary critics, given the cur-
rency and clarity of the term "pictorialism" or "literary pictorialism." While accepting his basic point, therefore, this study
will use "pictorial" in reference to literature in the ways previously defined, but will use the term "linguistic" rather than
"verbal" to signify aspects of the text distinctly not pictorial,
distinctly incapable of being imagined as a painting or other
form of the visual arts.

The work of art critic Rudolf Arnheim in *Visual Thinking*
similarly challenges the neatness of Lessing's dichotomy. As
Arnheim so persuasively discusses, psychologists "have no reason
to suggest that a gestalt shows up with automatic spontaneity."[50]
This view reintroduces time as an important element in the
perception of a work of visual art. In fact, says Arnheim:

the perceiving of a work of art is not accomplished suddenly.
More typically, the observer starts from somewhere, tries to orient

himself as to the main skeleton of the work, looks for the accents, experiments with a tentative framework in order to see whether it fits the total content, and so on. When the exploration is successful, the work is seen to repose comfortably in a congenial structure, which illuminates the work's meaning to the observer. (p. 35)

Even more explicitly, Arnheim notes that, "More clearly than any other use of the eyes, the wrestling with a work of visual art reveals how active a task of shape-building is involved in what goes by the simple names of 'seeing' or 'looking' " (p. 36). Time thus figures as surely in the experience of the visual arts (a spatial medium) as in the reading of a literary text, although the time involved is usually (though, I suppose, not always) briefer. Indeed, it makes little more sense to exclude temporality from the nature of the visual arts than to maintain that we perceive literature spatially when we regard an unopened book and feel its dimensions.

Thinking logically rather than experimenting scientifically, some literary critics have also modified Lessing's distinction. Jan Mukařovský points out that the prescriptive force of Lessing's separation of the arts by the essence of their material is not always helpful because "the real development of art shows that every art sometimes strives to overstep its boundaries by assimilating itself to another art."[51] One might use, as one piece of evidence for Mukařovský's point, the narrative thrust of much painting (and art criticism, like that of Pater), the attempt to make the "moment" rendered by the painting imply prior and future events. Taking a different approach, Michel Beaujour points out that both paint-pictures and word-pictures "frame scenes and objects, thus mediating their emergence out of the big, confusing mess of pre-reflexive experience . . . [and may be] variants of cultural clichés or commonplaces that transcend, precede, or cut across any simple opposition between the visual and the verbal. *Ut pictura poesis* may well be a more profound, more essential assertion (hence its success over the centuries in one form or another) than its opposite, which insists on the specificity and incommunicability of the various media and sense data."⁵²

One of the clearest challenges to Lessing in a way that facilitates certain kinds of comparisons of art and literature is the introduction to Ernest Gilman's *The Curious Perspective: Literature and Pictorial Wit in the Seventeenth Century*. Gilman begins by acknowledging that Lessing's argument "has a core of common sense that refuses to crack."⁵³ But he goes on to show that reading a painting and reading a text *do* have similarities, especially when we recognize that both interpretive activities involve seeing wholes, seeing parts, and reseeing wholes, even though the sequence of these acts and the amount of time elapsed between them differ in reading paintings and reading literary texts. As Gilman says: "Both experiences consist in two phases that might be called 'reading' and 'seeing'—a processional and an integrative, or reflective, phase which together generate understanding" (p. 10).

To make this point absolutely clear, I will quote from Gilman at greater length:

> The witness reads a literary text from page to page over time. But his understanding is ideally not complete until he "sees" the work as a whole, as if spatialized in his mind as a simultaneous pattern of significance. . . . This pattern may be thematic, formal, psychological, or a combination of these or other elements; it may take shape before he has finished the book, or perhaps not before he has read it many times; it will certainly grow richer and more clearly defined through re-reading. (p. 10)

Gilman goes on to note how the experience of a painting is, in a sense, identical:

> The witness sees the painting as a pattern but he does not understand it fully until he "reads" it . . . moving from one detail to another over time . . . perceiving the interrelationships of light, color, form, gesture, surface, space, point of view, and so on. The order of experience in painting (seeing first, then "reading") is

superficially the reverse of the literary experience, except that the final painting which, having been seen and "read" is finally known, is no longer identical with the square of canvas we happened to notice when we first walked into the room. (p. 11)

Gilman's point seems to me subtle and valid. It is capable of supporting broader speculations about the act of interpreting paintings and that of interpreting texts, and provides a start toward what this study calls interpretive uses of the visual arts in novels.

One more explanatory note may be helpful, this time concerning the popular idea of "spatial form" in narrative. Because the term derives from Lessing's distinction between the visual and literary arts, "spatial form" may seem to be an indispensable idea for this study. Actually, however, Joseph Frank's essay "Spatial Form in Modern Literature" (the origin of the concept) explicitly borrowed the term from Lessing without intending to imply analogies between the visual arts and the novel and without reference to either the ways that novels use the visual arts or the general idea of pictorialism.[54] Frank's heirs in the elucidation of "spatial form" sometimes seem to forget the lack of connection between the term and the visual arts, as when Joseph Kestner in a recent essay diagrams the narrative forms or points of view in novels and then uses metaphors drawn from the visual arts to describe these manifestations of "spatial form," implying, almost, that the diagrams are somehow the equivalent of the texts.[55] Essentially, I accept the idea of "spatiality" in narrative, so long as we recognize the term's essential status as a metaphor and as a description of the *interpretive process* as much as a description of the inherent qualities of the text, and so long as space does not become exclusive of time.[56] Such assumptions seem implicit, for example, in Gilman's use of the term "spatialization" in the quotation above. I also see "spatial form" as a way of designating one of the most valuable legacies of Formalist and New Critical ways of thinking about literature, ways suggested in part by the work of Modernist authors, rather than as a new and independent direction in literary analysis. As will be obvious from these remarks, I will hold the term "spatial form" to Frank's initial divorcing of it from the visual arts. And I do not see this book as extending the already significant domain of the term "spatial form," though there are affinities between some of Frank's findings and some of mine.

ONE

IN THE DOCUMENTARY MODE:
JAMES, LAWRENCE, WOOLF, AND
THE VISUAL ARTS

Henry James (1843-1916) is the oldest, most conservative of the novelists with whom I will deal, and his age and temperament largely determine the nature of his involvement with the visual arts. A consciousness of the visual arts surrounds all of James's life and career, but, as we shall see, that consciousness was more circumspect, less radical, less Modern, than that of either Lawrence or Woolf. As an autobiographer and critic, James provided unusually detailed records of his exposure to the visual arts, and of his likes and dislikes. And many of the details are little short of perfect in fitting the general picture just sketched.

We must rely on others to assure that our last words sound right to posterity, but can proffer to the world for ourselves our earliest, most vivid memories. Several of James's concern the visual arts. He recorded his first memory as a *framed* image seen *through* a carriage window and, as Viola Hopkins Winner notes, this remains a characteristic mode of perception for James, reflecting, perhaps, his later passion for observation.[1] As Winner also notes, the perception of things framed becomes a characteristic mode of perception for characters within James's novels: Isabel framed in the doorway for Ned Rosier's eye, for example.[2]

Other early memories include illustrations in novels (especially those of Cruikshank) and the desire to be himself a painter (from which he was dissuaded by the painter John La Farge).[3] In the autobiographical *A Small Boy and Others*, James also recalled an early visit to the Louvre's Galerie d'Apollon which recurred for him later in life in the form of a "dream-adventure" or nightmare. In the dream, James felt overwhelmed by the greatness and power of the art he beheld, which impressed themselves upon him, oddly, in terms of sound. In his biography of James, Leon Edel connects the experience to James's rivalry with his brother William and notes that in the Louvre, "Henry James discovered for the first time the meaning of 'Style.' "[4]

One other of James's noteworthy early impressions of art was his enthusiasm for Delaroche's *Les Enfants d'Edouard* (1831; plate 1) which depicts the young Princes in the Tower awaiting their doom at the hands of Richard III's henchmen.[5] In his autobiography, James later attributed his interest in the psychological to this painting; others have noted its anticipation of James's recurrent interest in the theme of terrified or confused children, of children under the shadow of evil. When we consider the status of this painting in Victorian England, however, other aspects of James's appreciation become prominent. As Roy Strong notes in *Recreating the Past: British History and Victorian Painting*, the theme of the menaced or victimized child or woman (especially when Royal) was a Victorian obsession, and this painting by Delaroche (and a similar one by Millais) was among the most popular in Victorian England.[6] In many ways, then, James's tastes in the visual arts typified those of his adopted country and especially those of the educated high bourgeois of his day. He admired the High Renaissance and the "grand style" in architecture. He admired too Titian, Leonardo, Michelangelo, Fra Angelico, Botticelli, Raphael, and Tintoretto, especially Tintoretto for his sense of light and movement and for the sense of the inner life manifested in the outer form. His tastes inclined always to painting rather than to sculpture, a preference reflected in the above list.[7]

Especially in his early and middle career, James wrote travel pieces, pieces sometimes collected in volumes with titles that evoke the visual arts, like *Portraits of Places*. These essays show a wide range of sensitivity to foreign places and richly evoke the sounds, smells, feelings, and forms of life in the locales described. But, as the very genre and titles imply, they are especially rich in *sights* that evoke the sense of place. Indeed, James shows an implicit awareness of a principle that we will frequently find associated with perceptual uses of the visual arts: the ability of a remembered sight to compose like a painting, to be recalled as a whole, and thereby to evoke a complete memory and understanding. Thus, in "Venice," James notes that when he hears the name of that city,

> I simply see a narrow canal in the heart of the city—a patch of green water and a surface of pink wall. The gondola moves slowly; it gives a great, smooth swerve, passes under a bridge. . . . A girl is passing over the little bridge, which has an arch like a camel's back, with an old shawl on her head, which makes her look charming; you see her against the sky as you float beneath. The pink of the old wall seems to fill the whole place; it sinks even into the opaque water.[8]

Then, "Afterward, in ugly places, at unprivileged times, you can convert your impressions into prose" (p. 17). The habit of mind James describes fostered his most extensive and felicitous uses of the visual arts and pictorialism in his novels.

In all of James's tastes, however, there is little unexpected, little out of the ordinary. He seems to articulate, with characteristic grace and accuracy, precisely the likes and dislikes that one might expect of his age and class. The same remains true in his evaluation of earlier nineteenth-century and contemporary painting. In 1868, James pronounced dislike for Ingres, but great liking for Delacroix, whom he called "the one really great modern painter of France." Later, he elaborated his praise for Delacroix, using criteria entirely typical of his attitudes toward art, and based almost entirely on subject or content, especially on dramatic or psychological interest: "I think there is no question that, on the whole, the artist we value most is the artist who tells us the most about human life."[9] Again like many Victorians and Edwardians, James favored the first generation Pre-Raphaelites—among whom he had personal friends, like Sir Edward Burne-Jones—but disliked Wildean aestheticism and artists like Beardsley.[10]

Like all nineteenth-century devotees of the visual arts, James's
crucial and most complex encounter came with the most radical
and mutating of nineteenth-century art movements, Impressionism and its various heirs, grouped since the 1910 English
exhibition under the name Post-Impressionism. Now wildly
popular and entirely acceptable, the Impressionists were once
considered little more than fools and madmen, and it requires
an act of historical imagination to share the nineteenth century's
outrage at the movement.

The name "Impressionism" was given, in derision, by a hostile
critic to the work of Claude Monet, Auguste Renoir, and Alfred
Sisley, but it has also come to designate some of the work of
Edouard Manet, Paul Cézanne, Edgar Degas, and Pisarro. Unlike the neutral term "Post-Impressionism," coined by Roger
Fry, the term was designed to ridicule the hallmark of Impressionist style: rapid brushstrokes to capture impressions of people
and landscapes, and to "suggest the scintillation of light and to
recreate it to a certain extent on canvas [as well as] to retain
rapidly changing aspects."[11] The Impressionists also tended to
paint subjects from the lower classes in more ordinary activities
than found in much earlier painting, especially that ruling in
the Salon. Our historical imaginations may be aided in understanding nineteenth-century fears by quoting from a review of
the Impressionists' exhibition by Louis Leroi, now known, ironically, as the man who christened Impressionism; his remarks
refer to Monet's *Boulevard des Capucines, Paris* (1873; plate 2)
and are in the form of a dialogue between a defender and
attacker of the movement:

> "There's impression, or I don't know what it means. Only be
> so good as to tell me what those innumerable tongue lickings in
> the lower part of the picture represent?"
> "Why, those are people walking along!" I replied.

"Then do I look like that when I'm walking along the Boulevard des Capucines? Blood and thunder!"[12]

James was less crude but hardly more enthusiastic about the Impressionists. His first encounter with the movement—and it is significant that he speaks of the movement as a monolith, uncharacteristically making little attempt to distinguish among its artists—[13] produced, in 1876, a cooly dismissive review which decided that "none of its members shows signs of possessing first-rate talent."[14] In the review, James especially criticized the Impressionists for declining the burden of arrangement that he himself found the artist's chief task: the Impressionists, noted James, "are partisans of unadorned reality and absolute foes to arrangement, embellishment, selection, to the artist's allowing himself, as he has hitherto, since art began, found his best account in doing, to be preoccupied with the idea of the beautiful. The beautiful, to them, is what the supernatural is to the Positivists— a metaphysical notion, which can only get one into a muddle and is to be let severely alone. Let it alone, they say, and it will come at its own pleasure; the painter's proper field is simply the actual, and to give a vivid impression of how a thing happens to look, at a particular moment, is the essence of his mission."[15]

James's remarks are wholly consistent with his general disposition toward painting. A work without photographically mimetic qualities, without a dramatic situation, was, for him, lacking some of the essential qualities of art. James's reactions to Whistler's work are instructive in this regard. He frequently praised Whistler and liked the traditional portrait of Whistler's mother. But, significantly, he ignored Whistler's titles—in this instance, *Arrangement in Black and Gray*—which urge our attention away from the subject portrayed to formal arrangement independent of subject. Interestingly, James's position here resembles his qualified admiration for Flaubert, whose technical achievements James thought brilliant and worth borrowing, but whose desire to write a novel about nothing, just style, and whose repeated choice of protagonists that James found "stupid" dismayed him.[16]

It is frequently said that James eventually accommodated the Impressionists and came to understand their emphasis on the perceiving eye so fully that he became a "literary Impressionist."[17] Yet it might be more accurate to say that he began to appreciate *some* aspects of *some* Impressionist paintings and arrived at an emphasis on the perceivng subject analogous to, though not, I think, derived from theirs. Such a view accords far better than others with the stinging criticisms of the Impressionists that appear quite late in James's writings, as in an essay on John Singer Sargent, James's friend and (in 1913) the painter of his portrait.[18] The remarks occur in an essay of 1893:

> From the time of his first successes at the Salon he was hailed, I believe, as a recruit of high value to the camp of the Impressionists, and today he is for many people most conveniently pigeon-holed under that head. It is not necessary to protest against the classification if this addition always be made to it, that Mr. Sargent's impressions happen to be worthy of record. This is by no means inveterately the case with those of the ingenuous artists who most rejoice in the title in question. To render the impression of an object may be a very fruitful effort but . . . [the Impressionists lie] not unjustly, as it seems to me, under the suspicion of seeking the solution of their problem exclusively in simplification.[19]

Such criticisms show the master skeptical of the French experimenters, long after their experiments had ceased to be the most radical things on the visual arts' horizon.

James wrote art reviews between 1868 and 1882, with brief resumptions in 1893 and 1897. His career as an art critic thus skirts the years in which he produced his most brilliant novels. His art criticism always reflects his taste for the representational, the dramatic, the art of content and moral. James thought, moreover, that the best art critics shared his tastes and assumptions. He notes with approval that the "best" of the French critics (named as Stendhal, Planche, Vitet, and Taine) "deal with painters and paintings as literary critics deal with authors and books. They neither talk pure sentiment (or rather impure sentiment), like foolish amateurs, nor do they confine their observations to what the French call the *technique* of art. They examine pictures (or such, at least, is their theory) with equal regard to the standpoint of the painter and that of the spectator, whom the painter must always be supposed to address."[20]

James's habits of mind concerning the visual arts predate his career as a writer. When he turned from painting to literature as his vocation, he felt that the two arts had identical aims: in fiction as in the visual arts "the picture was still, after all, one's aim." A similar view informs "The Art of Fiction," in which the author's ability to form impressions as "pictures" becomes a source of knowledge, and the comparison between painting and writing novels is strongly asserted. Said James:

> the analogy between the art of the painter and the art of the novelist, is, so far as I can see, complete. Their inspiration is the same, their process (allowing for the different quality of the vehicle) is the same. They may learn from each other.[21]

Appropriately, his later criticism and prefaces abound in metaphors and terms drawn from the visual arts as well as, more obviously, from drama. And yet these terms frequently lack the crispness and aptness of the terms he borrowed from drama, and they frequently seem misleading or confusing. James often, for example, describes literary pieces or individual sentences as "pictorial," using none of the meanings usually given to the term. The sentences and passages he so designates seem unimaginable as paintings or sculptures, but do share quaintness or a high degree of psychological awareness that, for James, seems to be what the term "pictorial" describes, along with a certain "unity" of elements into a suitable whole.

It is certainly true that James derived inspiration for his fictional theories from the visual arts. As Ellen Eve Frank shows in *Literary Architecture*, James often used architectural metaphors in his theoretical remarks about fiction, with the architectural images suggesting central features of James's work, like the balance between what Frank calls "internalities" (the characters' consciousnesses, for example) and "externalities" (like the authorial shaping of form). His ideal of organic form in fiction and his concern with point of view also evolve in part from his sense of paintings as organic wholes rendered (at least in the traditional art he knew and favored most) from a single and consistent vantage point. The "in part" in the preceding sentence counts heavily with me, however. For James simultaneously evolved his theories of fiction from his conception of drama and from his (often critical) reading of earlier novels, as well as from his experience of the visual arts, with these sources rather entangled in his theoretical writing. Perhaps because James tended so pervasively to make analogies between drama, the novel, and the visual arts, connections between his theory of fiction and the visual arts frequently become so large as to end in vagueness or else are tainted by analogies to drama as well. One should note, however, that in linking drama, the novel, and painting, James once again was in accord with his time: for the dramatic reenactment of paintings, as well as illustrations from novels—often in the form of the tableau-vivant, which itself imitates a painting—was common in nineteenth-century theatre.

Accepting James's very general theoretical conceptions at face value, several other critics have adequately stressed the importance of the visual arts in his novels, sometimes (as in the Frank and Taylor studies cited earlier) with strength in the discussion of theoretical analogies, but weakness in freshly illuminating the novels' texts. I have, consequently, remained aware of the limitations of James's relationships to the visual arts in my own study, an awareness also required by my focus on Modern art (so much of which dismayed James or came to him very late in life) and the Modern novel. At times, I may appear to underrate James's brilliance as a novelist, but—since I have read and frequently written on James's novels with the greatest pleasure and admiration—that is not at all my intention, and I hope not to be misunderstood. My discussions merely attempt to correct some misconceptions about James's relationship to the visual arts in both his critical writing and (most particularly) in his novels that I believe have diluted the meaningfulness of interdisciplinary approaches to his fiction.

Reading through James's art criticism, in fact, one is forcefully struck not only by his love of the visual arts, but also by his persistently *literary* approach to them, and by his lack of sympathy for the abstract, formal qualities of painting. Such blindspots are, in a sense, surprising, given the thrust of his literary criticism, with its great emphasis on shape and form and denunciation of the typical novelistic plot as bread and circuses. For James, however, painting at its best was a form of frozen drama; it was like a tableau on the stage, frozen and made permanent on canvas or paper.

The boundaries of James's involvement with the visual arts are charted perhaps most clearly in his reaction to the 1910 exhibition of Post-Impressionists. In *Roger Fry: A Biography*, Woolf provides an account. At the exhibition, after James had looked around a bit, Fry

> would take [James] down to the basement where, among the packing cases and the brown paper, tea would be provided. Seated on a little hard chair, Henry James would express "in convoluted sentences the disturbed hesitations which Matisse and Picasso aroused in him, and Roger Fry, exquisitely, with something of the old-world courtesy which James carried about with him," would do his best to convey to the great novelist what he meant by saying that Cézanne and Flaubert were, in a manner of speaking, after the same thing. (p. 180)

As a thinker of great power, James no doubt understood what Fry meant. But although he probably sensed that his sympathies *should* lie with the new art—especially given Fry's analysis of its import—that sympathy did not come naturally. Nor do I criticize James on this basis: of advanced age and conservative temperament, James had every reason not to revise his years of feelings about the visual arts, not to embrace what to him (and to many others at the time) seemed distasteful. But his distance from abstract, Modern art marked James's involvement with the visual arts, as we shall see in the remainder of this book. He brought the novel to the edge and beyond in all kinds of technical achievements. But he would always stop short of Woolf's and Lawrence's experiments and never use the visual arts as radically as they could.

II

D. H. Lawrence's involvement with the visual arts was more complicated and more intense than was James's. It also had more dimensions. Like James, Lawrence wrote travel literature rich in the visual evocation of place: *Sea and Sardinia* and *Etruscan Places*, for example. Like James, Lawrence was knowledgeable about the visual arts and wrote critically on them. His writing, however, took the form of comments in letters and rather rambling, personal essays rather than the more disciplined form of the art review practiced by James. He was also a painter himself, and attempted to embody in his art all that he thought painting should be and to protest against all that he thought painting should *not* be. Again unlike Henry James, Lawrence knew intimately Modern art, both in England and the Continent. He was frequently no more enthusiastic than James about Modern art—was, indeed, often vituperatively *unenthusiastic*—but he knew Modern art as James did not and internalized his reactions to it for use in his novels in ways impossible for James.

Surprisingly, James and Lawrence shared many tastes in and premises about the visual arts. Both clearly preferred painting to sculpture and liked the Italians of the High Renaissance very much indeed; both especially liked Titian. Lawrence also admired Rembrandt, Velasquez, Van Dyck, and Turner—some also favored by James.[22] And he overtly liked some artists that James clearly disliked, like Peter Paul Rubens; all those fleshy females clearly pleased Lawrence but displeased the more reserved James. An artist oddly ignored by James but central for Lawrence is William Blake, called by Lawrence in his essay "An Introduction to these Paintings," "the only painter of imaginative pictures, apart from landscape, that England has produced" (p. 560). Given the similarities in their philosophies (especially their common emphasis on the need to liberate the body into equal partnership with the now oppressive intellect) and of their prophetic stances, Lawrence's admiration for Blake seems apt. Indeed, Lawrence's paintings frequently recall Blake's, both in subject matter and overall coloration.

In view of the abyss of personality that severs Lawrence and James, their philosophies for the visual arts also emerge as remarkably similar. Their view of the visual arts is, in fact, one area in which the similarity between James and Lawrence asserted by F. R. Leavis holds good—both believed in the moral basis of art, in art's need to be quite firmly grounded in recognizable human experiences.[23] Lawrence's beliefs about the visual arts echo his beliefs about the novel. In "Morality and the Novel," Lawrence maintained, for example, that "the business of art is to reveal the relation between man and his circumambient universe, at the living moment," and that "Morality is that delicate, for ever trembling and changing *balance* between me and my circumambient universe which precedes and accompanies a true relatedness." He elsewhere asserted, apropos of the visual arts, that "The essential function of Art is moral. Not aesthetic, not decorative, not pastime and reaction. The essential function of Art is moral." Consequently, very much like Henry James, he habitually spoke of "what powerful life has been put into every curve, every motion, of a great picture" and of the great artist's "intense eagerness to portray an inward vision."[24] Like James's criteria, Lawrence's emphasize the content and effect of art rather than its purely formal qualities. In fact, like James's approach to the visual arts, Lawrence's faces the charge that he took a "literary approach" to painting and cared more for subject, psychological representation, and implied moral than for qualities of color or form.[25]

As was true for Henry James, Lawrence's basic beliefs about the visual arts grew from his early experiences with them. Although Lawrence (1885-1930) was younger than James and ready to regard twentieth-century art as *the* art of his day, he shared with James a comfortable, reassuring fondness for much traditional art and for some of the popular art of the Victorians and Edwardians. As a young man, he began by copying illustrations from magazines (much as Charlotte Brontë had) and was tutored by a local potter, George Leighton Parker, especially in geometrical drawing.[26] In her account of her relationship with the novelist, Jessie Chambers reported that Lawrence spent much of his free time painting, most of it in copying other artists as faithfully as he could.[27] He preferred working from flower pieces and landscapes, landscapes in traditional modes, like those of Corot. Especially favored were English landscapes by artists now thought minor, like Frank Brangwyn, found in a book of English watercolors given him on his twenty-first birthday by the Chambers family.[28]

Lawrence's letters during this early period frequently mention his activities as a copyist and allude to art and visits to art galleries. He found "some of Watts pictures ... commonplace and a trifle vulgar," thought Sargent "a man of startling brilliance—and a cold heart," and found Millais "only so-so."[29] On the other hand, he liked George Weatherbee's *A Fisherman's Treasure*, which showed "a fisherman's wife, holding her child, and looking out over the sea."[30] He also found Leighton's *Garden of Hesperides* "magnificent," and liked Ernest Waterlow and Adrian Stokes.[31] After a visit to the Dulwich Art Gallery with Louise Burrows, he expressed pleasure in Dutch pieces, in "charming Watteaus," "splendid Guido Renis," "great Murillos," and "many quaint interesting Poussins."[32] Art apparently formed one link between Lawrence and Burrows (the model for Clara in *Sons and Lovers*). In his letters to her he proposed visits to the National Gallery and to the Tate, especially (in 1911) to the new wing exhibiting Turner's art.[33] Later in his life, some of these early preferences remained intact, like the interest in

Turner. But he revised some of his early views, finding in Watteau, for example, no longer just "charm," but also a denial of the body.[34]

Lawrence's greatest enthusiasm in his youth was for a painting most of us today would find cliché-ridden and sentimental, Maurice Greiffenhagen's *An Idyll* (1891; plate 3). In 1908, Lawrence rhapsodized about the "splendid uninterrupted passion" of the piece, which made him feel "almost as if . . . fallen in love" himself.[35] In the next few years, he copied *An Idyll* four times. He especially favored (and this much is characteristic of Lawrence) the little swoon with which the woman in the painting surrenders to her lover's embrace. Like the Beardsley Lawrence showed to Jessie Chambers and later used at a crucial point in *The White Peacock*, the Greiffenhagen seemed to Lawrence to reveal the force of passion in a new and startling way.[36]

As for James, Lawrence's early acceptance of some traditional art and his basic belief that the visual arts, like the novel, must be grounded in a recognizable reality conditioned his responses to the innovations typical of the late nineteenth and early twentieth centuries. He does not comment in his letters on Impressionist and Post-Impressionist art until 1914, and we may assume, therefore, that his strongest exposure to this art came only after he was an established novelist and especially during the period of his loose association with Bloomsbury. Perhaps because he discovered Modern art rather late and in the context of Bloomsbury, his reactions to it were considerably mixed. He liked Renoir, for example, and loved Cézanne, the first for his awareness of the body, the second for more complex reasons to which I will return. He felt ambivalent, however, about Van Gogh, whose art "reveals, or achieves, the vivid relation between himself" and his subject, but whose landscapes make "a violent assault on the emotions, and repel a little for that reason."[37] As Harry Moore and Emile Delavenay note, there is a certain irony in Lawrence's expressing such views, since the landscape in novels like *The Rainbow* makes similar assaults upon the characters' emotions.[38] We also know that Lawrence admired Van

Gogh's attempt to capture the absolute but believed that the attempt had driven the painter mad; perhaps it was this questing after the absolute that made Ottoline Morrell comment (after her falling-out with the novelist) that Lawrence reminded her of Van Gogh.[39]

Without doubt, Lawrence's flirtation with Bloomsbury formed a crucial point in his involvement with the visual arts and influenced his later views on their development in the Modern period. Lawrence reacted to the artistic creeds of Bloomsbury (to be discussed shortly) as he did to the group in general: his initial interest turned to flaming and often quite vicious disdain. He especially connected Bloomsbury's artistic preferences with their well-known, dramatically involuted, sexual ones. A brief meeting with Duncan Grant produced, for example, various explosions in Lawrence and a thinly veiled attack on the painter in Chapter xvIII of *Lady Chatterley's Lover*. Invited to Grant's studio to view his art, Lawrence could not refrain from pointing out how *wrong*, how *trivial* everything he saw in Grant's canvases seemed, and he persistently ignored Frieda's hints that he really should pretend to like something.[40] Grant apparently remained silent before Lawrence's abuse, but his silence irritated the novelist mightily. For later, in *Lady Chatterley*, there appears the artist Duncan Forbes, of whom Lawrence's narrator comments:

> Duncan [Forbes] was a rather short, broad, dark-skinned, taciturn Hamlet of a fellow with straight black hair and a weird Celtic conceit of himself. His art was all tubes and valves and spirals and strange colors, ultra modern, yet with a certain power, even a certain purity of form and tone: only Mellors thought it cruel and repellent. He did not venture to say so, for Duncan was almost insane on the point of his art; it was a personal cult, a personal religion with him.[41]

Lawrence, of course, endows Mellors with far more reticence than he himself showed. And he transfers to Duncan "Forbes" qualities perhaps his own.

Grant was not the only Bloomsbury associate to be pillaried

in Lawrence's fiction. Ottoline Morrell's aestheticism is savagely attacked through Hermione Roddice of *Women in Love*; Gudrun in the same novel is based on the writer Katherine Mansfield; Halliday (owner of South Pacific and African statues) is based on another, peripheral, member of the group, Philip Heseltine, who threatened to sue Lawrence when the book appeared; and Minette or Pussum is based on Dora Carrington, involved with the painter Mark Gertler and with Lytton Strachey.[42] Such attacks on her friends and associates may have influenced Virginia Woolf's refusal to read most of Lawrence's work after *Sons and Lovers* and yet her willingness both to assess his achievements publicly and to pronounce him a less than great novelist in her letters.[43]

The aesthetic doctrines of Roger Fry and Clive Bell—frequenters and intimates of Bloomsbury—also annoyed Lawrence powerfully—so powerfully, that one wonders whether Lawrence's reactions against them may not have prejudiced his reactions to the Post-Impressionist and Modern art they championed. Some of that work might have otherwise appealed to him strongly—some of the expressionist works of Van Gogh, for example, or some of Gauguin, and some of Matisse (like, "The Dance," not so dissimilar to some of Lawrence's own paintings). But he hated Fry's and Bell's emphasis on color and form and reacted violently against a philosophy of art that downplayed representation, psychological content, and moral. In *Vision and Design*, for example, Fry maintained that art is "open at times to influences from life, but [is] in the main self-contained," a position that required abandoning his earlier ideal of "the dramatic idea" in art, an ideal quite similar to James's and Lawrence's. Despite his original preferences, however, by the teens and twenties, Fry repeatedly announced his desire "to disentangle our reaction to pure form from our reaction to its implied associated ideas."[44] Such pronouncements could only horrify Lawrence. Clive Bell's windier formulations of similar ideas probably especially annoyed Lawrence by their seemingly deliberate downgrading of all that the novelist held valuable.

Says Bell in *Art*: "The representative contents in a work of art may or may not be harmful; always it is irrelevant. For, to appreciate a work of art we need bring with us nothing from life, no knowledge of its ideas and affairs, no familiarity with its emotions. Art transports us from the world of man's activity to a world of aesthetic exaltation."[45] Lawrence rightly sensed that Bell's views, hyperbolic in the extreme, might be possible for a machine or a vegetable, but hardly possible for the average human viewer of art.

Lawrence felt something was rotten in the state of aesthetics, and he repeatedly tried to articulate its nature both in nonfiction and in novels like *Women in Love*. But his instinctive reaction was to link the aesthetic doctrines with secondary, involuted forms of sexuality. Just as, in Lawrence's history of Western art, fear of the body destroyed the tradition of painting, so the aestheticism of the Moderns seemed to Lawrence a form of intellectual onanism. He also connected the new attitudes with all that he loathed in conventional religions and in Christianity as a form of humbug:

> I find myself equally mystified by the cant phrases like Significant Form and Pure Form. They are as mysterious to me as the Cross and the Blood of the Lamb. They are just the magic jargon of invocation, nothing else. If you want to invoke an aesthetic ecstasy, stand in front of a Matisse and whisper fervently under your breath: "Significant Form! Significant Form!—and it will come. It sounds to me like a form of masturbation, an attempt to make the body react to some cerebral formula. ("Introduction," p. 567)

Lawrence's encounters with Modernist art theory via Bloomsbury beautifully illustrate how the combative stance suited Lawrence's genius. For even as he repudiated the overall aesthetics of Fry and Bell and savaged associates of Bloomsbury in his novels, Lawrence's debt to the group was profound. Their clarification of the principles of the new art facilitated Lawrence's own crystallization of his social theories (in the way described by Jack Lindsay and summarized in the Introduction to this book). It planted seeds in Lawrence's imagination that blossomed in *Women in Love*. For the same aesthetics that elevated form above content also brought to Lawrence's attention the primitive and Futurist art so important in that novel and so catalytic in Lawrence's realization of his views on art and contemporary society.

While the encounter with Bloomsbury doubtless quickened Lawrence's dislike for Modern art, he paradoxically felt an inherent interest in many of its movements because (as he says in a letter of 1914) of their "revolt against beastly sentiment and slavish adherence to tradition and the dead mind."[46] He persistently maintained, however, that the revolt had taken the wrong directions and now espoused harmful goals. In his fascinating but highly idiosyncratic history of art, "An Introduction to these Paintings," Lawrence maintained that the failures of Western art derive from the fear of syphilis (which came to Europe with the age of exploration) and a consequent alienation from the body and from instinct, the source, for Lawrence, of all true art (pp. 551-55). These tendencies culminated, Lawrence believed, in art's "grand escape into impressionism and pure light, pure colour, pure bodilessness" (p. 563). Post-Impressionism discovered the bankruptcy of the Impressionist ethic when it discovered that "There *was* substance still in the world, a thousand times be damned to it!" But still rooted in the fear of the body, art after the Impressionists took refuge, Lawrence believed, in images of the body mechanical and repugnant:

> This is the sulky and rebellious mood of the post-impressionists. They still hate the body—hate it. But, in a rage, they admit its existence, and paint it as huge lumps, tubes, cubes, planes, volumes, spheres, cones, cylinders, all the "pure" or mathematical forms of substance. As for landscape, it comes in for some of the same rage. It has also suddenly gone lumpy. (pp. 564-65)

As the quotation indicates, Lawrence (like many others in England) grouped movements like Cubism, Futurism, and abstraction under the heading "Post-Impressionism," a term now used more narrowly.[47] To Lawrence, moreover, the emphasis on abstraction and form was just a fad, and the innovation typical of Modern art was just "novel," "a new arrangement of clichés, soon growing stale" ("Introduction," p. 576).

Lawrence's reactions to the Futurists best typify his reactions to Modern art. In a letter written in 1914, the year when he began work on "The Sisters," eventually to become *The Rainbow* and *Women in Love*, Lawrence made some revealing comments about the Futurists and compared the methods, goals, and achievements of art and literature. Lawrence's immediate subject is material he had just read by Marinetti, Buzzi, and Soffici, three Italian Futurists. He declared: "It [the Futurist movement] interests me very much," and went on to explain why: "I like it because it is the applying to emotions of the purging of the old forms and sentimentalities." But Lawrence moved from this initial expression of interest to a critique of the movement: "They want to deny every scrap of tradition and experience, which is silly. . . . But I like them. Only I don't believe in them. . . . The one thing about their art is that it *isn't* art, but ultra scientific attempts to make diagrams of certain physic or mental states."[48] The posthumously published "A Study of Thomas Hardy" repeats Lawrence's position. In that essay, he saw the Futurists as aggressively re-introducing motion (for Lawrence a masculine principle) into Italian culture, thus trying to revitalize it. At the same time, however, Lawrence believed that the Futurists failed to take into account authentic "states of mind," settling instead for fake "lines of force" to indicate conflicts within the individual and within the culture.[49]

Several days after the letter quoted above, Lawrence wrote again of the Futurists, this time to Edward Garnett. This letter has frequently been quoted for the comments it offers on Lawrence's ideas of character as distinct from the "old stable ego." His comments arose out of differences with Marinetti's ideas of characterization:

When Marinetti writes: ". . . The heat of a piece of wood or iron is in fact more passionate, for us, than the laughter or tears of a woman"—then I know what he means. He is stupid, as an artist, for contrasting the heat of the iron and the laugh of the woman. Because what is interesting in the laugh of the woman is the same as the binding of the molecules of steel or their action in heat; it is the inhuman will . . . that fascinates me. . . . That is where the futurists are stupid. Instead of looking for the new human phenomenon, they will look only for the phenomena of the science of physics to be found in human beings.[50]

By subsuming human phenomena to mechanical, scientific ones, the Futurists—and most other Modern artists, in Lawrence's view—indicated but did not protest the increasing mechanization and alienation of human life. Lawrence believed his own art recorded but did not coolly accept the drift of modern culture toward dissolution. Rather it "howl [ed] in self-lacerating despair" at the situation of contemporary culture. The phrase comes from a letter in which Lawrence described his reactions to a painting called *The Merry Go Round* (1916; plate 4) by his friend, Mark Gertler.[51] The painting, which Lawrence described as "great, and true" but also as "horrible and terrifying," is generally thought to be the model for Loerke's factory frieze of peasants and artisans in "a frenzy of chaotic motion," in *Women in Love*.[52] I shall have more to say about Lawrence and the Futurists in later chapters of this study, but stress, for now, the importance of the Futurists in Lawrence's development.

Cézanne formed for Lawrence the great exception in Modern art. Lawrence believed that, unlike Impressionist and other Post-Impressionist art, the painter's work attempted to recapture the essence of flesh and matter—the appleness of the apple, if you will. Lawrence further believed that Cézanne's followers and critics like Fry and Bell belied the effort of Cézanne's work by blanketing it in notions like "significant form." The real battle in Cézanne, said Lawrence, was the battle against the "cliché": "The way he worked over and over his forms was his nervous manner of laying the ghost of his cliché, burying it" ("Introduction," p. 577). Lawrence's analogous technique was the repetition so typical of his mature style. Cézanne, said Lawrence, "*wanted* true-to-life representation. Only he wanted it *more* true-to-life. And once you have got photography, it is a very, very difficult thing to get representation *more* true-to-life: which it has to be" ("Introduction," p. 577). Cézanne, then, struggled to break clichés of form based upon clichés of perception and experience: "he wished to displace our present mode of mental-visual consciousness, the consciousness of mental concepts, and substitute a mode of consciousness that was predominantly intuitive, the awareness of touch" ("Introduction," p. 578). Cézanne did not always or even usually succeed, but Lawrence endowed his struggle with value, as he did with regard to his own life and fiction.

As Lawrence's comments on both the Futurists and Cézanne indicate, the novelist was remarkably up-to-date in his awareness of the visual arts, although what he found in contemporary art almost always displeased him. Lawrence was more emphatic than James with regard to the new art, and it provided him with vital fuel for the synthesis of his own theories about culture and consciousness. In the writing on Cézanne, for example, we see Lawrence grappling toward a theory of integrated consciousness through the centrality of the visual image conceived and communicated tactilely, a theory that is, as we shall see, crucial in his uses of the visual arts in his novels. Like Bloomsbury, Modern art functioned as a negative influence for Lawrence both in his novels and in his own paintings, but as an important influence.

Lawrence's own work as a painter has prompted mixed evaluations. All agree that he had a gift for color, but lacked adequate training in formal composition. To judge from his letters and critical comments about painting, it is fair also to say that Lawrence deliberately avoided highly realized formal qualities in his art, believing that such qualities deadened the instinctive sources of painting. Evaluators like Harry Moore suggest that "with training he might have gone far," but, while this may be true, Lawrence's paintings, for his purposes, go quite far enough.[53]

Essentially, Lawrence's paintings recapitulate the same concerns and preoccupations evident in his fictions. A man and a woman, slim and naked, dance freely against a generalized background consisting only of diagonal lines suggesting vegetation. A goat, on two feet, joins in the dance, but suggests little of lechery, in *Dance Sketch* (1928, plate 5).[54] A blond woman, solid like most women in the art and naked to the waist, is chastely embraced by a dark, mustachioed man as a young boy looks on approvingly in *A Holy Family*. Once again, the setting is generalized, though vaguely Mexican, and surprisingly (though apropos of the title) the couple's heads are surrounded by haloes. In both these paintings and in most of the others, the influence of Modern art, except as a negative one, is largely absent. Possible exceptions here may be the somewhat flattened perspective (reminiscent of Manet), and the softened primaries so typical of Blake and of some Post-Impressionists.

In *The Kiowa Ranch, New Mexico* (1925), Lawrence revises violent Expressionist and Futurist images of horses (like Franz Marc's and Boccioni's), portraying a genial, almost Edenic relationship between horses and riders. A woman leads two men— the first in western dress, the other probably in Mexican (he wears a wide-brimmed hat like a sombrero)—on an outing. All three are integrated and at peace with their surroundings, and relatively small in scale as compared to the majestic plains and hills. A mood of order and calm prevails here as in *A Holy Family*. The painting bears comparison with some of Gauguin's works, like *Riders on the Beach* (1902), which also idealize the relationship of man, horse, and nature,[55] though I have no precise evidence that Lawrence knew the earlier painting.

In a more mischievous mood, Lawrence paints four nuns who giggle at the sight of a man, naked from the waist down, asleep near a hayloft. Again, the colors are clear, softened primaries, but the mood is playful. Curiously, *Boccaccio Story* (like *Dance Sketch*) was among those seized by the police in 1929 and threatened with burning (a fate Lawrence resented immensely and against which Bloomsbury also strongly protested), the chief criterion being the exhibition of pubic hair.[56] In a final example, *Red Willow Trees* (1927, plate 6) the forms of naked men and bending willows assume marked identities of both form and coloration, illustrating an idea infrequently but strikingly expressed in Lawrence's novels: that humanity is only one form in which nature embodies the life force, and a replaceable form at that.[57] Coincidentally, the juxtaposition of men and willows, with the implication of identity, figures prominently in Woolf's *The Waves*.

All the paintings just described share a characteristic surprising to one familiar with Lawrence's finest fiction. They are almost entirely *ahistorical*, with their generalized settings suggesting no particular time and place. *The Kiowa Ranch* is a partial exception here, but even its setting would be vague—suggesting only some kind of frontier—without the title. Moreover, in each of the paintings, the historical facts of time or setting have little relevance for characterization, meaning, or message. I find it significant that Lawrence's paintings lack the historic specificity of Lawrence's novels, and portray, moreover, scenes and concepts quite idyllic, generally more idyllic than those in the fiction. I will return to this comparison later, when discussing the extent to which pictorial elements or elements based on the visual arts embody ideals in Lawrence and Woolf.

Two paintings rather atypical of Lawrence's work refer to the contemporary scene and deserve mention. In one of these paintings, *Rape of the Sabine Women* (1928, plate 7), the reference is only implied and indirect. In it, the only figure presented individually and frontally—perhaps a disgruntled Sabine—skulks in a corner, evidently disgusted with the action before him, and looks very much like Loerke in *Women in Love* or like Lawrence himself. The painting's tones are murkier than usual for Lawrence, and the abduction proceeds without vitality or zest. Romans and Sabines are indistinguishable forms twisted and distorted in what Lawrence jokingly called "A Study of

Arses." Inevitably, the painting suggests less the subject painted earlier by Poussin than the state of sexuality in contemporary society as Lawrence conceived it. The ambiguous groping of male for male or female in an anonymous heap suggests that the "Rape" is really about sexuality in the modern dystopia, in contrast to many of the other paintings, which deal with sexuality in an ahistorical utopia.

The other painting, *Flight Back into Paradise* (1927, plate 8), "represents an anomaly in Lawrence's oeuvre, for it is the only painting in which one is forced to confront the pressures of modernism."[58] In it, a figure identified in a letter as Eve attempts to dodge out of a gray-blue-red cityscape that recalls the cities of the Futurists. She is hindered both by the forms of the city, which unravel into a tapelike substance that ensnares her legs, and by two menacing males (identified in a letter as Adam and the Angel at the gate). The two human bodies are distorted in ways that recall Modern art. The painting features, in addition, a device popular among the Futurists—the use of strongly painted lines to suggest directions of force and movement. The easy, comfortable sexuality often found in Lawrence's paintings is, as in the "Rape," gone in this one: "Adam" glares at "Eve," and the cityscape features menacing red smokestacks, acknowledged by Lawrence as modernity's "tribute" to the phallus it everywhere else tried to deny.[59]

Largely on the basis of his experiences as a painter, Lawrence believed in the power of the visual arts more profoundly than did Henry James. He frequently made, in fact, statements attributing special powers to the visual arts that any respectable novelist would wish somehow to share. In "An Introduction to these Paintings," Lawrence maintained that

> real works of art are made by the whole consciousness of man working together in unison and oneness; instinct, intuition, mind, intellect all fused into one complete consciousness, and grasping what we may call a complete truth, or a complete vision, a complete revelation. ... A discovery, artistic or otherwise, may be

more or less intuitional, more or less mental; but intuition will have entered into it, and mind will have entered too. The whole consciousness is concerned in every case.—And a painting requires the activity of the whole imagination, for it is made of imagery, and the imagination is that form of complete consciousness in which predominates the intuitive awareness of forms, images, the *physical* awareness. (p. 574)

Painting especially had the potential to embody Lawrence's ideals because of its use of imagery and the *source* of that imagery, identified in "Making Pictures" by Lawrence as something like the Jungian collective mind: "The picture must all come out of the artist's inside, awareness of forms and figures. We can call it memory, but it is more than memory. It is the image as it lives in the consciousness, alive like a vision, but unknown."[60]

In the same essay, he expands on the value of the visual arts, associating art with knowledge:

The only thing one can look into, stare into, and see only vision, is the vision itself: the visionary image. . . . I believe one can only develop one's visionary awareness by close contact with the vision itself: that is, by knowing pictures, real vision pictures, and by dwelling on them, and really, dwelling in them.[61]

The visual arts and especially painting, then, hold a key to the perceptual and interpretive processes for Lawrence because they decisively require of the viewer a condition of all vital discovery: the integration of various mental faculties. Lawrence's realization of this principle leads, I believe, to some of his most venturesome uses of the visual arts and pictorial elements in his novels, which I will discuss later under the headings of ideological, perceptual, and hermeneutic uses of the visual arts.

III

Perhaps the easiest way to get a sense of the role that the visual arts played in Virginia Woolf's life (1882-1941) is to browse through John Lehmann's amply illustrated *Virginia Woolf and her World*.[62] In the many photographs and illustrations, there is art everywhere—Virginia as subject for Vanessa and the others; Leonard as same; portraits of various friends by Roger Fry and Walter Sickert; paintings in the nonrepresentational mode as the backgrounds for photos; many letters exchanged about designs for book jackets, furniture, or art ordered from the Omega workshops managed by Roger Fry; exchanges about exhibitions or paintings by Vanessa; paintings given by Vanessa to the Woolfs and gladly acknowledged. Art formed, then, part of the very texture and fabric of Woolf's life. It was second nature for her, so much so that her overt comments about it are fewer and less systematic than either James's or Lawrence's. Art was, moreover, the special province of her beloved sister Vanessa, a province adjacent to but not identical with hers. Her remarks are frequently, then, less passionate than James's and far less passionate than Lawrence's, in part because she tended to share the tastes of her group rather than to carve out tastes and preferences of her own.

In her years as Virginia Stephen, at least those spent in her father's house, Virginia's exposure to the avant-garde in art was limited. The Stephens, a conspicuously literary family with roots in the Victorian era, did have artists visit frequently, but artists who were also eminent Victorians, like the painter Watts. Apparently from the beginning, Virginia and Vanessa divided the arts between them; Virginia was to be a writer, Vanessa, a painter—a division that avoided (as Vanessa saw it) at least one source of jealousy between them.[63] Vanessa was loved so passionately by Virginia and their friendship was so constant and consistent a feature of both their lives, however, that Vanessa's tastes inevitably became Virginia's. And even as a young apprentice, Vanessa's sympathies sheered away from painters like Watts to lodge with the French Impressionists and their American followers, Whistler and Sargent.[64]

The relative absence of a full grounding in the traditional forms of art constitutes, then, a significant difference between

Woolf's involvement with the visual arts and those of James and Lawrence. She of course knew the Old Masters and was even shown some of them on trips abroad with cognoscenti like Roger Fry, but her deepest, most basic sense of art was of the art championed by Bloomsbury and practiced by her sister— twentieth-century art, rooted in the Impressionists and Post-Impressionists and advancing eagerly into Cubism, abstraction, and other innovations. Like James and Lawrence, she was always alert to points at which the visual arts could clarify her ideas about the nature of fiction. But because the art she knew best and admired most differed from theirs, the uses to which she put the visual arts also sometimes differed substantially.

The key Bloomsbury figures in the visual arts were Roger Fry, Vanessa Bell, Clive Bell, Duncan Grant, and Walter Sickert, of whom the first two were the most influential for Woolf. Fry doubtless was the thinker who most shaped her views, and the crucial events the same as were crucial to them all: the 1910 exhibition, "Manet and the Impressionists," and the 1912 show of Post-Impressionists and young heirs in England and on the continent. To judge from her diaries and letters, one guesses that the full impact of these events did not dawn for Virginia until years later, when she had transferred some of the lessons taught by the visual arts into the medium that concerned her far more passionately, literature. The letters and diaries mention the exhibitions only briefly and with occasional flipness, as here, in 1916: "I predict the complete rout of post-impressionism, chiefly because Roger, who has been staying with us, is now turning to literature, and says pictures only do 'to look at about 4 times.' "65 But the words she heard spoken and saw written about the new art movements powerfully affected her and lay dormant in her consciousness.

The words were chiefly those of Roger Fry, words she remembered well enough to record, twenty years later, in her biography of the art historian. Fry's chief legacy was, I believe, a view of the new movements that emphasized their *continuity* with the older efforts from the Renaissance to the nineteenth century, conveniently grouped under the heading of realism. Fry saw Impressionism, Post-Impressionism, and all that followed as a reaction to a realism that had gone as far as it could, and he conceived of the movements he was now introducing to England as expansions of traditional conceptions of how to render reality through "the reestablishment of purely aesthetic criteria in place of the criterion of conformity to appearance [and] the rediscovery of the principles of structural design and harmony."[66] In *Roger Fry: A Biography*, Woolf reconstructed Fry's dialogues around the time of the exhibition in this way:

> Were you puzzled? But why? And he would explain that it was quite easy to make the transition from Watts to Picasso; there was no break, only a continuation. They were only pushing things a little further. He demonstrated; he persuaded; he argued. The argument rose and soared. It vanished into the clouds. Then it swooped back to the picture. (p. 152)

From Woolf's account, it becomes apparent that Modernism as she conceived it was not nihilistic toward the past, though not nostalgic for it either. As Woolf recalled the exhibitions in her 1937 biography of Fry, it also becomes apparent that the exhibition fostered her sense of being on the *progressive*, avant-garde side of the controversy and hence reinforced her feeling of being on the frontiers of new developments in culture. In that biography, she noted with wicked zest the damning judgments of conservative art critics who "assumed, somewhat rashly," that "the verdict of Time ... would be in their favor" (p. 155).

When we turn to Woolf's criticism of the novel with her background in the visual arts in mind, the role the Impressionist, Post-Impressionist, and Modern art vocabulary played in helping her to formulate ideas about fiction becomes apparent. One of her first pieces, *Kew Gardens*, prompted Arnold Bennett to question "the possibility that some writers might do in words what the Neo-Impressionists have done in paint."[67] Woolf replied in a way that suggests that she did, indeed, conceive of her work in this way. We may also see the influence of Impressionist theory in her famous essay "Modern Fiction." In the essay, Woolf defined reality as the Impressionists did and set the same goals for fiction that they had set for painting. She protested that fidelity to details of furniture, dress, and setting and to the demands of a "story" obscure the very realities novels should try to express:

> So much of the enormous labour of proving the solidity, the likeness to life, of the story is not merely labour thrown away but labour misplaced to the extent of obscuring and blotting out the light of the conception. ... If a writer were a free man and not a slave, if he could write upon his own feeling and not upon convention, there would be no plot, no comedy, no tragedy, no love interest or catastrophe in the accepted style, and perhaps not a single button sewn on as the Bond Street tailors would have it.

The verbal contrast between "solidity" and "reality" and the image of light may well derive from the Impressionists. Woolf then made a now famous proclamation:

> Life is not a series of gig-lamps symmetrically arranged; life is a luminous halo, a semi-transparent envelope surrounding us from the beginning of consciousness to the end. Is it not the task of the novelist to convey this varying, this unknown and uncircum-scribed spirit, whatever aberration or complexity it may display, with as little mixture of the alien and external as possible? We are not pleading merely for courage and sincerity: we are sug-gesting that the proper stuff of fiction is a little other than custom would have us believe it.[68]

Once again, the imagery of the passage—especially of life as a "luminous envelope, a semi-transparent envelope"—may have been suggested to Woolf by the Impressionists. And surely her overall creed resembles theirs at many points. In the review of Arnold Bennett's *Books and Persons* cited earlier, moreover, Woolf had also connected Impressionism to the revision of "ines-sential and infantile realisms," much as her vocabulary does here.

In "The Art of Fiction" and "Roger Fry" Woolf entered the debate about the separation of art and life initiated by Fry and Clive Bell in the visual arts and continued, with gusto, by D. H. Lawrence. She saw Fry as never quite having divorced life and art as strongly as the rhetoric of *Vision and Design* implies that he wished to do; implicitly, Woolf believed that art derives strength from life experience:

> I want to say that his [Fry's] understanding of art owed much to his understanding of life, and yet I know that he disliked the mixing and mingling of things. He wanted art to be art; literature to be literature; and life to be life. . . . He detested the storytelling spirit which has clouded our painting and confused our criticism.[69]

She also, however, in "The Art of Fiction," could speak for the elevation of art over life, seeing E. M. Forster as too tied to the criterion of "life" in his famous study of fiction, *Aspects of the Novel*. She chided Forster, noting that

> a wise and brilliant book like Mr. Forster's can be written about fiction without saying more than a sentence or two about the medium in which a novelist works. Almost nothing is said about words.[70]

Woolf believed that Forster erroneously feared that, with an emphasis on language, "the story might wobble, the plot might crumble, ruin might seize upon the characters. The novel might, in short, become a work of art" (p. 112). Clearly, Woolf's novels never entirely abandon "life," though they go very far indeed in minimizing "plot" and "character" and emphasizing "words." Her comments here almost look like a program for the "Time Passes" section of *To the Lighthouse* or for *The Waves* and like a polemic for such fiction only as "art." Once again, I believe we may see controversies originally centered on the visual arts adopted by Woolf and applied to her evolving aesthetics and theory of fiction. The influence is more profound than anything found in Henry James's involvement with the visual arts and vaguer but equally important as what we have seen in D. H. Lawrence's involvement with them.

In the Introduction to this book, I quoted several passages from Woolf's *Roger Fry: A Biography* and "Walter Sickert" exploring analogies between the visual and verbal arts. Such analogies were a habit of mind for her. Throughout the 1920's, as she worked on *To the Lighthouse* and *The Waves*, she referred in her diary to her books as "canvases." She frequently speculated, moreover, on the translation of one art into another, as we saw her doing in her review of 1917. When she saw an exhibition of her sister's, for example, she wrote:

> I went to your show and spent an hour making some extremely interesting theories. . . . I had forgotten the extreme brilliancy and flow and wit and ardour of these works. . . . I think you are a most remarkable painter. But I maintain you are into the bargain, a satirist, a conveyer of impressions about human life: a short story writer of great wit and able to bring off a situation in a way that rouses my envy. I wonder if I could write the Three Women in prose.[71]

Note in this quotation how Woolf saw the anecdotal and narrative as an *addition* to the achievement of a "remarkable painter" and not (as James or Lawrence would) as the *essence* of that achievement.

Vanessa shared her sister's sense that, while their media differed, something in their goals was similar:

> Will it seem to you absurd and conceited or will you understand at all what I mean if I tell you that I've been working hard lately at an absurd great picture [*The Nursery*, 1930-1932] I've been painting off and on the last 2 years—and if I could only do what I want to—but I can't—it seems to me it would have some sort of analogous meaning to what you've done. How can one explain, but to me painting a floor covered with toys and keeping them all in relation to each other and the figures and the space of the

floor and the light on it means something of the same sort that you seem to me to mean.[72]

Virginia replied to her letter, "I'm frightfully interested about your picture."[73] As one final example, I offer a letter to Duncan Grant in 1938, in which she said: "Like all painters, your sense of words is plastic, not linear, and I am on the side of the plastic myself."[74]

Yet, despite her interest in analogies between the media, Woolf sensed that the painter's work—so much more easily free of anecdote and narrative than hers—differed profoundly from the writer's. She felt able to approach *some* paintings, like Walter Sickert's, literarily. In fact, her essay on his work stresses the stories implied by his paintings. But other kinds of paintings— particularly in the nonrepresentational, abstract style experimented with by Bell and Grant—seemed to her substantially different from the world of the writer. Not *unassimilatable*, but different. Thus, she despaired on one occasion of lecturing on art, that "sublime silent fish world."[75] Again, she noted that her nephew had better be a writer, not a painter, given his propensity for the human and satiric. She also seemed to feel that the painter, especially of abstract or extremely varied art, gives himself away less than the writer, produces, in a sense, a less personal kind of art. Her comments occur in an introduction to a catalogue of Vanessa's work:

One asks, Does she show any special knowledge of clothes? One replies, Stark nakedness seems to please her as well. Is she dainty then, or austere? Does she like riding? Is she red haired or brown eyed? Was she ever at university? Does she prefer herrings or brussels sprouts? Is she—for our patience is becoming exhausted—not a woman at all, but a mixture of Goddess and peasant, treading the clouds with her feet and with her hands shelling peas? Any writer so ardently questioned would have yielded something to our curiosity. One defies a novelist to keep his life through twenty-seven volumes of fiction safe from scrutiny. But Mrs. Bell says nothing. Mrs. Bell is as silent as the grave. . . .

her pictures claim us and make us stop. They give us an emotion.
They offer a puzzle.[76]

The quotation may reveal more about Woolf's views of her
sister than of visual artists in general. But I think that we may
generalize some of what she says for all visual artists.

Woolf recognized, I believe, that abstract art had little to do
with the traditional forms and concerns of novels, but she recognized as well that her own concerns and forms were not very
traditional. In fact, as I shall discuss later, the abstract idiom—
so common in the painters she knew best, but so alien, apparently, to the world of the novel—suggested to her a method by
which she could render extreme, mystical, other-worldly states
of consciousness not traditionally explored in fiction. Such uses
of the visual arts differ from most of what we find in James
and Lawrence and—as we shall see—touch the most profound
bases of Woolf's fiction.

Virginia Woolf also assimilated the visual arts into her evolving theories of perception and memory. It becomes increasingly
clear through the 1920's, both in and out of the novels, that
Woolf more and more conceived of perception and memory as
having a strong visual component, frequently serving as the
trigger for a more defined, verbal comprehension. Thus, in her
diaries, Woolf notes: "Lytton once said,—I connect it with a
visit to Kew Gardens—that we can only live if we see through
illusion. & that reminds me (it is odd by the way how small a
thought is which one cannot express pictorially, as one has been
accustomed to thinking it: this saying of Lytton's has always
come pictorially, with heat, flowers, grass, summer & myself
walking at Kew)."[77] Again, she records: "I shall spend my day
at the British Museum. (This is one of those visual images,
without meaning when written down, that conveys a whole state
of mind to me)."[78] In the essay "Three Pictures," she expresses
an impasse in the interpretive process in this way: "It had been
merely a voice. There was nothing to connect it with. No picture
of any sort came to interpret it, to make it intelligible to the

mind."[79] Despite their antithetical attitudes toward the visual arts as they were developing in the first decades of the twentieth century, then, Woolf and Lawrence here reach a point of commonality: both inclined quite naturally toward what I call perceptual and hermeneutic uses of the visual arts, because both had made visually perceived images important parts of their theories of consciousness.

IV

It will be apparent from this survey of the three authors' involvement with the visual arts that they represent different kinds and degrees of involvement, especially with developments from the Impressionists forward. I will not, then, argue in the pages that follow for a uniform or monolithic use of the visual arts in the emerging Modern novel. Indeed, such conformity would be surprising given the diverse backgrounds, interests, and assumptions of James, Lawrence and Woolf.

The chapters to follow will, however, illustrate the various segments on my continuum of the ways in which novels can use the visual arts and pictorial elements and cumulatively indicate points of similarity in the three novelists' uses of the visual arts or pictorialism. The chapters will frequently build upon or refer back to the information both documentary and comparative found in this chapter. We will begin with a study of decorative uses of the visual arts in *Roderick Hudson* and *The Tragic Muse* and a brief glance backward at some earlier instances of decorative uses, some with the potential (though a failed potential) to move up the continuum that governs this study.

PAINTBRUSHES, CHISELS, AND RED HERRINGS: DECORATIVE USES OF THE VISUAL ARTS AND PICTORIALISM IN SELECTED NOVELS BY JAMES AND EARLIER NOVELISTS

Some of the surest approaches to the visual arts and pictorialism in the novel ought to be studying the presence of characters who are artists, or language rich in the metaphors of art, or clear references to historical works of art, or the actual inclusion of illustrations in novels. In many cases, however, these approaches prove to be red herrings in the interdisciplinary study of art and the novel, despite our preconceptions and the efforts of able scholars. Indeed, many of the artists and art metaphors in the two novels by James to be discussed in this chapter—*Roderick Hudson* and *The Tragic Muse*—ultimately have rather little to do with either James's views on the visual arts or with the presence of pictorialism in the novel. They may illuminate James's conceptions of artists or cognoscenti of the arts as general types, but they say little about the particular nature of the visual arts and their potential function in fiction. Similarly, direct references to the visual arts in most earlier fiction have led to dead-ends for the investigating critic. Some seem susceptible only to excursions in the documentary mode; others have interesting potential but remain, as they function in the text, only latent in that potential. And the study of illustrations, as it has commonly been done, has provided a wealth of documentary information but left the misleading impression that to study illustrations is identical to studying the interdisciplinary role of the visual arts

in fiction.¹ Before we turn to more dynamic uses of the visual
arts and pictorialism, we will do well to recognize a few red
herrings.

II

In the novel that bears his name, Roderick Hudson is a sculptor
by trade but a genius by essence. Rowland Mallet, a patron,
critic, and connoisseur of the arts, first recognizes and labels the
special qualities borne by Roderick. He immediately notices that
Roderick's work "had taken form under the breath of genius,"
and he wonders if "for men of his friend's large easy power
there was not an ampler moral law than for narrow mediocrities
like himself."² Roderick too comes to believe that the artist must
be allowed a freer, more romantic, less responsible life than
other men, saying "I think that when you expect a man to
produce beautiful and wonderful works of art you ought to
allow him a certain freedom of action, you ought to give him
a long rope, you ought to let him follow his fancy" (p. 224). So
much emphasis on genius as the ruling quality of the visual
artist is surprising, since James's critical writing on the visual
arts never severs genius from the capacity for dedication and
hard work, and his theory of fiction called for far more per-
spiration than inspiration. Perhaps, as a sculptor, Roderick differs from the writers and painters more typically James's subjects.
More likely behind this emphasis on "genius," however, is either
a young Henry James relying too hard on clichés in his portrait
of Roderick or a way of characterizing *Rowland* and *Roderick*
rather than of characterizing the visual artist in general. Their
reliance on genius may well reflect romanticism and weakness,
qualities that lead Roderick to an early death and condemn
Rowland to loving a series of women devoted to other (often
deceased) men. James himself knew that problems existed in his
presentation of the inspired, erring Roderick as the type of the
artist: "The very claim of the fable is naturally that he *is* special

... but that is not for a moment supposed to preclude his appearing typical (of the general type) as well."[3]

More troubling than James's portrait of the artistic temperament in this novel is the role assigned to Roderick's productions. He sculpts a number of remarkable pieces: the boy cup-bearer that introduces him to Rowland, the "Adam" sculpted soon after arrival in Rome, his portrait of Christina Light, and that of his mother stand out. The treatment of the "Adam" is representative and significant. The work finished and displayed is pronounced by all "miraculous." Its production and, more tellingly, its appearance, are never described in any kind of detail, however, and the only clue for visualization that James gives is the vague indication that the statue was "life size." A few details are provided for the other statues, but none is described so as to enable visualization.

Most tellingly, the "Adam," once mounted in Rowland's library, serves no real function in the novel. It decorates the place, surely, but no one in the novel thinks about it again, and for no one does it serve as a significant item in the consciousness. If such oblivion is the fate of "miraculous" works of art, pity those of less inspired statues! Just as the statues serve merely as decorations for Rowland's library, works of art in this novel tend to be purely decorative. They have no real significance, no real influence, no real function. They simply indicate Roderick's genius, and Roderick's genius produces further miraculous art in a closed, self-perpetuating circle.

Roderick's very identity as a sculptor is similarly decorative rather than functional. The few discussions he has about art are general in the extreme, leading back always to the general sense that Roderick's "genius" carries with it the grave danger of self-indulgence and weak will. His longest discussion about art—with the sculptor Gloriani—concerns the impossibility (as the older man sees it) of sustaining artistic production by inspiration. In response to Roderick's claim that he will create marble images "expressing the human type in superhuman images," Gloriani replies: "Your beauty, as you call it, is the effort of a man to quit the earth by flapping his arms very hard. He may jump about or stand on tiptoe, but he can't do more. Here [in the cup-bearer] you jump about very gracefully, I admit; but you can't fly; there's no use trying" (p. 119). Their conversation then turns to the subject of artists undone by women as Roderick displays "Eve," companion piece to "Adam." The conversation and action rather heavily foreshadow the remainder of the novel but touch, in no authentic way, James's theories of art. If they did, the novel's moral might be: if you see a young sculptor in decline, *cherchez la femme*.

Unfortunately, this cliché provides a program for the remainder of the novel. Roderick loses Christina Light to the rich but pitiable Prince Casamassima. He announces, almost immediately, his permanent loss of inspiration and determination to hit the skids. When he sees Christina again, by chance, in Switzerland, he proceeds to arrange his suicide by climbing a treacherous mountain in a blinding storm. What are we to make of all this? That Christina embodies beauty and that, having lost her, Roderick cannot pursue it in sculptural form? Little in the novel supports so vastly allegorical a reading. That Roderick is less a genius than a moonstruck young man? Perhaps—but that returns us to James's double difficulty: making Roderick both a special case *and* a representative artist. Here again, James sensed his problem, noting in the preface to the novel that "It [Roderick's collapse] has all begun too soon, as I say, and too simply, and the determinant function attributed to Christina Light, the character of well-nigh sole agent of his catastrophe that this unfortunate young woman has forced upon her, fails to commend itself to our sense of truth and proportion" (pp. xiv-xv). We might, like Maurice Beebe, see a theory of the artist's need for detachment from ordinary life, and especially from love and passion, reflected in Roderick's decline. But James's own critique seems to be truer than Beebe's:[4] as a serious illustration of a theory of art, *Roderick Hudson* risks making the theory look ridiculous.

One final aspect of the dilemmas presented by the novel when

we try to take seriously its use of the visual arts concerns Rowland
Mallet. As an evaluator of art, Rowland must have some merit
or the central premise of the novel collapses: if Roderick is not,
as Rowland believes, a young man of singular talent, why on
earth should we wish to read a many-paged novel about his
decline and fall? And so, we must assume, Rowland recognizes
the fine in art when he sees it and lives surrounded by eminent
paintings and sculptures, worthy to endow the museum he
dreams of some day establishing in his native city. And yet, for
a man so adept at identifying the fine in art, he appears a
singularly dense emotional being. Apparently attractive to
women, he yet fails to pursue the two women he loves (first his
cousin Cecilia and then Mary Garland), and he fails utterly to
notice what others easily remark: that both Augusta Blanchard
and Christina Light value his good opinion and covet his company. In fact, James underscores Rowland's lack of perception
by having his situation at the end of the novel echo that which
begins the work; he still haunts Northampton to be near a
secretly loved woman, though that woman is now Mary Garland
rather than Cecilia. Contact with art, then, does not help very
much in guiding Rowland through experience, and his skill as
a connoisseur of the arts promises little for his connoisseurship
of that more general category, life. In germ here is a major
Jamesian theme: the gulf between the appreciation of the beautiful and the recognition of the vital and the good. But the theme
is weakly developed and, once again, reveals nothing about the
visual arts supposedly at the heart of the novel.

A test suggested earlier, in the Introduction, for Lawrence's
Sons and Lovers might usefully be applied also to *Roderick Hudson*. The Introduction described the use of Paul Morel's career
as painter as decorative in that novel, noting that it ultimately
mattered little that Paul was a painter. The same test, applied
to *Roderick Hudson*, yields a similar conclusion. Roderick might
have been a young man of inspiration in other fields as well—
poetry, science, mathematics, music—without that changing the
novel very much. Christina Light could still serve to inspire and

then destroy. Works of music or scientific discoveries could still be alluded to and named—and then forgotten—as are the works of sculpture completed by Roderick. He could still debate with Gloriani about the possibility of sustaining work on the basis of inspiration alone and not on the homelier bases of routine, or schedule, or making a living. In fact, Roderick's career and death remind one of Romantic heroes who were not sculptors—like the poet Byron or the fictional Dr. Frankenstein. The paintbrush or rather, in this case, the sculptor's chisel is a red herring indeed.

III

Like *Roderick Hudson*, *The Tragic Muse* seems an indispensable novel for pursuing the subject of the visual arts and pictorialism in James's fiction. The novel's hero, Nick Dormer, finds himself drawn to painting far more than to the political career he has begun quite brilliantly. Under the urging of the Wildean Gabriel Nash, he decides to pursue painting, not politics, and thereby loses a seat in Parliament, a rich and beautiful fiancée, and the adoration of his family. His career choice thus decisively influences his future, and, appropriately, the novel devotes long sections to his progress as a painter. In *The Tragic Muse*, then, the visual arts seem to have greater importance than in *Roderick Hudson* or in *Sons and Lovers*, with a career in the arts necessary to account for the course of Nick's life. And yet very little of Nick's work lives for the reader, and astonishingly little of this novel is pictorial. Its uses of the visual arts finally emerge once again as decorative.

The book abounds in moments that should be pictorial, that *should* exercise the characters' and the reader's pictorial imaginations but ultimately do not. Early in the novel, for example, Peter Sherringham takes Miriam Rooth to the Louvre, as a form of cultural education suitable for her intended role as great actress. On these occasions "she had remarkable flashes of perception. She felt these things, she liked them, though it was always because she had an idea she could use them. ... 'That's the dress I mean to wear when I do Portia.' Such were the observations apt to drop from her under the suggestion of antique marbles or when she stood before a Titian or a Bronzino."[5] So little description of a visit to the Louvre or of the Titian and Bronzino seems unpictorial with a vengeance, and though we might say that James eschews the pictorial in this instance to render the quality of Miriam's sensibility—blank to the visual arts except as applicable to the emotive—the same kinds of omissions occur where pictorialism seems almost mandatory. Though he spends much time painting them, for example, Dormer's paintings remain mere adjuncts in the text—neither visually described nor visually imaginable. And the novel includes numerous passages in which Nick sketches the company, but no description accompanies the action, so that poor Nick might as well be knitting. As for *Roderick Hudson*, James showed awareness of his lapses in *The Tragic Muse*. He notes in his preface to the New York Edition: "It strikes me, alas, that he [Nick] is not quite so interesting as he was fondly intended to be. ... For to put the matter in an image, all we then—in his triumph—see of the charm-compeller is the back he turns to us as he bends over his work" (p. xxi). James refers, of course, to failures in characterizing Nick and in making him interesting, but his remarks point as well to the blankness of Nick's canvases for the reader.

Even those moments when we supposedly enter the consciousness of the artist in the process of conceiving his paintings seem weak in clues to stimulate the visual imagination. Take, for example, this encounter of Nick with the dying Mr. Carteret:

> The rich old man was propped upon pillows, and in this attitude, beneath the high spare canopy of his bed, presented himself to Nick's picture-seeking vision as a figure in a clever composition or a "story." He had gathered strength, though his strength was not much in his voice; it was mainly in his brighter eyes and his air of being pleased with himself. (VIII, p. 161)

When we consider the kinds of visually sensitive description that James *might* have provided here, the book's minimal pictorialism seems striking. Few adjectives, no adverbs, no hands, no lines on face, no smile or posture or expression to explain his air of "being pleased with himself," no frills or color on those bedclothes, no color anywhere, not much of anything to help our "picture-seeking vision." The words "a figure in a clever composition or a 'story' " (in the unrevised edition, "or a novel") tell here: the visual and the verbal are equivalent in James's rendering of Nick's consciousness. At times, Nick Dormer does seem invested with a high artistic mission as a painter, as when he realizes that the "language of art, the richest and most universal" language "made the indestructible thread on which the pearls of history are strung" (VIII, p. 391). His reflections most often, however, could refer with equal ease to literature.

Very few passages in the novel even approach the pictorial, but those few result from James's placing himself strongly in the character's circle of vision and writing what the character sees. For example, in a description of a London street, as Miriam remains "looking about her," we are told she was in "a straight blank ugly street, where the small cheap grey-faced houses had no expression save that of a rueful unconsoled acknowledgement of the universal want of identity" (VIII, p. 298). This is not much in the way of pictorialism, and its incipient pictorialism quickly slips into a phrase highly linguistic ("save ... identity"), but it goes further than much of what we find in the book.[6]

If we return for a moment to *Roderick Hudson*, we shall see the same technique used, on two occasions, more strikingly and more pictorially. In each case, the pictorialism results from the description's being grounded *in the eye of a character*. First, there is Roderick's initial glimpse of Christina Light, accompanied by her fantastic poodle: the beast "was combed and decked like a ram for sacrifice; his trunk and haunches were of the most transparent pink, his fleecy head and shoulders as white as jeweller's cotton, his tail and ears ornamented with long blue ribbons. He stepped along stiffly and solemnly beside his mistress, with an air of conscious elegance" (p. 94). Amused at so startling a sight, Roderick (whose eye presents and arranges what we see) begins to smile, but stops when Christina turns her head and reveals "A pair of extraordinarily dark blue eyes, a mass of dusky hair over a low forehead, a blooming oval of perfect purity, a flexible lip just touched with disdain, the step and carriage of a tired princess—these were the general features of his vision" (p. 95). Perhaps pressed into presenting the details noticed over a period of seconds by Roderick's eye, James here gives the reader's visual imagination more to go on than in the preceding instances. One might argue that Christina is beautiful in a rather general way, but the passage offers enough visual detail to make us capable of imagining it as a picture.

The most pictorial passage in *Roderick Hudson* and *The Tragic Muse* is a set piece in the first novel, this time with Rowland Mallet as the beholding eye. Here, the conception is definitely pictorial, and the "picture" includes elements of framing and of light from a single, dramatic source:

> Coming back to the drawing room he [Rowland] paused outside the open door; he was struck by the group formed by the three men. They were engaged in discussion of the so admirable Eve, and the author of the figure had lifted up the lamp and was showing different parts of it to his companions. He was talking with the confidence that never failed and yet never betrayed him—the lamplight covered his head and face. Rowland stood looking on, for the group appealed to him by its romantic symbolism. Roderick, bearing the lamp and glowing in its radiant circle, seemed the beautiful image of a genius which combined sincerity with power. Gloriani, with his head on one side, pulling his long moustache like a genial Mephistopheles and looking keenly from half-closed eyes at the lighted marble, represented art with a mixed motive, skill unleavened by faith. . . . Poor little Singleton, on the other side, with his hands behind him, his head thrown back and his eye following devoutly the course of Roderick's charming extravagance, might pass for an embodiment of

aspiring candour afflicted with feebleness of wing. In all this, Roderick's was certainly the *beau rôle*. (p. 123)

Although this description is pictorial in its use of frame, its sensitivity to composition, and its attention to lighting, Rowland's consciousness (like James's) betrays itself as essentially literary in its approach to the visual arts. Rowland does not merely see a composition of three men balanced in a particular way; he endows the figures with allegorical significance not unknown in painting, but not demanded by the medium, either. Such thinking in terms of drama and symbol, rather than in terms of composition, form, color, and technique, typifies Rowland's approach to art (see also p. 26). The work of art is never worth as much in itself as it is when seen as the representation of something else. As a "painting," however, this one belongs in a line of paintings that comment on the nature of painting (a popular nineteenth-century sub-genre). And the use of a single source of light reminds one of effects in Caravaggio and in de la Tour.

Even in novels essentially unpictorial, with only decorative uses of the visual arts, then, James approaches pictorialism in descriptions of things explicitly seen, especially things seen whose essence takes time to register on the mind of the perceiver. We shall see this aspect of his fiction develop in later novels, and I shall describe it as one of the elements in James's fiction most involved with and tied to the visual arts. And yet, although suggesting the pictorial when compared to other passages in *Roderick Hudson* and *The Tragic Muse*, the passages just discussed make rather small claims for the uses of the visual arts and of pictorialism in fiction. As was true of the statues so masterfully carved by Roderick, these scenes are rendered and then forgotten—they linger in neither the characters' minds nor in the reader's—an effect quite different from what we will see in Lawrence and Woolf and some of James's better fictions. Again, the many verbal allusions to artists and to works of art in these novels prove separable from their most important qualities of theme and form. The brush and the chisel are once again red herrings.

IV

Although attention to artists and to language rich in art metaphors has been among the most pervasive and persistent of red herrings in interdisciplinary criticism on the novel, the instances given from James's work certainly do not exhaust the kinds of decorative uses of the visual arts found in novels before the twentieth century. As noted in the Introduction, the emphasis of this study is on the early decades of that century. But it will be helpful to look back at the end of this chapter at decorative uses of the visual arts and pictorialism in some eighteenth- and nineteenth-century novels, helpful in establishing the kinds of decorative uses typical of novels and helpful too in indicating why earlier novels often hover at the beginning of the continuum.

Among the clearest of documentary relationships in the early history of the novel is that between Hogarth and Fielding. If, as is frequently said, Fielding fathered the line of fiction leading from Thackeray through Dickens, then Hogarth must be considered, at the very least, a favorite uncle. As Mario Praz puts it, "just because it is so easily translatable into words, Hogarth's painting is closely connected with the literature, particularly the satiric literature of his age."[7] Indeed, Hazlitt included Hogarth in his *Lectures on the English Comic Writers* and Hazlitt's fellow Romantic Charles Lamb noted that "His greatest representations are indeed books; they have the teeming, fruitful, suggestive meaning of *words*. Other pictures we look at—his prints we read."[8] If Lamb is right, we may see in Hogarth one source for Victorian painting's emphasis (much like the Victorian novel's) on anecdote, narrative, and moral, an emphasis that almost makes "between 1830 and 1860, English painting . . . a branch of literature."[9]

Fielding worked with Hogarth in his theatrical career, and he frequently pays homage to the artist in his novels. In his preface to *Joseph Andrews*, Fielding defined "his own art in terms of the painter," and his comic theory and practice bear relation to Hogarth's,[10] as does his generally satiric stance. Like Thackeray in *Barry Lyndon*, moreover, Fielding used *A Rake's Progress* as a source: it shapes Mr. Wilson's history in *Joseph Andrews* and the Man of the Hill's narrative in *Tom Jones*.[11] Even more directly, he alludes to Hogarth in his novels. When, for example, he introduces Bridget Allworthy, Fielding invokes Hogarth: "I would attempt to draw her picture; but that is done already by a more able master, Mr. Hogarth himself."[12] Again, upon the announcement of Sophia's disappearance, Fielding evokes the newsbearer's demeanor in this way: "O, Shakespear! had I thy pen! O, Hogarth! had I thy pencil! then I would draw the picture of the poor serving-man, who, with pale countenance, staring eyes, chattering teeth, faultering tongue, and trembling lips ... enter'd the room."[13] As Moore points out in *Hogarth's Literary Relationships*, "Hogarth had drawn exactly such a servant in the last picture of the *Marriage*."[14]

Critics generally greet direct correspondences of this kind between the visual arts and literature with delight, as proof that interdisciplinary studies "work." It is not difficult, however, to see a loss rather than a gain from such direct, tangible uses of the visual arts. In the two instances above, Fielding invokes Hogarth at moments when he himself might create a visual impression in words. He refers the reader's visual imagination to a prior-existing picture, thus asking it to perform an act of memory, rather than a creative act of collaboration with the author. In effect, the evocation of the novel's action in terms of a picture existing outside the novel sidetracks the process of pictorialism and constricts the reader's visual imagination. In *Tristram Shandy*, the great eccentric, Laurence Sterne, offers what might be a critique of Fielding's practice. When introducing the "concupiscible ... Widow Wadman," Sterne presents the reader with his now famous blank page and exhorts him to act: "To conceive this right—call for pen and ink—here's paper ready to your hand.—Sit down, Sir, paint her to your own mind—as like your mistress as you can—as unlike your wife as your conscience will let you—'tis all one to me—please but your own fancy in it."[15] Although the jest of the blank page could not be repeated, Modern novelists characteristically, as we shall see, make the gesture toward actively involving the reader that Sterne does at this point in *Tristram Shandy*.

Also eighteenth century is the celebrated conjunction of the visual arts and literature around aesthetic theories of the sublime and beautiful. As implemented by painters like Claude Lorrain, Salvador Rosa, and Giovanni Battista Piranesi, these theories decisively fueled the novels traditionally called gothic. The influence of the architectural painter Piranesi on the late eighteenth-century novel has been described in this way: "In the disproportion between Piranesi's mighty daedalean buildings and his little figures of men at the foot of them, is to be seen the germ of the ruling idea of *The Castle of Otranto*" by Horace Walpole.[16] We might add that the almost obligatory monumental settings of the gothic novel—castles and monasteries far more often than houses in town—derive also, in part, from Piranesi. Similarly, the overall use of landscape and of figures in the landscape in gothic novels derives from Claude and Rosa and "was part of the movement away from neoclassic ideals of order, restraint, and reason towards an admiration for the picturesque, the sublime, and the emotional in art."[17] Both the paintings and the literature had, moreover, a common source: theories of the sublime, newly current in England with the translation of Longinus' *On the Sublime* and with Edmund Burke's "A Philosophical Enquiry into the Origin of Our Ideas of the Sublime and Beautiful."

Many gothic novelists fully and unabashedly mined theories of the sublime and drew freely upon landscape painters for their novels. Ann Radcliffe is among the most indebted to these sources outside her own discipline. In *The Mysteries of Udolpho*, for example, Emily and Valencourt experience a sublime mountain landscape:

From Beaujeu the road had constantly ascended, conducting the travellers into the higher regions of the air, where immense glaciers exhibited their frozen horrors, and eternal snow whitened the summits of the mountains. They often paused to contemplate these stupendous scenes, and, seated on some wild cliff, where only the ilex or the larch could flourish, looked over dark forests of fir, and precipices where human foot had never wandered, into the glen—so deep, that the thunder of the torrent, which was seen to foam along the bottom, was scarcely heard to murmur. Over these crags rose others of stupendous height, and fantastic shape; some shooting into cones; others impending far over their base, in huge masses of granite, along whose broken ridges was often lodged a weight of snow, that, trembling even to the vibration of a sound, threatened to bear destruction in its course to the vale. Around, on every side, far as the eye could penetrate, were seen only forms of grandeur—the long perspective of mountain-tops, tinged with ethereal blue, or white with snow; valleys of ice, and forests of gloomy fir. The serenity and clearness of the air in these high regions were particularly delightful to the travellers; it seemed to inspire them with a finer spirit, and diffused an indescribable complacency over their minds. They had no words to express the sublime emotions they felt.[18]

As is well known, Radcliffe never actually visited the sites she described, but depended instead on secondary sources like paintings and essays. Extraordinarily arranged and "pat," her landscapes serve as virtual catalogues of effects designated by Burke as sublime. In the quoted passage, a typical example, Radcliffe emphasizes contrasts of height, color, and texture, according to Burke's observation that extremes of height and depth and contrasts in texture produce a feeling of sublimity. Thus, we have eternally white summits, precipices, crags of "stupendous height and fantastic shape," and so on. Later on in the same passage, other elements of Burke's sublime—including silence and obscurity—enter the description. The landscape, moreover, is lavishly described not just for its own sake but for the effect it produces on the characters: the full passage frequently refers to the delight, tears, and awe produced in the company by the scenery. Once again, Radcliffe readily displays her debts, as the characters' reactions follow Burke's program for how the sublime affects the perceiver.

Radcliffe's use of visual stimuli based upon the historical visual arts anticipates later developments in the use of visual stimuli to precipitate the character's emotions and thoughts. But, in novels like *Udolpho*, the effect is rather mechanical and hence no more than decorative in terms of the continuum that governs this study. The same limitations mark Radcliffe's tendency to make paintings or statues prominent objects in her plots, a tendency she shared with other gothic novelists, like Walpole. Thus Emily spends much time in *Udolpho* tempted to look behind the black veil that covers a painting in the villainous Montoni's castle. When, around mid-novel, she yields to her temptation, she faints. Unexplained until the end of the novel, the event invites readers to think that the picture behind the veil somehow crystallizes all the horrors of Montoni and his castle. In fact, however, as we learn at the end of the novel, the painting was not really a painting. After removing the veil, Emily fainted before what appeared to be a decomposing corpse. But the corpse was not a corpse either, as we also find at the end of the novel. It was a wax statue, commissioned as a *momento mori* by one of Montoni's ancestors.

One could argue that the visual arts—in the form of the "painting" and "statue"—play a vital role in *Udolpho*. But to my knowledge, and with my full approval, no one ever has. For the art objects are mere props—obligatory, mechanical items merely decorative in overall resonance and effect and, therefore, similar to works of art in *Roderick Hudson* and *The Tragic Muse*. Radcliffe might have linked the art objects to deeper themes: the authentic contemplation of death, the qualities of human obsession, for example. But she does not. Indeed, her uses of the visual arts and pictorialism almost parody those we will examine in Modern novels, in which art objects or scenes experienced pictorially trigger complex perceptual and hermeneutic processes. In *Udolpho*, the characters react programmatically to visual stimuli, and the reader unproblematically understands all such allusions to art and the visual. Radcliffe's uses of visual stimuli derived from the visual arts in developing her characters' consciousnesses are thus merely decorative gestures of homage to leading painters, and to the theories of Burke and other eighteenth-century aestheticians. But they are historically important gestures that presage stronger links between the visual arts, pictorialism, and the novel. As was the case for Fielding, even strong, documentary connections between the visual arts and the novel do not guarantee that novels will use the visual arts and pictorialism in ways other than decorative. Indeed, such overt or familiar references, like James's use of artist figures, can in themselves constitute formidable red herrings in interdisciplinary studies.

V

Charlotte Brontë's *Jane Eyre* makes a more aggressive movement up the continuum, but fails to sustain that movement, resulting in a rather complex instance of decorative uses. True to her creator, who responded strongly to the visual arts,[19] Jane Eyre frequently reports with visual detail what characters and places look like, often describing them as "pictures," and noticing actual pictures when she encounters them. Thus, she reports present on the walls of a local inn some standard paintings of the day: "a portrait of George the Third, and another of the Prince of Wales, and a representation of the death of Wolfe."[20] When she first arrives at Thornfield, "a cozy and agreeable picture presented itself to my view. A snug, small room; a round table by a cheerful fire; an arm-chair high-backed and old-fashioned, wherein sat the neatest imaginable little elderly lady, in widow's cap, black silk gown, and snowy muslin apron" (pp. 114-15). From the recessed portion of Rochester's drawing room, she observes and renders pictorially Blanche Ingram and other female guests "framed" by the archway, first giving a picture of the whole and then focussing on details (see pp. 214-17). Again, Rosamund Oliver forms a picture of perfect beauty: she boasts

> a youthful, graceful form: full, yet fine in contour ... as sweet features as ever the temperate clime of Albion moulded; as pure hues of rose and lily as ever her humid gales and vapoury skies generated ... regular and delicate lineaments; eyes shaped and coloured as we see them in lovely pictures, large, and dark, and full; the long and shadowy eyelash which encircles a fine eye with so soft a fascination, the pencilled brow which gives such clearness; the white smooth forehead ... the cheek, oval, fresh and smooth; lips fresh too, ruddy, healthy, sweetly formed; the even and gleaming teeth without flaw; the small, dimpled chin; the ornament of rich, plenteous tresses. (p. 463)

As if to reinforce our sense of the pictorial, Jane frequently draws with considerable accuracy characters in the novel, characters including Rochester, Blanche Ingram, and Rosamund Oliver.

Like her pictorial descriptions, however, Jane's drawings usually have a limitation to modern tastes: they depend quite strongly on notions of type. In the description of Rosamund just quoted, for example, many of the formulations ("eyes shaped and coloured as we see them in lovely pictures," "the [not "a"] smooth white forehead," "the even and gleaming teeth without flaw") make a notation toward physical features that the reader would, apparently, have encountered often before.[21] Other characters match other types: Blanche dark and majestic like Diana; St. John, the very type of classical Greek masculine beauty; Rochester, the very picture of a gothic hero/villain. Much of the eighteenth-century and earlier heritage of describing characters by types lingers, then, in *Jane Eyre*'s pictorialism, and while the reader needs a visual imagination to enjoy Jane's narration, that imagination's most basic task is to translate indications of type into an appropriate, somewhat general, mental picture.

Other aspects of the novel more complexly stress Jane's visual imagination and call upon the reader's. Certain scenes, like that when the escaped Bertha tears Jane's wedding veil, demand for their full effect the reader's sympathetic re-enactment, parallel to Jane's re-enactment in memory, of how the moments felt because of how they looked. The incident (pp. 357-59) depends for its rather thrilling effect on details like Bertha's "roll of the red eyes and the fearful blackened inflation of the lineaments," and on the gradual approach of the scene's sole illumination— Bertha's candle—to Jane's bed. As in James's novels, *Jane Eyre's* pictorialism often arises when we see through a character's eyes.

Pictures also figure prominently in two other incidents at Thornfield. First, the whole extended description of charades shows a link between drama, tableau-vivant, and picture in the nineteenth century. Most important, however, are Jane's drawings of shadowy ladies and cormorants, icebergs, and jewels by which Rochester begins to confirm his sense of Jane's hidden powers. The drawings all express the greatness of Jane's imagination and support the idea that the visual imagination, to Brontë, was among the most important of mental faculties.

The affinity between novelistic pictorialism in the nineteenth century and the dramatic tableau-vivant informs the novel's least merely decorative use of the visual arts and of pictorialism and yet its hardest to concisely define. J. Hillis Miller has recently discussed the important subject of repetition in the novel, a technique novelists have long used to highlight meanings.[22] *Jane Eyre* uses numerous repetitions and echoes—many partly visual—to reinforce its meanings. Among the most basic is the interplay between beings dark, demonic, and Dionysian and beings light, angelic, and Apollonian. Among the less obvious is the use of repeated "rhyming" pictures to suggest the essential quality of Jane's attachment to Rochester, especially "pictures" in which the man leans physically on the woman for support.

At Jane and Rochester's first meeting, we encounter the first of these "pictures." After Rochester has fallen from his horse, he needs assistance to remount. Not possessing "an umbrella that he can use as a stick" and unable to catch the bridle of Rochester's horse, Jane lays aside her muff and serves herself as a prop: "He laid a heavy hand on my shoulder, and leaning on me with some stress, limped to his horse" (p. 140). Jane then restores to him his riding whip, lost in the fall, and picks up her muff. Only slightly and fleetingly pictorial (hence the need to put "pictures" in quotation marks), the moment might fail of visual imagination or be forgotten but for its repetition. It bears comparison, I believe, to a very quick tableau-vivant in an ongoing drama, repeated with variations through a play and memorable largely because of its repetition. The numerous sexual props in the scene both add to its fun and suggest dramas of male and female identity largely responsible for the wide appeal of *Jane Eyre*. The two figures separate from gender-linked items (like the muff and the riding crop) to meet in androgynous terms of support offered and accepted. Jane restores Rochester to his masculine horse, but does so with energy and power themselves masculine in the Victorian world.

The same gestures are repeated when Rochester hears from Jane of Mason's arrival and leans on her in his momentary despair. Brontë does not insist that we visualize this scene (and, in fact, provides few pictorial details), but she does prompt the reader's visual memory by having Jane say, " 'Oh! lean on me, sir,' " and Rochester reply, " 'Jane, you offered me your shoulder once before, let me have it now,' " (p. 255), a reference to the horse-mounting scene. Once again, sexual reversals obliquely enter if we visualize the scene, which, once again, Brontë does not insist we do. Rochester has been dressed, after all, in the garb of a female gypsy and the slighter Jane once again emerges as the physically stronger. Visualization helps the reader, however, both to make the indicated connection to the earlier scene and to appreciate this scene's gender-reversals.

The final appearance of this quasi-pictorial motif comes at the end of the novel as, freshly betrothed at Ferndean, Jane and Rochester wend their way homeward. To do so, Rochester "stretched his hand out to be led. I took that dear hand, held it a moment to my lips, then let it pass round my shoulder: being so much lower of stature than he, I served both for his prop and guide" (p. 573). Once again, the fleeting "picture" "rhymes" with that at their first meeting and that when Rochester hears of Mason's visit. The repetition encourages us to give a pictorial reality to all three. Once again, as well, the sexual politics in this scene intrigue: the best relationships between men and women in this novel involve the negation of sexual stereotypes. As in the earlier scenes, aberrant sexual notes are present here, though not emphasized by Brontë: we might, if we visualize the scene, remember that Rochester wears Jane's pearl necklace around his neck, and Rochester's crippled status has prompted more than one critic to cry "castration."[23]

Jane Eyre's repetitions with a strong visual component bear affinities to what we shall see later in this study. They are, however, less vitally a part of the novel, with pictorialism neither as extensive as in later novels nor as highlighted by the novelist. Characters do not, moreover, explicitly use the visual recollection of moments to make sense of their experience (as in perceptual uses of the visual arts or pictorialism), though they are, certainly, capable of doing so. Readers might use these visual clues in the interpretation of the novel (as in hermeneutic uses), especially its more subversive themes like gender-reversals, but they also might easily obtain similar interpretive data from other aspects of the novel. *Jane Eyre* represents, then, a peculiar case in relation to the continuum introduced in this study. For while it is difficult to imagine the novel without its many references to the visual arts and instances of pictorialism, few of those references or instances really are complexly ideological, perceptual, or hermeneutic. And its perceptual uses refer almost exclusively to fairly straightforward qualities of Jane's memory, as she attempts to recreate her youthful experiences for the reader. The movement up the continuum is definitely present in Brontë's novel, but is so spasmodic and unsustained that the novel rarely transcends the decorative in its uses of the visual arts and pictorialism.

VI

Another area in the classical novel's history seems especially fertile for interdisciplinary exploration: the inclusion of illustrations in novels, especially nineteenth-century novels initially published in serial form. As the handsome volume by Gordon N. Ray, *The Illustrator and the Book in England, 1790-1914*, testifies, the nineteenth century was a golden age in English book illustration.[24] All kinds of books were strikingly illustrated during this period: books of songs and melodies, the Bible, books of history, Tennyson's *Poems* and *Idylls of the King* (these by artists like Hunt and Beardsley), classics of eighteenth-century literature (like Goldsmith's *Poems* or Pope's "The Rape of the Lock"), Carroll's *Alice in Wonderland*, travel literature, *The Arabian Nights*, Virgil's *Eclogues*, Chaucer's *Works* (strikingly illustrated by Edward Burne-Jones), Keats's *Works*, essays like Carlyle's *Sartor Resartus*, and, of course, children's books like Barrie's *Peter Pan* and Potter's *Tale of Peter Rabbit*. Significantly, classic literature (like Virgil and Chaucer) would be, as a matter of course, published with contemporary illustrations in the nineteenth century. Even poetry, a form we do not usually associate with illustrations, was quite frequently accompanied by plates during the late eighteenth and the nineteenth centuries. But the best known of illustrated volumes—and the most pertinent to this study—remain novels, often illustrated with the author's collaboration or, at least, with his tacit consent.

The study of illustrations in novels has produced some fine books, books usually rich in factual information and strong in what I call the documentary approach. On Dickens, for example, the following very good and even excellent studies come to mind: John Harvey's *Victorian Novelists and Their Illustrators*, Albert Johannsen's *Phiz: Illustrations for the Novels of Charles Dickens*, Edgar Browne's *Phiz and Dickens*, Q. D. Leavis' essay on illustrations in *Dickens the Novelist*, Michael Steig's *Dickens and Phiz*, and J. Hillis Miller's excellent, suggestive essay "The Fiction of Realism: *Sketches by Boz, Oliver Twist*, and Cruikshank's Illustrations."[25] And yet, the study of illustrations, while not exactly a red herring in interdisciplinary approaches to the novel, has sometimes been a fairly robust pink. For (with important exceptions, like Miller's essay), such criticism has tended to oversimplify the theoretical implications of illustrations in the process of the reader's understanding the text and realizing its visual potential.

In general, most critics have shared Q. D. Leavis' sense (with regard, once again, to Dickens) that "illustrations are frequently indispensable even to us, the highly trained modern reader, in interpreting novels correctly because they encapsulate the themes and give us the means of knowing with certainty where [the author] meant the stress to fall."[26] Thus, John Harvey shows how the illustrations of *David Copperfield*—prepared by H. Hablot Browne (or "Phiz"), who illustrated ten of Dickens' novels—make thematic comments on the novel and can be "read" like the drawings by Hogarth that are their most important source. Sometimes the illustrations make thematic comments through background pictures—as when an illustration showing the redeemable Martha being comforted by the still innocent Emily has hanging in its background a Magdalen scene and (to the far right and half hidden) a scene of Eve being tempted by the devil, foretelling Emily's future. The illustrations also comment harshly on Dora as, in "Our Housekeeping," Dora is identified with her dog, Jip, who sits untidily amidst the untidiness of the Copperfields' dining table and room (p. 548). Like Dora, Jip has long, shiny dark hair, and his central location suggests that all the disorder in the Copperfield household radiates from the child-wife.[27]

All these points are well taken, and yet they raise a significant problem in regarding the illustrations to *David Copperfield* (and other well-known illustrations, like those to *Vanity Fair*) as ideological or hermeneutic uses of the visual arts: the illustrations reiterate ideas plainly available in the text without use of the visual arts or pictorialism, ideas that would emerge quite easily even if the illustrations were omitted. Only one critic I have encountered gives a significantly new reading of the novel based upon the illustrations—Michael Steig in *Dickens and Phiz*. Working from the fact that Little Emily and Martha appear in a disproportionate number of plates, Steig suggests that Dickens' work is more interested in "fallen" women than in domestic angels like Agnes, and that David's attitudes to these women are significantly unresolved. The observation is excellent, as is Steig's general premise that illustrations in novels offer a "reading" of the novel similar to a critical interpretation rather than to a definitive version of the text. Accepting Steig's premise, we can say that illustrations *can* emphasize aspects of the novel's themes that might otherwise escape notice and that, when they do so, they perform helpful functions parallel to ideological or hermeneutic uses of the visual arts or pictorialism within the text itself.

Even my admiration for Steig's perceptions, however, fails to persuade me that Q. D. Leavis does not overstate her case in praise of illustrations. I expect that Steig, for example, could have reached his conclusions about Little Emily and Martha by focussing on the roles of women characters rather than on the illustrations. I will, in fact, advance an iconoclastic position by suggesting that even the fine illustrations to *David Copperfield*—while interesting, valuable, and eminently nice to have—neither rival the text in any serious way nor provide an adequate representation of the text to the reader. The worthiness of illustrations, moreover, obviously decreases in novels depicted by lesser artists than Phiz or illustrated without the author's approval and collaboration, approval and collaboration of the kind provided by Dickens.

In *David Copperfield*, for example, characters rarely emerge in the illustrations with the subtlety and force of characters in the novel. Traddles, to take one instance, continues to look merely ridiculous in the illustrations long after the text has revealed his unusually fine, sterling qualities. And the women in the novel—Agnes, Emily, and Dora—look so astonishingly alike that only their situations in the plates, and not their forms or faces, distinguish them. Similarly, I find myself less than satisfied with Phiz's heroic attempt to capture the novel's strong retrospective first-person form by including David in all the plates, usually as an observer watching the other characters. He wears a variety of facial expressions, from confusion, to dismay, to tranquillity, to amazement, to tearfulness, expressions appropriate to the novel's dramatic shifts in mood. And he ages appropriately as the novel proceeds, a plausible device for capturing the retrospective mood, if not a totally successful one.

David's role in several of the drawings is especially problematic. Hands clasped and eyes agog in the illustration of Mr. Peggotty holding his reclaimed niece (plate 9), for instance, David reduces rather than heightens the effectiveness of the moment. The element of melodrama is simply too pronounced, with David's response pre-empting the reader's. Many of the plates, indeed, remind one of dramatic tableaux-vivants, with David indicating the desired audience response. Overall, Phiz's illustrations of faces tend to be rather weak, though (especially in a novel like *Bleak House*) he sometimes achieves considerable success with the illustration of place and the evocation of mood.

The failings that I instance in the illustrations are partly Browne's, but partly inherent in the necessary relationship of illustration to novel, particularly when the novel was written by a writer of brilliant visual imagination. The illustrations seem, finally, inadequate to the text even though they—perhaps because they—linger in the reader's imagination and often shape his later conception of the novel much as the film of a novel often influences a viewer's subsequent experience of the text.[28] When writing of Cruikshank's illustrations for Dickens, J. Hillis Miller notes that illustrations shut off the novel's reference to a real world, resulting in "a continual back and forth movement" between illustration and text.[29] The illustrated novel's constriction of the reader's visual imagination seems to me equally significant and comparable to the effect of Fielding's references to Hogarth, described earlier. For illustrations severely limit the range of the reader's visual imagination as it comes into contact with the author's. Often, indeed, the author's visual imagination sprints ahead of the illustrations, suggesting more than the plates actually record and yet tempting the reader to accept the plates as an accurate and adequate representation of how people and events in the novel "really looked." Though originally intended to help readers to visualize novels, illustrations can thus lull the reader's visualizing faculties. Here phenomenology provides corroboration; for the act of perceiving (as one perceives an illustration in a text) is less free than the act of imagining (as one imagines a pictorial rendering).[30]

Consider the two following examples, one involving details omitted by the illustration, the other the distortion of the text's spirit. When David enters Mr. Peggotty's boat—the home around which so much of *David Copperfield*'s sentiment centers—we are given the following description:

> It was beautifully clean inside, and as tidy as possible. There was a table, and a Dutch clock, and a chest of drawers, and on the chest of drawers there was a tea-tray with a painting on it of a lady with a parasol, taking a walk with a military-looking child who was trundling a hoop. The tray was kept from tumbling down, by a Bible; and the tray, if it had tumbled down, would have smashed a quantity of cups and saucers and a teapot that were grouped around the book. On the walls there were some common colored pictures, framed and glazed, of Scripture subjects; such as I have never seen since in the hands of pedlars, without seeing the whole interior of Peggotty's brother's house again, at one view. Abraham in red going to sacrifice Isaac in blue, and Daniel in yellow cast into a den of green lions, were the most prominent of these. Over the little mantel-shelf, was a picture of the Sarah Jane lugger, built at Sunderland, with a real little wooden stern stuck on to it; a work of art, combining composition with carpentry, which I considered to be one of the most enviable possessions that the world could afford. (p. 26)

The accompanying illustration, "I am Hospitably Received by Mr. Peggotty" (plate 10), shows all the major characters (Ham, Mr. Peggotty, David, Mrs. Gummidge, Peggotty, and Little Emily), enclosing them in a circular arch and in a circle of fond glances that suggest, quite nicely, the vessel's snugness, its ideal and loving protectiveness. But the plate omits all the wonderful details noticed by David, details helpful in establishing the family's simple tastes and wholesome mores. Several items in the description allude, for example, to the family's simple Christianity. Others have a *Biedermeier* quality that, for the Victorians, signified home.[31] All make credible the family's humane and yet extreme reaction to Emily's seduction. More important, the household items are actually more present in the text than the group scene given an artificial "reality" by the illustration: the boyish David quite literally notices most the things that surround the family rather than its individual members.

Another example, from *Great Expectations*, will make it clear that my reservations about illustrations refer to more than the special qualities of Phiz's style. *Great Expectations* was not accompanied by illustrations in serial form, reflecting both the greater sophistication of Dickens' reading public and the novel's intensive use of the first person form which, as we saw in *David Copperfield*, is so minimally captured in that novel's illustrations. When published in book form, the novel was accompanied by drawings done by Marcus Stone, drawings inadequate and not highly regarded, perhaps commissioned "in order to provide the orphaned son of Dickens' old friend with a job."[32] In the Scribner Gadshill edition, however, illustrations by Charles Green in the non-caricature, realistic style typified by Millais and popular after 1860 accompany the text.[33] The style certainly emphasizes detail, and yet it proves inadequate to the spirit of Dickens' novel.

Think for a moment of the wonderful opening chapters of *Great Expectations* and try to find scenes for illustration. If your memory is like mine, some of the following possibilities will arise: the inverted landscape of the marsh as Magwitch turns Pip upside down; the prodigious bread-eating contest of Joe and Pip; the Pumblechookian gathering around the Christmas table. Perhaps most of all, the striking picture of Magwitch left alone on the marshes that ends chapter one suggests itself for illustration:

> The marshes were just a long black horizontal line then, as I stopped to look after him; and the river was just another horizontal line, not nearly so broad nor yet so black; and the sky was

just a row of long angry red lines intermixed. On the edge of the river I could faintly make out the only two black things in all the prospect that seemed to be standing upright; one of these was the beacon by which the sailors steered—like an unhooped cask upon a pole—an ugly thing when you were near it; the other a gibbet, with some chains hanging to it which had once held a pirate. The man was limping on towards this latter. . . .

What, however, is the first illustration in the novel? A close-up of the soldiers who interrupt the Christmas dinner drinking brandy—a scene that in no way captures the essence of the novel or foretells its future development, and a scene rendered so as not to capture even Pip's immense suspense as the soldiers drink.

Such illustrations—indeed illustrations in general—may be harmless enough, may sometimes even be helpful to readers who have difficulties visualizing as they read. But, like eyeglasses improperly used, they dull the average reader's visual imagination, accustoming him to relying on illustrations and not on his own faculties. Paradoxically, however, the reader of Dickens who does not go beyond the illustrations in collaborating with the author's pictorial imagination is only a partially responsive reader. Dickens' illustrations were consistently among the best in the business, and yet these illustrations do not fully capture the richness of the text, and perhaps no illustrations could. Their limitations help to show how illustrations can inhibit the reader's exercise of the pictorial imagination so necessary in appreciating certain kinds of fiction. Moreover, they suggest the unsuitability, in general, of the usual styles of illustration to novels in which psychological processes, or certain narrative points of view (especially first person or the strong authorial narration in novels like *Middlemarch*), or the symbolic, semiotic quality of things require emphasis. Nineteenth-century illustrations tend to emphasize plot and character. They also tend to fudge the question of point of view and to reduce the resonance of objects as signs or symbols. The thing pictured in a textual graphic tends to seem complete in itself—mimetic, not semiotic or symbolic.

VII

Hardy's *Tess of the D'Urbervilles* provides another and even more striking example of what is gained and what is lost when novels are accompanied by illustrations. A very late nineteenth-century novel, *Tess of the D'Urbervilles* appeared in *The Graphic* of 1891 in weekly installments with twenty-five illustrations, including two in impressive double-page format.[34] Like all Hardy's novels and most illustrated novels after 1860, its plates followed the dramatic, realistic style of Millais, which had all but discredited the earlier, caricatural style of Thackeray, Cruikshank, and Phiz, and was itself being displaced by the art-nouveau of artists like Beardsley. Earlier novels by Hardy (like *Far From the Madding Crowd*) had appeared in prestigious periodicals which included illustrations but emphasized text, journals like Leslie Stephen's *Cornhill* magazine. The subject matter of *Tess* made it difficult to place, however, and, after rejections by *Murray's Magazine* and *Macmillan's*, Hardy accepted an offer from *The Graphic*, a journal aimed at a less literary audience, and one noted more for its illustrations than for its literature.[35]

In the case of *Tess*, then, the role of illustrations in accommodating the imaginations of relatively unskilled readers and in defining and thereby limiting the more visually acute reader's pictorial imagination would have been prominent, as *The Graphic*'s readers relied on the expected illustrations more than most readers. Publication in *The Graphic* also involved some other artistic compromises for Hardy. First, as was the magazine's policy, he had no say in the illustrators or illustrations for the novel (though he did not always exercise such control, even when available, as it was at the *Cornhill*). *The Graphic* chose to use four artists of differing abilities and even differing styles: Hubert Herkomer (the main illustrator, and the most talented), Borough Johnson (who largely followed Herkomer's lead), Daniel Wehschmidt, and J. Syddall (the last two generally inferior artists). Most seriously of all, Hardy acquiesced—with some unhappiness—to the magazine's insistence that portions of *Tess* be bowdlerized to suit the serial-reading public. The bowdlerized text excluded all mention of Tess's illegitimate child and hedged a great deal about the nature of her relationship (both early and late) to Alec. Such suppressions risk making nonsense of some aspects of the novel. Thus, the serial version of *Tess* with illustrations is a seriously compromised version, a fact which may have influenced later decisions that most book editions of the novel omit the illustrations that accompanied the serial version, a situation different from that of *David Copperfield*, which is usually printed with its illustrations.

Comparing the illustrations to the final text provides an interesting case of the merits and demerits of illustrated novels. As Arlene Jackson notes, the illustrations serve to highlight aspects of plot and characterization in the novel that might easily be missed on a quick reading, especially by a relatively unsophisticated reader and especially, one might add, over the six-month period required to read the novel in its serial form. Thus, the opening illustration, a double-page picture of Tess returning from the May Day celebration as "There stood her mother, amid the group of children, hanging over the washing tub," emphasizes both the innocence and voluptuousness of Tess, clad in white, and the warmth of her family group.[36] The initial perception of Tess in her family helps to make sense of her repeated sacrifices for the hapless Durbeyfields and also contrasts with the scenes of familial deracination later in the novel. A later illustration of Joan Durbeyfield poised atop the wagon that is to move her and her belongings to a new, unfamiliar home, for example, emphasizes the contrast between the old, family-centered village life with which the novel begins and the new life of the English rural migrations with which it ends. As Jackson also notes, other paired illustrations emphasize the ironic reversals in the novel's plot. In the plates for August 22 and September 26, 1891, for example, Angel Clare accosts Tess, blocking her path and reaching out to her, first in the fields of Talbothays and then (in the second plate) on the stairway of the household. In the second plate, Tess is illuminated by the light

of a candle. In a later plate (of October 10, 1891) Tess is once
again illuminated by a fire's glow, this time as she pleads with
Clare to accept her post-nuptial confession as the equivalent of
his own. This time, however, Tess is on her knees to Clare,
reaching out to *him*, and *he* recoils as she had in the August 22
illustration. Their situations have been reversed, one of life's
little ironies.

Clare's characteristic gestures in the illustrations reinforce a
similarity between Angel and Alec (present also in the initial
vowel of their names—two Adams?), the sense in which both
men meddle with Tess to her harm. For, in each illustration in
which he appears, Alec reaches out to Tess, often impinging on
her space and causing her to recoil, as when he dangles before
her a tempting strawberry or (in the best, though melodramatic,
illustration) when he surprises Tess in her father's garden as she
works by firelight (plate 11).

In what I have said thus far, it may appear that the illustrations
for *Tess* are inoffensive or neutral when poor, and helpful when
good, in emphasizing aspects of theme and form. In their en-
tirety, however, the illustrations repeatedly distort the novel by
de-emphasizing nature—placing characters always in the foreground—while Hardy's text frequently offers a "cosmic view,"[37]
in which characters appear peripherally or in small scale against
the landscape. Involved in an enterprise that requires "talking
up" the illustrations, Jackson notes the point and then drops it.
I think, however, the weakness of the illustrations in portraying
nature's role in the novel worth pursuing as a clue to more vital
aspects of *Tess*'s involvement with the visual arts and pictorialism, an involvement obscured and even belied by its illustrations, because, as I noted when discussing *David Copperfield*,
nineteenth-century illustrations tend to emphasize plot, action,
and characterization and to de-emphasize point of view and the
semiotic quality of things.

An early critic who noted Hardy's ability to create pictures
which "can later epitomize a whole work in a single memory"
makes a valid point, but one I would make plural: a novel like

Tess includes a number of such "pictures," among the most notable being the panoramic landscapes in which the main characters are, at first, unrecognizable.[38] Consider the following "picture," for me among the most memorable in the novel. It describes Tess and Marian at work in Flintcomb-Ash:[39]

> The swede-field in which she and her companion were set hacking was a stretch of a hundred odd acres, in one patch, on the highest ground of the farm, rising above stony lanchets or lynchets—the outcrop of siliceous veins in the chalk formation, composed of myriads of loose white flints in bulbous, cusped, and phallic shapes. . . . Every leaf of the vegetable having already been consumed, the whole field was in colour a desolate drab; it was a complexion without features, as if a face, from chin to brow, should be only an expanse of skin. The sky wore, in another colour, the same likeness; a white vacuity of countenance with the lineaments gone. So these two upper and nether visages confronted each other all day long, the white face looking down on the brown face, and the brown face looking up at the white face, without anything standing between them but the two girls crawling over the surface of the former like flies.
>
> Nobody came near them, and their movements showed a mechanical regularity; their forms standing enshrouded in Hessian "wroppers"—sleeved brown pinafores, tied behind to the bottom, to keep their gowns from blowing about—scant skirts revealing boots that reached high up the ankles, and yellow sheepskin gloves with gauntlets. The pensive character which the curtained hood lent to their bent heads would have reminded the observer of some early Italian conception of the two Marys.
>
> They worked on hour after hour, unconscious of the forlorn aspect they bore in the landscape, not thinking of the justice of their lot. (p. 253)

Information about Hardy's particular likes or dislikes in the visual arts is unfortunately spotty, or else we might be able to identify precise sources for this pictorial rendering—in Courbet, or Van Gogh, or in Turner's paintings and book illustrations, for example.[40] But even if the source was simply his native

1. *Les Enfants d'Edouard*, Hippolyte Paul Delaroche, 1831
(The Wallace Collection, London)

2. *Boulevard des Capucines, Paris*, Claude Monet, 1973
(The Nelson-Atkins Museum of Art, Kansas City, Missouri;
Acquired through the Kenneth A. and Helen F.
Spencer Foundation Acquisitions Fund)

3. *An Idyll*, Maurice Greiffenhagen, 1891
(Walker Art Gallery, Liverpool)

4. *The Merry Go Round*, Mark Gertler, 1916
(Ben Uri Art Gallery, London)

landscape rather than actual paintings (as we may be sure the source was, in part, given Hardy's "map" of "Wessex"),[41] the visual acuity of the presentation still emerges as both striking and meaningful. In bold, simplified outlines, a painting of the scene would divide roughly in half between the representation of the sky and representation of the earth as "nether and upper visages [that] confronted each other all day long, the white face looking down on the brown face, and the brown face looking up at the white face, without anything standing between them but the two girls crawling over the surface of the former like flies." Although the image of the faces is metaphoric, it can be imagined as a painting. The uniform tone of sky and earth suggests large blocks of unbroken color, approaching, almost, abstract art, except for the presence of the tiny figures.

The pictorial rendering's emphasis on sky owes much, I believe, to the example of artists like Turner, who often emphasize the sky and de-emphasize the human figure, as in, for example, *Snow Storm: Hannibal and his Army Crossing the Alps* (1812, plate 12). Indeed other passages in *Tess* (like the arctic birds passage) have been traced to Turner's influence.[42] Other models for such experiments in Lilliputian human scale—like Piranesi, and Salvador Rosa, muses of the gothic novel—come readily to mind, but Hardy's emphasis on the grandeur of nature is more ominous and threatening than theirs, or even Turner's, with both sky and earth terrifyingly vast, blank, and indifferent. Rather than being stirring and dramatic, this landscape numbs the senses of the figures in the "picture" and includes no reminders of man's aspirations, like the ruins and abbeys frequently included by the earlier visual artists. In visual impact, the sky and field quite genuinely trap and bind the two girls. The fly image—so striking here—repeats an earlier reference (in a rhyme both verbal and visual) to Tess, "not quite sure of her direction," standing "still upon the hemmed expanse of verdant flatness like a fly on a billiard-table of indefinite length, and of no more consequence to the surroundings than that fly" (p. 92). At the base of the "picture" are the "stony lanchets or lynchets" with their strangely phallic shapes—an indication that earth in this novel is less motherly than convention will have it and more threateningly male.

Equally important as the dominance of sky and earth is the anonymity of the figures, even when we focus on them as we might on the slide of a "detail" in a larger work. Thus far in the sequence, the characters remain unnamed, and their garb matches their lack of particularized identity. Voluminously draped and hooded, the women work on "unconscious of the forlorn aspect they bore in the landscape." This last comment marks, I think, one crucial difference between the ways that Hardy uses this pictorial rendering and the ways that James, Woolf, and Lawrence most often use theirs. In the Modern novelists, the "picture" is usually presented *through the character's eyes* and acts upon the consciousness of the character. Indeed, such will be the case for virtually every example from Modern fiction that I will examine in this study. In *Tess*, however, the character remains ignorant of his place in the picture presented to the reader. The characters neither "see" that picture nor "know" anything from it about their "forlorn aspect." The pictorial thus becomes a technique that is part of the author's overt communication with the reader via the narrative voice. No perceptual use of pictorialism as described in the Introduction to this study operates here since the characters are left out of the process of interpretation; and while an ideological or hermeneutic use arguably does operate, the meaning of the picture is essentially given to the reader through the use of didactic language, like the descriptions of the earth as "desolate drab," the sky as a "vacuity," and the girls as "flies."

The hermeneutic processes of insinuation and visual rhyme described in the Introduction, moreover, unfold over the course of the novel, while the meaning of this pictorial representation is altogether given both here and earlier in the novel by linguistic pointers. The pictorial representation quite strikingly summarizes several other sequences in the novel (some pictorial, some not), each of which gives the same interpretive information. One of those other scenes—the portrait of Tess in the verdant field, confused as to her direction and no more significant than a fly—has already been mentioned. Another is the reaping scene at Marlott, which provides ideas about animals, men, and nature identical to those in the scene just examined at Flintcomb-Ash, though in a more mellow landscape.

In Hardy, then, the pictorial usually summarizes information given plainly in the exposition, frequently information given *before* the "pictures." In James, Lawrence, and Woolf, on the other hand, as we shall see, the "picture's" meaning is translated only later and gradually into words and sometimes never glossed at all, but left to the reader's contemplation through the processes I call insinuation and visual rhyme. While both are pictorial, the methods differ fundamentally in sequence, effect, conception of audience, and the extent to which "pictures" are believed to tell fully definable stories.

If I am right about how the pictorial operates in Hardy's novel, its effect falls somewhere between the definition for the reader's visual imagination typical of early fiction's overt references to works of art and of the illustrated novel, and the freer appeal to the reader's visual imagination in, say, Lawrence's best novels. The reader of all but the inferior illustrated version of *Tess* would have to use the visual imagination vigorously to read the book properly, but he would have much of the work of glossing the "pictures" so conceived done for him by the authorial voice. The novel's ideological use of the visual arts and pictorialism is, then, qualified by the glossing of the third-person narrator, with those uses reiterating elements already present in the text rather than encoding something new (an effect comparable to that of illustrations in *David Copperfield*).

VIII

The elements in this chapter, though various, have not been miscellaneous. All have been designed to separate decorative uses of the visual arts from other, more complex and significant uses, especially from uses described as ideological, perceptual, and hermeneutic in the Introduction to this study. Despite the high percentage of characters and language in *Roderick Hudson* and *The Tragic Muse* based on the visual arts, almost every use of the visual arts in these novels emerges as decorative and not as ideological or interpretive. Similarly, references to the visual arts or instances of pictorialism based on historic works of art in Fielding and Radcliffe remain essentially decorative and can—like the inert presence of artist figures or the superficial language of the visual arts—be red herrings in interdisciplinary study. The presence of artist figures, descriptions based on works of art, or references to historical works of art need not, then, always be important in making sense of a novel. The function and effect of such elements always serve as more reliable indicators of their importance than does their mere presence. The point is worth emphasizing because the respect typically accorded the visual arts by literary critics frequently leads us into seeing any reference to the visual arts as especially meaningful.

Two other principles that have emerged from this discussion are worth reiterating for the remainder of this study. First, even persistent references to the visual arts do not guarantee that a novel will be, to any significant extent, pictorial. *Roderick Hudson* and *The Tragic Muse* amply demonstrate that. Uses of the visual arts and uses of pictorialism are separate techniques, although they may occur and frequently do occur in the same novel. Second, as the examples from *Roderick Hudson, The Tragic Muse, The Mysteries of Udolpho, Jane Eyre*, and *David Copperfield* suggest, novels have from very early in their history tended to move toward perceptual uses of the visual arts or pictorialism whenever the author moves into the eye of the perceiver or uses visual stimuli as triggers for the characters' emotions or thoughts or memory (devices more frequent in, though not restricted to, first-person or third-person subjective narration, uncommon forms in the nineteenth century, and devices also frequent in autobiography). But as in the "rhyming pictures" of *Jane Eyre*, sustained perceptual or hermeneutic uses of the visual arts and pictorialism are unlikely without the author's persistent, self-conscious linking of visual stimuli to mental processes, and the highlighting of visual elements through the techniques that I call in the Introduction insinuation and visual rhyme.

Finally, my discussion has tried to show that the discussion of illustrations—as it has commonly been done—has been, if not quite a red herring, then at least only part of what needs to be done. For illustrations involve losses as well as gains for the texts they accompany, reducing the symbolic resonance of the text and sometimes obscuring important qualities, like point of view. They can, moreover, handicap the free appeal to the reader's visual imagination necessary in movement to the far end of the continuum that governs this study. Indeed, several key statements made around the turn of the century suggest that the *decline* of illustrated novels (a casualty of World War I)[43] coincided with other developments in literature that reduced the appeal of illustrations and fostered the kinds of dynamic engagement with the visual arts and pictorialism that we shall see in later chapters, especially those which examine the ideological and interpretive segments of the continuum. In 1898, for example, the poet and leader of the Symbolist movement, Mallarmé, said that "Je suis pour—aucune illustration" (I favor omitting illustrations). His reason: "tout ce qu'évoque un livre devant se passer dans l'esprit du lecteur" (everything that a book evokes must be created in the imagination of the reader).[44] When the possibility arose of having illustrations in the New York Edition of his novels, James discouraged them. He insisted that each volume have only one illustration, a frontispiece, and eventually arranged that the illustration be a photograph of a place or object appropriate to the fiction as an "optical symbol" rather than as a graphic representation. James always resented illustrations to his fiction and, in his preface to *The Golden Bowl*, explained why: the "text putting forth illustrative claims (that is producing an effect of illustration) by its own intrinsic merit," illustrations would "elbow" the text "by another and competitive process." Moreover, said James, "Anything that relieves responsible prose of the duty of being, while placed before us, good enough, interesting enough and, if the question be of picture, pictorial enough, above all *in itself*, does it the worst of services."[45]

Lawrence and Woolf (and other Moderns, like Conrad, Joyce, and Proust) also published their novels without illustrations, in part because (in most cases) their novels appeared when illustrations were no longer the norm.[46] But if they *had* been asked to approve illustrations for their texts, they would probably have shared James's sentiments. For illustrations in nineteenth-century novels imply (sometimes falsely, as I tried to show earlier) the interchangeability of text and picture, the sense in which novels can be a series of pictures and pictures can tell stories as novels do. Modern instances of pictorialism emphasize, on the other hand, the difference between pictures and novels, even when both are narrative and tell stories.

The difference will perhaps be clearer if we try to imagine how we would illustrate a novel like *The Golden Bowl* or *To the Lighthouse* if we were graphic artists commissioned to draw plates for the text. If we followed nineteenth-century precedents, the best we could do would be to present static images of characters in various combinations and settings. But such illustrations would, in an especially obvious way, miss the essence of the novels. For that essence involves not *what* happens, or where it happens, or how the action *looks* so much as how characters feel or what they are thinking at any given moment. And such matters are most aptly rendered in words, not pictures. We shall see in subsequent chapters—as we leave the decorative and move up the continuum that governs this study—that the Modern novel's uses of the visual arts and pictorialism were implicated in the redefinition of the nature of narrative from the nineteenth to the early twentieth centuries,[47] and epitomize in many ways the essence of the Modern novel as written by James, Lawrence, and Woolf.

THREE

THE SISTERS' ARTS: VIRGINIA WOOLF AND VANESSA BELL

Virginia Woolf's sister, Vanessa Bell, provided the model for the heroine of Woolf's second novel, *Night and Day*. In that novel, the heroine, Katharine Hilbery, articulates a principle relevant to current issues of women's need for productive work: "I want to assert myself, and it's difficult, if one hasn't a profession."[1] Neither Virginia nor Vanessa had much cause to echo Katharine's lament. Virginia enjoyed, of course, an extraordinarily brilliant and varied career as publisher, essayist, reviewer, and—above all—as novelist. Vanessa had a less brilliant but still remarkable career as a painter. Vanessa also had, however, something Virginia perceived as a lack in her own life: children, and handsome, talented children at that. In Woolf's novels and in her newly available diaries and letters, it becomes clear that Vanessa posed for Virginia significant conflicts. Readers of Woolf have long recognized the importance of Virginia's mother, Julia Stephen (model for Mrs. Ramsay), in her daughter's life and work.[2] I would like here to explore some of the roles that Virginia's other beloved female relative, Vanessa, played in Virginia's attitudes toward her own work, toward the visual arts that constituted her sister's arena, and especially the connections between the two. I will, therefore, need to explore aspects of Woolf's biography—like the conflict in her mind between the value of career versus that of having children—before making clear how this biographical material pertains to my topic of the visual arts and pictorialism in novels.

II

The richest sources for investigating Vanessa's roles in Virginia's life are, without doubt, Woolf's diaries and letters. Though incalculably valuable and suggestive, however, neither autobiographical document nor the two together tell the whole, the complete, story. The early diaries and letters are marked by a relative lack of color in Virginia's early life and are generally of less interest than the later. In Woolf's most productive years, however, an increasing guardedness enters the entries and letters. Woolf's sense that the documents belonged to a great writer and might well become public began, I believe, to enter their composition. Though casually written, the diaries do not, for example, record very often deep feelings about Leonard and Vanessa, the two people undoubtedly closest to Woolf in her lifetime. Either she did not conceive of a diary as the place to record feelings about relatives, or she expected that the diaries and letters would eventually be read by Leonard and others— as in fact happened—and, therefore, to some extent censored her entries. We also know of other self-censorings: Woolf's diaries are, for example, far less frank in their account of her affair with Vita Sackville-West than are Vita's own.

The letters present even greater problems of reliability. Almost always playful in tone, they rarely allow the reader to say with certainty that *here* Virginia was really serious. Crucial figures like Leonard and Vanessa were, moreover, so often present in Woolf's life that her most significant exchanges with them probably occurred in conversation, not in writing. Vanessa's letters (unpublished, but available in original form to scholars)[3] make the limitations of the correspondence clearer than Woolf's. Repeatedly, she suggests that "it is difficult to go into details in writing" or postpones discussion of something important until "when I see you."[4] Interesting as Woolf's letters are, indeed, few exchanges impress the reader as really frank, really honest. One of the few is the remarkable exchange in the mid-twenties between Woolf and the Raverats, Jacques and Gwen, shortly before and after Jacques' death from a lingering illness. It seems likely that the pressure of death prompted Woolf's openness in this exchange, and since many of her comments in these letters concern Vanessa and the trade-offs between career and children, they will be quoted later.

In the volume of the *Diary* that corresponds to the writing of *To the Lighthouse* and *The Waves* (Volume Three), several issues dominate. The first two issues are financial matters (how much each book cost to produce, how much each book made in profits, how those profits would be spent), and relationships with servants, especially the troublesome Nelly. The third issue, of most interest here, is the intensity of Vanessa's presence in Woolf's consciousness and the extent to which Vanessa seemed to her sister a "complete" woman. Woolf's comparisons of herself to her sister focus on Vanessa's possession of children and bespeak genuine pain. In 1926, for example, while finishing *To the Lighthouse*, Woolf wrote: "Oh its beginning, its coming— the horror—physically like a painful wave swelling about the heart—tossing me up. I'm unhappy unhappy! Down—God, I wish I were dead. Pause. But why am I feeling this? Let me watch the wave rise. I watch. Vanessa. Children. Failure. Yes; I detect that. Failure failure. (The wave rises)."[5] A few days before, Woolf blamed herself for her childlessness: "A little more self control on my part, & we might have had a boy of 12, a girl of 10: This always rakes me wretched in the early hours" (p. 107). Ironically, though not accidentally, such powerful statements of failure coincide with her most brilliant and creative period as a writer—the years in which *To the Lighthouse* was finished and *The Waves* begun. Not accidentally, because these were also the years when Woolf entered her mid-forties and knew that Leonard's decision that they not have children was irrevocable.

Often, Woolf recorded events in Vanessa's life with attention to things missed in her own, as in the following: "Angelica goes to school for the first time today I think; & I daresay Nessa is crying to herself—one of the emotions I shall never know—a child, one's last child—going to school, & so ending the 21 years of Nessa's children—a great stretch of life; how much fuller than I can guess—imagine all the private scenes, the quarrels, the happiness . . . as they grew up" (p. 255). Virginia here reminds me of Lily Briscoe, fascinated by the Ramsays but unable (despite her intelligence and imagination) to conceive what they say to each other when alone. Most tellingly, Woolf perceived herself as dependent on her sister as her sister was not dependent on her. With Vanessa returned after an absence, Woolf wrote: "My earth is watered again . . . as if her happiness were a million or two in the bank" (III, p. 186). Vanessa here shares one of Mrs. Ramsay's symbols—the fountain, the balm and center of life. The sharing of images suggests what the letters confirm: Mrs. Ramsay was modelled not just after Julia Stephen, but also after Vanessa Bell. Shortly after sending Vanessa a copy of *To the Lighthouse*, Woolf confided to her sister, "Probably there is a great deal of you in Mrs. Ramsay; though, in fact, I think you and mother are very different in my mind."[6]

Woolf's emphasis on her sister's happiness in the above quotation overlooks—as, indeed, do her letters and diary entries in general—the oddities and strains in Vanessa's life. Vanessa was, after all, separated from a philandering husband who still remained her husband for all public purposes. She was living with Duncan Grant, who was to prove a lifelong companion, but who was also to take homosexual lovers throughout their life together—a situation Vanessa was able to manage by befriending the young men in question, but one which caused great unhappiness and trouble. Although Grant was the father of Bell's daughter, Angelica, the child was kept ignorant of her parentage until young adulthood, a situation which laid the seeds of dissent between mother and daughter when Angelica ultimately became the lover and then the wife of Bunny Garnett, who had been Duncan's devoted lover at the time Angelica was born. The most comprehensive study of Vanessa Bell to date is Frances Spalding's biography, and it puts emphasis on the turbulence and disappointments in Vanessa's life and notes—in connection

with typically adoring and admiring quotations like that above—
that Virginia tended not to see the problems in Vanessa's personal life, perhaps because her sister's "outwards serenity pre-
vented even those close to her from seeing that she was not
always happy."[7] An equally plausible reason, I think, was that
Woolf's lack of passion for men would have made her relatively
indifferent to the facts of Vanessa's sexual life. What she envied
most was not her sister's involvement with men like Roger Fry
and Duncan Grant (though she was capable of a mighty and
lacerating flirtation with Clive Bell in the years after his marriage
to Vanessa), but the general plenitude of her sister's life, a plenitude that, in Virginia's mind, centered on her children.

Woolf's laments over her childlessness suggest that the truer
status of career in her emotions was defined not just by Katharine
Hilbery's remark in *Night and Day* about the need for fruitful
work, but also by the novel's subsequent treatment of careerism.
In the novel, Katharine breaks her engagement to the effete
William Rodney (based on Clive Bell) and turns instead to Ralph
Denham, her social inferior, but a man who relishes her idiosyncracies rather than wishes them gone. Ralph will, presumably,
foster Katharine's ambition to be a great mathematician (a stand-
in, to Woolf's mind, for the headiness of abstract art).[8] But the
whole issue of Katharine's career really drops out of the novel
after Katharine and Ralph announce themselves as a couple. The
real career woman in the novel, Mary Datchet, loved Ralph
Denham but lost him to Katharine. Late one night, Ralph and
Katharine contemplate the light in Mary's window:

> "That is the light in Mary's room" said Ralph. . . .
> "Is she alone, working at this time of night? What is she
> working at?" she wondered. "Why should we interrupt her?"
> she asked passionately. "What have we got to give her? She's
> happy too," she added, "She has her work." Her voice shook
> slightly, and the light swam like an ocean of gold behind her
> tears. . . .
> They stood for some moments, looking at the illuminated

blinds, an expression to them both of something impersonal and serene in the spirit of the woman within, working out her plans far into the night—her plans for the good of a world that none of them were ever to know. (pp. 505-06)

Poor Mary: work is really a kind of booby prize, after all. The people having fun, having love, are outside looking up at, but not wishing to be, conscientious Mary, scribbling her feminist tracts.

III

Parallel volumes of the *Letters* provide further information, both about the issues of career and children and about how Virginia regarded her sister's career as a painter. Volume Two of the *Letters* begins with the newly wed Virginia Woolf confident that her marriage will produce children and announcing to both Vanessa and Violet Dickinson of a baby that "we want to have one" (p. 23). By the end of this volume (the year 1922) and Virginia's realization that she will be childless, an unhealthy— though teasing—emphasis on Vanessa's maternity emerged. Virginia rhapsodized about Vanessa's pregnancy with Angelica (see p. 261) and she made several comments cast so as to suggest that the coming baby would be her own child and not merely her niece. On the matter of the baby's gender, for example, Woolf said, "I should prefer the variety of a daughter—how I should adore her!" (letter to Vanessa, 11, p. 299). Or again, with a playfulness that seems excessive, Woolf warned her sister: "I want to set on foot a scheme of mine which I may tell you is to confuse her mind from the first as to her maternity; she is going to think me something more than an Aunt—not quite a father perhaps, but with a hand (to put it delicately) in her birth" (11, p. 335). During the same period, she played odd games about being Vanessa's child herself (see 11, p. 312), or about being "the Ape" desirous of kissing Vanessa's "most secluded parts" (11, p. 124).

Volume Three of the *Letters*, like the parallel volume of the *Diary*, shows Virginia Woolf wrestling with the now recognized fact of childlessness. She repeated to Jacques Raverat her sense, so frequent in the diaries, that Vanessa's life, much richer than her own, caused Vanessa to neglect her. Her sister, she complained,

> often shocks me by her complete indifference to all my floating loves and jealousies, but with such a life, packed like a cabinet of drawers, Duncan, children, painting, Roger—how can she budge an inch or find a cranny of room for anyone? (III, p. 164)

Again, after reading Jacques Raverat's last letter to her and hearing of his death, she wrote to Gwen Raverat to say how important it was to her that Jacques had praised her last novel, *Mrs. Dalloway*:

> I don't think you would believe how it moves me that you and Jacques should have been reading Mrs. Dalloway, and liking it. I'm awfully vain I know; and I was on pins and needles about sending it to Jacques; and now I feel exquisitely relieved; not flattered: but one does want that side of one to be acceptable— I was going to have written to Jacques about his children, and about my having none—I mean these efforts of mine to communicate with people are partly childlessness, and the horror that sometimes overcomes me. (III, p. 172)

In her next letter, she reported that her prolonged flirtation with Clive Bell early in her sister's marriage (the period of greatest strain between the sisters) "turned more of a knife in me than anything else has ever done" (III, p. 172).[9]

Virginia's comments to Vanessa about her children must have been even more persistent and intense than the letters show. Tired of it all, Vanessa wrote to Virginia: "I wonder how you'd really like the problem of children added to your existence. I don't feel at all equal to dealing with it myself."[10] To which Virginia replied, "I'm sure . . . that I should make a vile mother

... motherhood seems to me destructive and limiting" (III, p. 366). Throughout their lives, in fact, Vanessa did not present motherhood to her sister as eminently desirable. During her first pregnancy, Vanessa wrote: "I am honestly terrified sometimes of the responsibilities of having any children. I'm not sure it doesn't mean having the most terrible millstone round one's neck."[11] After the birth, she anticipated that Virginia would have lots of ammunition for ridiculing her as someone who was "losing all her individuality and becoming the usual domestic mother." After her second child, Quentin's, birth, Vanessa wrote to her sister, "If ever I have another baby, which God forbid, I shall give it ten months instead of nine in which to arrive."[12] Perhaps drawing upon her dual authority as elder sister and experienced mother, however, Vanessa frankly offered Woolf advice on suitors, marriage, and children, telling the newly married Virginia that the question of children usually settles itself and wondering, in the middle teens, "why Leonard has gradually come to think childbearing so dangerous."[13] Years after a major breakdown by Virginia had shelved the issue of children permanently, Vanessa told Virginia that she need not "regret that your nephews and nieces aren't your offspring. There seems to me to be an added excitement in the fact that you're round the corner and not in the house."[14]

Heeding her sister, Virginia knew that the business of motherhood can absorb the personality and impede professional accomplishment. And she duly noted Vanessa's diapers, and bottles, and fatigue, and trouble with governesses. At times, moreover, she questioned the value of both career and children: "there is nothing—nothing for any of us. Work, reading and writing are all disguises; and relations with people. Yes, even having children would be useless" (Diary, III, p. 232). Note, however, the force of the "even" in the sentence just quoted.

In later years (those after 1930) Woolf felt increasingly able to assert her greater professional success against Vanessa's more varied life (an assertion Vanessa entirely accepted). But Vanessa remained the adored, the aloof, the sought-after, the powerful

in Virginia's conception of her. Tellingly, Virginia's characteristic stance toward her sister altered significantly in her letters
only late in their relationship, with the great trouble in Vanessa's
life as a mother—the death of her son Julian in the Spanish
Civil War.

The letters also provide a continuing commentary on how
the sisters regarded each other's careers. Each invariably supported the other strongly, but each was also quick to suspect
her sister of secret and devastating criticisms. Virginia frequently
called upon Vanessa to illustrate the jackets for her books (*Kew
Gardens* was, in fact, decorated throughout by Vanessa) and to
provide decorative items for her home—testimony to Woolf's
confidence in her sister's art. She reported with pleasure having
heard Vanessa called "the best [living] woman painter," noting
that "I like you to be praised, chiefly because it seems to prove
that I must be a good writer" (*Letters*, III, p. 34). Oddly, however,
comments about Bell's art often circle around to Virginia herself,
as in the letter just quoted. For example, in 1928, Woolf praised
one of Vanessa's paintings and then wondered whether she could
reproduce the effect of the painting in words (*Letters*, III, p.
498). Or, in 1937, she wrote to Vanessa: "I thought the show
[at the Le Fevre Gallery] a great triumph. ... 'What a very
gifted woman your sister is!' as an unknown lady remarked.
Yes, I'm jealous" (*Letters*, IV, p. 126).

In one of the most significant exchanges, what Vanessa described as Virginia's "faculty of being able to create an atmosphere of tense thundery gloom" is evident.[15] Virginia wrote her
sister about a show, in 1926, at the Leicester Galleries:

> It is my opinion you want. What I think is this: there is a divinely
> lovely landscape of yours of Charleston: one of flashing brilliance,
> of sunlight crystallised, of diamond durability. This I consider
> your masterpiece. I do not think the big picture of Angelica, etc.
> in the garden quite succeeds. I expect the problem of empty spaces,
> and how to model them, has rather baffled you. There are flat

passages so that the design is not completely comprehended. . . .
A mistress of the brush—you are now undoubtedly that; but still
I think the problems of design on a large scale slightly baffle you.
(*Letters*, III, pp. 270-71)

With, once again, her characteristic doubling back to herself,
Woolf ended: "But I was hugely impressed, and kept on saying
that your genius as a painter, though rather greater than I like,
does still shed a ray on mine. I mean, people will say, what a
gifted couple! Well: it would have been nicer had they said:
Virginia had all the gifts; dear old Nessa was a domestic character—Alas, alas, they'll never say that now" (*Letters*, III, p.
271). In this letter, too, the idea of a trade-off between professional and domestic success emerges clearly.

Apparently dependent on her sister's praise and sensitive to
her sister's criticism—though not as dependent or as sensitive
as Virginia herself—Vanessa complained. And her complaints
were justified: in the above letter Woolf attacked, after all, Bell's
intelligence as a painter and her overall sense of design, praising
her essentially as a clever craftsman. Somewhat disingenuously,
Virginia explained herself in her next letter: "I'm much amused
you should cast a days thought after my criticism—considering
how it was fired off with my feet on the fender in 6 seconds
precisely. I see I did not express my enormous admiration of
both your gifts: which was even more direct and ardent than
usual. No pictures now painted give me so much pleasure"
(*Letters*, III, p. 274). The exchange ended there, and yet one
wonders whether Vanessa could truly have been satisfied. Note
that Virginia implies that she gave her comments on Vanessa's
paintings only "6 seconds" of thought, and that Virginia found
"pleasure" but not "art" or "genius" in her sister's work. While
Virginia's work was—as time has shown—the greater, Virginia's comments still seem pinched and ungenerous.

In contrast, Vanessa's letters uniformly and generously tes-
tified to her faith in her sister's genius, even before much evidence of that genius existed in print. Vanessa went so far as to

grant Virginia the "special exemption" from women's laws sought by Lily Briscoe: she several times told her sister that a writer of such genius need not, after all, marry, even as she encouraged the marriage to Leonard Woolf, whom she described as "the only person I have ever seen whom I can imagine the right husband for you."[16] Virginia still vividly expected Vanessa's disapproval, however, even when such disapproval failed to come. When she sent Vanessa a copy of *To the Lighthouse*, she was especially anxious. Vanessa could, after all, have proven an especially harsh critic: she knew the originals for Mr. and Mrs. Ramsay as well as Virginia herself did, and she knew much about Lily's vocation in the novel, painting. In a letter of May 15, 1927, Woolf created an extraordinary dialogue between Vanessa and Duncan Grant in which the two bemoan the book as insufferably boring. In actuality, Vanessa's response (received by Virginia a few days later) contained the fullest, most sincere praise:

> in the first part of the book you have given a portrait of mother which is more like her to me than anything I could ever have conceived of as possible. It is almost painful to have her so raised from the dead. You have made one feel the extraordinary beauty of her character, which must be the most difficult thing in the world to do. It was like meeting her again with oneself grown up and on equal terms and it seems to me the most astonishing feat of creation to have been able to see her in such a way. ... I am excited and thrilled and taken into another world as one only is by a great work of art.... (*Letters*, 111, appendix, pp. 572-73)

Of Woolf's use of Lily as painter, Vanessa said this: "surely Lily Briscoe must have been rather a good painter—before her time perhaps, but with great gifts really? No, we didn't laugh at the bits about painting" (p. 573). Vanessa's praises were thus all that Virginia could have desired. They never had the double-edge of Virginia's praises, nor did they raise the issues of jealousy, competition, and power as Virginia's frequently did. The most that one can say against Vanessa is that she sometimes underestimated her sister's desire for a husband and, later, for children. But even that underestimate seems innocent and without malice.

The fascination of Vanessa for Virginia and her sense of loving competition with her has several parallels in the fiction, most notably in *To the Lighthouse*. In that novel, Mrs. Ramsay poses for the unmarried Lily Briscoe a question similar to that posed by Vanessa for Virginia: is my work enough when compared to *all that*? Critics have, correctly but too simply, tended to see Lily as based largely on Woolf herself: their ages are similar, so too are their attitudes toward Mrs. Ramsay, and both are artists. And yet Lily is not a writer like Virginia Woolf; she is a painter, like Vanessa. I am not suggesting that we glibly substitute the idea that Vanessa is Lily for the more current idea that Lily represents Woolf herself; Woolf's identification of Vanessa with Mrs. Ramsay would make such a substitution illogical at best. But each fictional woman—Lily, like Mrs. Ramsay—is a composite of autobiographical imperatives, the remembered attributes of more than one person, and sheer invention. And it is suggestive to note that Lily's concerns as a painter are very like Vanessa's, especially since she triumphs as a painter in ways that Vanessa, in Woolf's opinion, did not.

At the end of *To the Lighthouse*, Lily achieves some significant things. First, she manages to absorb the meaning of Mrs. Ramsay while maintaining her independence, an achievement that comes from recognizing that Mrs. Ramsay created harmonies in human relationships similar to the harmonies Lily creates in paint. Second, she finally finishes her painting by drawing a line down its center, a line that connects the mass on one side (the house and the step where Mrs. Ramsay had sat with James) with the mass on the other (the trees that border the garden).

Woolf's overall conception of Lily's painting owes much, I believe, to Bell's art, especially to her use of verticals. One of the few critics to comment on the formal qualities of Vanessa's paintings, Richard Morphet, notes that she "seems to have had an obsession with verticals; her work gives the impression that even in subjects so far from built structures as portraits and still lifes, she would seize any opportunity that reasonably presented itself of introducing a vertical into a painting."[17] As in Lily's painting, the vertical line establishes a balance between representation (of, in Lily's painting, Mrs. Ramsay and her garden) and abstract meaning (in Lily's painting, the harmony of things). For Bell, the vertical similarly served as "one means of directing attention to a representational picture's equal reality as a two-dimensional *design*, tied to a flat, rectilinear surface."[18] Here, as elsewhere in Vanessa's work, the formal problems addressed by the painter have analogues for the novelist—for example, in Woolf's careful explorations of the balance between mimesis and stylization in her fiction. Bell explored the use of verticals in paintings like *Street Corner Conversation* (1913) and *Abstract Painting* (1914, plate 13).[19] They also structure a painting of 1908 that may have directly influenced Woolf's creation of Lily's painting, *Adrian and Virginia Stephen on the Lawn* (c. 1909-1910, plate 14). In this painting, Adrian and Virginia sit in a garden and the center is occupied by a two-story building, rendered in a way that emphasizes its verticality.

In a recent article, Harry R. Harrington astutely paused to consider just what completing Lily's painting involves for the artist.[20] It involves, in fact, superimposing views seen from two different directions into one harmonious whole. That is, Lily paints what she sees when facing *away* from her easel in search of Mr. Ramsay—the lighthouse—as though it exists in the scene that she sees as she faces her easel and looks *toward* the house. A good Modern artist, Lily places a lighthouse in the middle of a garden in the interest of form and in defiance of traditional realism. Her act successfully solves two problems that often vexed Modern artists: first, how to combine two or more perspectives harmoniously, in a way true to form and subject, and, second, how to fill the middle of a picture, flattening it, and making it two-dimensional in a way that would clearly announce its modernity, its difference from traditional art in love with the laws of perspective.

Interestingly, Virginia criticized Vanessa's work for having failed to solve these problems in a letter, previously quoted, written while she finished *To the Lighthouse*. Her criticism was, as I have discussed, sufficiently harsh to have flattened Virginia had Vanessa criticized her writing in such basic ways. With regard to an unidentified painting of Angelica and objects in a garden—perhaps similar to a painting sometimes mistaken for it, the much earlier *The Tub* (1917, plate 15), which used Mary Hutchinson as model—Woolf had written: "I expect that the problem of empty spaces and how to model them, has rather baffled you. There are flat passages, so that the design is not completely comprehended." Note that the painting on which Woolf commented—like that Lily paints—is of figures in a garden. It explores, moreover, a technical problem that Vanessa had repeatedly tackled in her career: filling the canvas without having the main subject located in the center of the canvas. Once again, there may be an analogy here between Woolf's fictional and Bell's painterly techniques. Woolf's effort to provide a portrait of Mrs. Ramsay in this novel through many different eyes, without in any usual sense having her serve as heroine, composes the novel, in a sense, around an absent center. She underscores the venturesomeness of her technique by having the "heroine" die midway through the novel. Paintings like *Studland Beach* (1913-1914) and *The Bedroom* (1912) by Bell use precisely this off-center composition, relying on color and line to fill the canvas and balance the eye's attention between the main subject and the overall design.[21] To tell Vanessa that her "middles" were insufficiently modelled was, therefore, to criticize a central and important technical aspect of Bell's art. Lily's feat in the novel, moreover, allows Lily to successfully master problems that Vanessa (according to Virginia) had not mastered in ten or more years of work. Was Vanessa's art a direct source for Lily's? And is there some oneupsmanship in Lily's solving problems that Vanessa did not (according to her sister) solve with real paint and canvas? I believe we can safely answer "yes" to both questions.

Vanessa never trespassed into Virginia's territory, literature. But Virginia made numerous incursions into Vanessa's province, painting. In novels like *The Years* and *The Waves*, as we have seen, description and metaphor (especially in the prologues to each section) draw upon Impressionist and Post-Impressionist art. Woolf creates, in words, effects previously realized only in paint, as she borrows the Impressionist sense of color, light, and temporality. As I discussed in Chapter One, Woolf also wrote on the visual arts, and, in her diary, she repeatedly referred to her books as "canvases." Moreover, as was discussed in Chapter One and will be explored further in Chapter Four, during the 1920's Woolf arrived at a theory of memory as essentially pictorial that informs both her diary and her novels. Bernard in *The Waves* best articulates this theory of thought and memory as pictorial when he notes that "visual impressions often communicate . . . briefly statements we shall in time come to uncover and coax into words." And Lily Briscoe provides extended examples of this process in Part III of *To the Lighthouse* as she "coaxes" into meaning moments partially rendered in paint or remembered as "pictures." I shall have more to say about both these instances, in a non-biographical context, in Chapter Four.

In Woolf's conception, the balance between the visually conceived object and the verbally articulated meaning is extremely taut. In one sense, the picture is superior to words insofar as it can instantaneously communicate complexes of ideas (a crucial aspect of visual art to theorists like Lessing). But, in another sense, the picture will remain private and mute unless its meaning is unpacked in Woolf's medium, words. Significantly, Lily is only able to have her final vision and to express it in paint by unpacking the meaning of her earlier painting. She must complete a verbal process through which she understands the essence of Mrs. Ramsay as a purple triangle, the symbol of harmony and balance, before she is ready to complete another picture which will again encode verbal processes into a single image.

One could argue, moreover, that Lily's painting would have little meaning for the reader—certainly not enough to end the novel triumphantly—if we did not have all the viewpoints on its meaning and significance given us by the novel.

It is likely, then, that the sister arts became one field on which Virginia worked out her sense of competition with Vanessa. For, while Virginia's use of the visual arts no doubt pays tribute to the importance of Vanessa's art, it also, in the instances I have given, tends to *appropriate* Vanessa's art and *absorb* it into Woolf's own. It uses the theory of painting as grist for Woolf's fictional mill. Virginia could not really appropriate Vanessa's children, "confuse them as to their maternity" as she jokingly planned, though she was a lavishly giving aunt. But without real malice she could appropriate Vanessa's work and thereby be compensated, at some level, for what she felt was the greater plenitude of her sister's life. If, at the end of *To the Lighthouse*, Lily entirely accepts her own path and relinquishes her fascination with Mrs. Ramsay as a supreme mother, Lily's solution was not simply Woolf's own. The diaries and letters show Woolf wrestling to uphold her belief in the value of her work during and after the completion of *To the Lighthouse*. They also show that when doubts about the value of her work came most strongly, they came via Vanessa and Vanessa's children.

My exploration of this biographically motivated use of the visual arts skirts areas psychoanalytic, and I feel in some danger of contributing to the notion that Virginia Woolf was a poor neurotic wretch. That is not at all my intention. For Virginia's loving rivalry with her sister and her ambivalence over the relative worth of career and children seem to me quite normal, especially for a writer who, in *A Room of One's Own*, correctly notes how rare was the woman of literary achievement who was also a wife, and how even rarer was the woman of literary achievement who was also a mother. Moreover, many of the letters and diary entries quite frankly raise her possible envy of Vanessa and her use of professional matters as consolation for her childlessness. Not *all* of what I have said in this chapter would, then, surprise Virginia Woolf.

Another pair of women in Woolf's novels share a conflict similar to that of Virginia and her sister and express the ambivalence of their relationship. I am thinking of Susan and Jinny in *The Waves*. Jinny is the cosmopolite, whose career is that of a brilliant society woman; Susan is the homebody who farms and walks the fields with her sons. When the two are reunited at a dinner party after many years, they assess each other's appearance. Jinny feels a reproach to her way of life in the depth of Susan's eyes and in the honest roughness of her hands. Susan hides her hands, with their "square-tipped fingernails," under the table, ashamed of her domesticity before Jinny's elegance and beautiful dress. Like Jinny's relationship to Susan, Virginia's with her sister involved a "hatred almost indistinguishable from love." Their love was openly expressed, especially by Virginia. Their sense of competition came out more obliquely, in the battlefields of the heart and between the lines of Woolf's letters, diaries, and novels. And Woolf's uses of the visual arts reflect both her love for and envy of her painter-sister.

FOUR

ART, IDEOLOGIES, AND IDEALS IN FICTION:
THE CONTRASTING CASES OF
VIRGINIA WOOLF AND D. H. LAWRENCE

As we saw in Chapter One, both Virginia Woolf and D. H.
Lawrence thought highly of and deeply about the visual arts.
Woolf's interests centered not so much in actual works of art
as in ideas about art associated with movements after Impressionism, ideas she could integrate with her evolving theory of
fiction. Lawrence's passions derived from actual paintings, and
he frequently denounced what he found in Western art, in its
past and, most especially, in its present, and often used his strong
ideas about Modern art in his novels. Given the intense, though
different, involvement of the two, we might expect their uses
of the visual arts and of pictorialism in fiction to be ideological:
such uses should have to do with the central themes and forms
of their novels, and with their informing views of consciousness,
society, and reality. And, in fact, such is the case for both authors
in several of their best volumes. But the ideological implications
of such references and instances of pictorialism differ radically
in Woolf and Lawrence. Congruently with her admiration for
Modern art, Woolf alludes to such art when touching upon states
of mind that she admired, and Modern art frequently provides
the idiom in which she can express some of her ideal values.
Congruently with his suspicions about Modern art, Lawrence
most frequently alludes to such art to embody things that he
disliked about contemporary mores and culture, and he tends
to use linguistic, unpictorial language as the idiom to express
ideal moments in his novels.

I I

One of Woolf's first pieces, a short descriptive essay with rudimentary plot, called *Kew Gardens*, shows quite dramatically how the visual arts helped her to shape her ideas about nature and facilitated her development as a writer. In the Introduction, I noted that *Kew Gardens* stimulated discussion by Arnold Bennett and by Woolf herself about the possibility that the methods of the Impressionists could influence the methods of the writer. Precisely such an influence operates in this short piece, set in the gardens that we know from Woolf's letters she always remembered in a rich, finished, visual impression.[1] Indeed, in some editions, the essay is a composite work, accompanied by decorative borders of floral and abstract shapes done by Vanessa Bell. The piece begins with a sketch of nature that recalls the Impressionists, the following description of flowers: "The petals were voluminous enough to be stirred by the summer breeze, and when they moved, the red blue and yellow lights passed one over the other, staining an inch of brown earth beneath with a spot of the most intricate color."[2] The sentence emphasizes color and light and endows light with the ability to alter the coloration of brown earth. Its focus on a single inch of ground distorts a more panoramic "realistic" view, and its "intricate spots of color" remind us of those created by the Impressionists and Post-Impressionists, and especially those of Seurat.

The passage proceeds to introduce images that stay with Woolf until late in her career, recurring prominently, for example, in the prologues to *The Waves*:

> The light fell upon the smooth grey back of a pebble, or the shell of a snail with its brown circular veins, or, falling into a raindrop, it expanded with such intensity of red, blue and yellow the thin walls of water that one expected them to burst and disappear. Instead, the drop was left in a second silver grey once more, and the light now settled upon the flesh of a leaf, revealing the branching thread of fibre beneath the surface, and again it moved on

and spread its illumination in the vast green spaces beneath the
dome of the heart shaped and tongue shaped leaves. (p. 68)

The pebbles, the snail shell, and the fibres of the leaf are all
objects that recur frequently in Woolf's writing, assuming over
the span of her career a rich variety of associations. As Lisa
Ruddick notes in another context—when discussing the tendency of a small number of objects to reappear in the texture of
To the Lighthouse—"the constant return to a few physical props
. . . allows each object to become irreversibly combined in the
reader's mind. Each time the object reappears in the narrative
it triggers simultaneously a multiplicity of associations."[3]

The same process Ruddick describes for the reader of *To the
Lighthouse* also applies more generally to Woolf's novels and to
the way her mind works: she returns over and over to certain
objects during the course of her career, especially to objects whose
visual memory could stimulate whole trains of thought. Many
of those objects, like the fibres of the leaf, are associated for
characters like the child Louis in *The Waves* and the boy George
in *Between the Acts* with the oceanic state of oneness with nature.[4]
Also remarkable in this quotation from *Kew Gardens* is what
we might call its microscopic focus. The ray of light guides us
from item to item, demanding our attention as light highlighting
small details might in a painting. And light has the same ability
to transform objects previously noted in my discussion of the
prologues in *The Waves*; here, for example, the green of the
leaves colors the air beneath it.

The sentence which ends the paragraph from which I have
been quoting makes a crucial shift from nature to people:

> Then the breeze stirred rather more briskly overhead and the
> colour was flashed into the air above, into the eyes of the men
> and women who walk in Kew Gardens in July.
>
> The figures of these men and women straggled past the flower-
> bed with a curiously irregular movement not unlike that of the
> white and blue butterflies who crossed the turf in zig-zag flights
> from bed to bed. (pp. 68-69)

The sentences juxtapose men and nature deliberately and with calculation. Repeated such associations in the pages that follow reinforce our initial sense that Woolf means to assert the equality and identity of nature and human beings as components of a visually conceived scene ruled and dominated by light.

Two other passages from *Kew Gardens* make essentially the same point, also in an idiom probably suggested to Woolf by Impressionist art and by discussions of such art to which Bloomsbury exposed her:

> Thus one couple after another with much the same irregular and aimless movement passed the flower-bed and were enveloped in layer after layer of green-blue vapour, in which at first their bodies had substance and a dash of colour but later both substance and colour dissolved in the green-blue atmosphere. (p. 77)

> Yellow and black, pink and snow white, shapes of all these colours, men, women, and children were spotted for a second upon the horizon, and then, seeing the breadth of yellow that lay upon the grass, they wavered and sought shade beneath the trees, dissolving like drops of water in the yellow and green atmosphere, staining it faintly with red and blue. (p. 78)

Characters and atmosphere, human beings and light, have equal weight and solidity—or the lack of weight and solidity—in these quotations. As in Impressionist art, objects bathed in light dissolve in the eye of the spectator. And the passage emphasizes adjectives of color in its attempt to cross the boundaries of the visual arts (a consequence Mukařovský sees as frequent in such attempts).

Woolf's verbal "pictures" seem unequivocally guilty of the sins that Lawrence found so prominent in the work of the Impressionists: the reduction of the body to sheer light, its dissolution in the general atmosphere, as in the final metaphor of the quotation from *Kew Gardens*. We can easily imagine, then, Woolf and Lawrence reacting differently to a painting like Monet's *Boulevard des Capucines, Paris* (1873, plate 2), a centerpiece of the Impressionist ethos, discussed in the Introduction to this study. Woolf would probably find in the painting's placement of human bodies on the same level with inanimate things like trees and carriages the visual embodiment of an idea that haunts her psyche and her novels: the idea, as expressed by Mrs. Ramsay, that "if one was alone, one leant to inanimate things; trees, streams, flowers; felt they expressed one; felt they became one; felt they knew one, in a sense were one."[5] Indeed, it is entirely possible that such paintings prodded her own ability to express this mystic sense in her novels and to sometimes identify it in sections of *The Waves* with the undifferentiated flow of urban traffic. Lawrence, on the other hand, would react antithetically to the same implications of the painting. Like the hostile French critic Leroi, he would insist that men be men and background be background, that perhaps not even trees and carriages and certainly not men should be "innumerable black tongue-lickings" as they appear in Monet's painting. The representation of human beings as though they were inanimate things seemed to Lawrence symptomatic of the illnesses that he diagnosed in Modern culture, not expressive of mystic, transcendent states of mind.

These differences between Woolf and Lawrence are, I believe, absolutely fundamental in comprehending both their differing reactions to Modern art and the different uses to which they put the visual arts and pictorialism in their novels. Woolf found in the abstracting tendencies of Impressionist, Post-Impressionist, and later art the visual equivalents to deeply felt aspects of her own philosophy, aspects of which we may justly call mystical. Lawrence found in the same art the downgrading of the vital, distinct individual that was for him the most sinister aspect of modern culture. Even when rendering states of mind similar to that felt by Mrs. Ramsay, therefore, Lawrence rarely merges the individual with nature. Indeed, the perceiving mind may be awed by the vastness of nature, but it remains separate from and aware of nature, as in this moment from *The Rainbow*, when Tom Brangwen experiences the sky as his child is being born:

A great, scalding peace went over him, burning his heart and his entrails, passing off into the infinite. . . . But his heart in torture was at peace, his bowels were glad. He went downstairs, and to the door outside, lifted his face to the rain, and felt the darkness striking unseen and steadily upon him.

The swift, unseen threshing of the night upon him silenced him and he was overcome. He turned away indoors, humbly. There was the infinite world, eternal, unchanging, as well as the world of life.[6]

The passage is remarkable in its evocation of the infinite "eternal, unchanging world" sensed also by Mrs. Ramsay, but equally remarkable in its presentation of Tom's emotions as the central control of the passage and in its crediting of "the world of life" even when faced with the humbling infinite. When exploring one relationship of Lawrence to the visual arts, Jack Stewart notes the expressionist mode frequent in Lawrence, stressing the emotional perception of landscape at moments like the one above in *The Rainbow* and noting words (like "threshing" for the sky) that evoke the expressionist skies of Van Gogh. Stewart's first point is persuasive, but his second point is insufficiently grounded in what I have called the documentary mode. Lawrence had extremely mixed feelings about Van Gogh. He was impressed by the painter's quest after the absolute, and yet "worried" by the painter's "surging earth." The artist's landscapes were among the "lumpy" Post-Impressionist landscapes he disliked (see Chapter One), and his use of expressionist images would, therefore, be more complex than Stewart implies.[7]

More significant, however, in limiting the applicability of any analogy to the visual arts is the scene's emotional, not visual, emphasis. The passage insists on the nonvisual quality of Tom's experience: Tom "*felt* the darkness striking *unseen* upon him"; he feels the "swift, *unseen* quality of the night"; even that Van Goghesque "threshing" sky is "unseen." The words stressed distance the experience from visual stimuli and frustrate any attempt to read the scene as pictorial. Indeed, Lawrence seems to conceive of such moments as distinctly *unpictorial* and *unvisual*, and he may have sensed this emotional, not visual, quality of the text when he wrote repeatedly to Edward Garnett about the unusual style of the novel that became *The Rainbow*, describing it as "written in another language almost."[8] I will return later to the subsuming of the visual to the emotional in most sequences of *The Rainbow* and in *Lady Chatterley's Lover*, but note it here as a central and important contrast with Woolf.

III

The identity between man and nature explored in the pictorialism of the early *Kew Gardens* persists as one of Woolf's major concerns in novels like *To the Lighthouse* and *The Waves*. The theme assumes special importance in *The Waves*. Confined almost entirely to the minds and utterances of its six characters, *The Waves* is not, in its essence, a pictorial novel. The novel abounds in images that could be "translated" into paint, but it so overloads the visual imagination with rapidly changing, rapidly substituted images that pictorialism, as we normally define it, shortcircuits. I offer as an example a passage from the novel, one from Bernard's consciousness describing Percival's ability to unite his friends:

> We who yelped like jackals biting at each other's heels now assume the sober and confident air of soldiers in the presence of their captain. We . . . who have sung like eager birds each his own song and tapped with the remorseless and savage egotism of the young our own snail-shell till it cracked . . . or perched solitary outside some bedroom window and sang of love . . . now come nearer . . . shuffling closer on our perch. (p. 123)

Individual components of this passage (the jackals, the soldiers, the birds) might be imaginable as a painting, but all the elements together would coexist so awkwardly in a single painting that the passage does not, in overall effect, invite visualization. By repetition and incremental revelation of meaning, moreover, Woolf invests particular objects with abstract, symbolic, and idiosyncratic meanings that no single painting would be likely to duplicate. How could a painting of birds tapping snail shells suggest, for example, "the remorseless and savage egotism of the young," unless in title or subtitle? No juxtaposition of birds and youths would be in itself likely to produce the effect of so highly linguistic a phrase.

The Waves' pictorialism is, then, sparing (confined largely, in fact, to passages in its prologues like those quoted in the Introduction), and its references to the visual arts only intermittent. Still, it is an important novel for my study since it uses the visual arts and pictorialism theoretically in ways often highly significant, though not always concrete or immediately apparent. The theory behind the overall form of *The Waves*, for example, bears comparison to that behind some Impressionist art. Its overall form juxtaposes prologues portraying a beach scene and a room slightly before dawn to slightly after dark, with chapters covering stages in the characters' lives from early childhood to old age and death. The idea of a *series* of perspectives on the same scene or objects was a favorite of the Impressionists and Post-Impressionists, most notably of Monet and Cézanne. In their series, different light yields, in effect, vastly different paintings of the same object, even when that object is viewed from the same angle of vision. In Woolf's literary equivalent, the prologues to *The Waves*, light also plays a transforming role, but light more specifically as a function of time—dawn followed by morning, followed by mid-day, followed by sunset, and so on, rather than time captured at random in a sequence of paintings.

Time becomes moreover, the literary equivalent of painterly light in the novel proper's progressive revelation of the characters' personalities and lives. As the agent which brings out the differences in the characters as they move (in sections two through five) from childhood to young adulthood, time functions as light does in this passage from the middle prologues:

Tables and chairs rose to the surface as if they had been sunk
under water and rose, filmed with red, orange, purple like the
bloom on the skin of ripe fruit. The veins on the glaze of the
china, the grain of the wood, the fibres of the matting became
more and more finely engraved. Everything was without shadow.
A jar was so green that the eye seemed sucked up through a
funnel by its intensity and stuck to it like a limpet. Then shapes
took on mass and edge. Here was the boss of a chair; here the
bulk of a cupboard. And as the light increased, flocks of shadows
were driven before it and conglomerated and hung in many-
pleated folds in the background. (p. 110)

Like other objects in the middle prologues (the prologues that
correspond to the period of youth and personality development),
the jar has "its exact measure of color" and exists "without
shadow." Woolf writes of "atoms of grey-blue air," currants of
"polished red," grass "in one fluent green blaze" (p. 149). And
the colors' intensity reminds one of the signature colors of Manet
and some of the Post-Impressionists.

As we read the novel, we automatically transpose what happens to the objects in the prologues into an analogy of what
happens to the characters in the chapters. Thus, near the end
of the novel, when the setting sun in the prologues melts "brown
masses into one huge obscurity" (p. 236), we are prepared for
the chapters that follow, in which the characters' diverse experiences in mid-life converge in the disappointments of old age
and the expectation of death. In *The Waves*, then, and especially
in its prologues, objects stand-in for characters and light for
time. Woolf's overall conceit expands the ideas broached in *Kew
Gardens* concerning the identity of men and nature, and it uses
the Impressionist and Post-Impressionist idiom more complexly
and with greater insistence.

The novel's overt references to the visual arts similarly show
a predilection for what we might call the theory of art rather than
for particular, individualized paintings or sharp instances of
pictorialism. Woolf divides art into two categories: representa-

tional, realistic art, and nonrepresentational, nonrealistic art. The categories perform rather different functions for the characters and promote very different states of mind. Bernard most extensively summarizes the two kinds of art during his visit to the National Gallery immediately after hearing of Percival's death. Pressed by normal social detail into abandoning his meditations on Percival, Bernard decides to "go up these steps into the gallery and submit myself to the influence of minds like mine outside the sequence" (p. 155). Bernard believes that certain forms of art lead us outside of the "sequence," the normal, detail-laden rounds of experience. We may see here some of Fry's and Bell's aesthetic theory at work, with Bernard, or Woolf, or both, attributing to the experience of art the ability to transform and transcend ordinary experience.

As the passage continues, it defines more specifically what kinds of art remove us from "the sequence" by contrasting what Bernard sees in the actual paintings with the imaginary picture of Percival's death that haunts him:

> Here are pictures. Here are cold madonnas among their pillars. Let them lay to rest the incessant activity of the mind's eye, the bandaged head, the men with ropes, so that I may find something unvisual beneath. Here are gardens; and Venus among her flowers; here are saints and blue madonnas. Mercifully these pictures make no reference; they do not nudge; they do not point; they thus expand my consciousness of him and bring him back to me differently. (p. 156)

Paradoxically, the experience of paintings in the Italian room of the National Gallery *alleviates* Bernard's vivid visual impression of Percival's death scene—a realistic, detailed, particular impression—and leads him to "something unvisual beneath"—the realization of Percival as his opposite, balancing his infirmities and making them less painful. The visual arts provide, then, not so much particular visual stimuli for Bernard as a setting for meditation away from the particularities of the world of sight. The key to this paradox resides in *how* Bernard perceives the art before him. He sees "madonnas among their pillars," "saints and blue madonnas"—descriptions of form and color as much as of subject. He also sees subject in these paintings as impersonal and abstract, not as particular. For Bernard, the madonna is not the Biblical figure or a recognizable face; she is the emblem of all grief or, even more abstractly, simply a figure among pillars. Perhaps tutored by Fry and Bell, Woolf, through Bernard, to a large extent reads Renaissance art in terms of modern, abstract art. Interestingly, Woolf here bears comparison to Lawrence, who comments in "A Study of Thomas Hardy" on a Raphael Madonna in the National Gallery—perhaps the same painting Bernard beholds—as "a geometric figure, an abstraction ... a great ellipse crossed by a dark column."9 The world of the Renaissance masters is not, for Bernard, representational; it is that of "the ruffled crimson against the green lining; the march of pillars; the orange light behind the black," a world of "silence [and] sublimity," not of referential particularity (p. 157). Years later, in Bernard's closing soliloquy, he remembers precisely this abstract quality of the paintings. He saw: "Madonnas and pillars, arches and orange trees, still as on the first day of creation, but acquainted with grief, there they hung" (p. 264). And he confesses that he sometimes still returns to the National Gallery to submerge himself anew in the meditative, abstract frame of mind: "This freedom, this immunity, seemed then a conquest, and stirred in me such exaltation that I sometimes go there, even now, to bring back exaltation and Percival" (p. 264). Art perceived nonrepresentationally provides, then, a stimulus for impersonal meditation, one analogous to that experienced by Mrs. Ramsay when merging with the stroke of the lighthouse.

The idea of two kinds of art also illuminates other aspects of the novel. Each of the characters in *The Waves* carries with him a collection of favorite mental "pictures" that summarize the essence of his anticipated or remembered life. No neat schematization of these pictures is entirely possible, since *The Waves* is not the neatest, most consistent, of novels. But it is generally true that characters weak in the universal, oceanic sense (like

Susan) incline toward representational "pictures" like seven-
teenth- through nineteenth-century genre paintings, while characters strong in the universal, oceanic sense (like Rhoda and
Louis) incline more to abstract "pictures." A typical "picture"
cherished by Susan looks like this:

> I shall have maids in aprons; men with pitchforks; a kitchen
> where they bring the ailing lambs to warm in baskets, where the
> hams hang and the onions glisten. I shall be like my mother,
> silent, in a blue apron locking up the cupboards. (p. 99)

The choice of a homely, nonallegorical setting, the piling-up of
domestic or still-life details, and finally the particularity, silence,
and stillness of the mother image mark this as a picture of life
lived *in* the sequence, not outside it. Rhoda's characteristic "pictures," on the other hand, show the same abstract concerns (often
in terms of the same or similar objects) important to Bernard
in the National Gallery. Typically Rhoda's is this picture: "Pools
lie on the other side of the world reflecting marble columns.
The swallow dips her wings in dark pools ... I ... long for
marble columns and pools on the other side of the world where
the swallow dips her wings" (p. 105). The recurrence of the
column or pillar emphasizes pure form like that perceived by
Bernard in Renaissance madonnas, and the pool and swallow
have a mystical, symbolic vagueness. Typically, too, at oceanic
moments, Rhoda feels the universe resolve itself into the balancing of abstract shapes. Thus, at the second dinner party, when
"the still mood, the disembodied mood" overtakes the characters,
Rhoda feels that "A square is stood upon the oblong and we
say, 'This is our dwelling-place. The structure is now visible.
Very little is left outside'" (p. 228; see also pp. 163-64). Here
again the nonrepresentational harmony of abstract art provides
Woolf with the idiom for expressing what cannot ordinarily be
expressed in words—nonverbal, mystical states of mind, and a
sense of universal harmony.

Elsewhere I have argued that *The Waves'* origin in Woolf's

vision at Rodmell of a fin in a waste of waters provides the central metaphors for the novel and controls its process of closure.[10] My earlier concerns unite with my present ones in this instance, since the fin image occurs to Bernard as a "bare visual impression . . . unattached to any line of reason," whose meaning can only be translated at length, and with time, into words (p. 189). In accord with the mystical states it describes, Bernard's visual impression—triangular in shape—mirrors Rhoda's impression of the swallow's wing cutting a triangular wedge into a pool of water. Woolf seemed, then, to find in abstract compositions a fitting representation of what she called the "essence of reality," a universal, oceanic sense that overarches the social, familial, time-bound reality in which individuals normally live.

The only other critic to comment on the use of geometric shapes in The Waves—Jean Alexander in The Venture of Form in the Novels of Virginia Woolf—elaborately relates geometric shapes to Rosicrucian and other mystical philosophies which, she admits, Woolf may or may not have known except via the collective unconscious.[11] A drama of abstract shapes closely related to the novel's mystical ideology does, I believe, exist in The Waves. But it seems more sensible to relate that drama to Woolf's experience of the visual arts—an experience directly referred to in the text and one that emphasized nonrepresentational, abstract art of the kind that Vanessa Bell and Duncan Grant knew and sometimes painted, of the kind that, says Bernard, takes us out of the "sequence" and into abstract, meditative states of mind that Woolf valued highly.

IV

Some ideas similar to those just described for The Waves also inform To the Lighthouse, the novel which precedes The Waves in Woolf's canon and one in which references to the visual arts and instances of pictorialism are far more central than in the later novel. One of the two major heroines in To the Lighthouse,

Lily Briscoe, is a painter and, along with the proposed and achieved journey to the lighthouse, her painting forms one of the iron rods that unifies the novel. Lily's vocation as artist has recently aroused discontent in some readers. Joyce Carol Oates, in a recent essay in the *New York Times Book Review*, sees Lily's artistic vocation as "insufferable and . . . improbable."[12] And my students frequently describe Lily, her painting, and its completion in the last lines of the novel as "nice, but corny." And yet Lily's vocation as a painter helps to express the novel's central themes and concerns in a way we cannot discount. I have argued that the painter's or sculptor's trade is expendable in *Sons and Lovers, Roderick Hudson*, and *The Tragic Muse*. It is not at all expendable in *To the Lighthouse*, and to dismiss it is to greatly endanger the value of the novel as a whole.

As in *The Waves*, mental "pictures" become in *To the Lighthouse* a way of defining experience, of knowing others; these "pictures" thus approach perceptual uses of pictorialism. Simple instances of knowing through visually imagined or remembered "pictures" include the scrubbed kitchen table Lily always sees when she thinks of Mr. Ramsay's work and the potato skins that come to mind and eye for Mr. Bankes'. They also include the picture of Minta eating a sandwich on the stairway while Paul stands above, by which Lily "knows" the Rayleys. More complex is the "trick of the painter's eye" that causes Lily repeatedly to see Mrs. Ramsay after her death as "putting her wreath [of white flowers] to her forehead and going unquestioningly with her companion, a shade across the fields" (p. 270). The "picture" implicitly touches a number of suggestions made earlier about Mrs. Ramsay in the novel: that she exhausts her life in the service of her family, that she may acquiesce to, even welcome, death as the ultimate opportunity to lose personality as she does when meditating with the stroke of the lighthouse. My favorite "picture" in *To the Lighthouse* is, however, one in a nineteenth-century anecdotal mode appropriate to its subjects, Mr. and Mrs. Ramsay. Lily recalls seeing Mr. Ramsay raise Mrs.

Ramsay from a chair and thereby imagines the scene of their betrothal:

> Lily could see him.
> He stretched out his hand and raised her from her chair. It seemed somehow as if he had done it before; as if he had once bent in the same way and raised her from a boat which, lying a few inches off some island, had required that the ladies should thus be helped on shore by the gentlemen. An old-fashioned scene that was, which required, very nearly, crinolines and peg-top trousers. Letting herself be helped by him, Mrs. Ramsay had thought (Lily supposed) the time has come now. Yes, she would say it now. Yes, she would marry him. And she stepped slowly, quietly on shore. (p. 295)

The interplay of gesture and expression and the need for old-fashioned details of clothing and background control this imaginary "picture."[13] And the picture—in Lily's mind for ten years—becomes one way for her to meditate on the marriage of Mr. and Mrs. Ramsay, one way to begin decoding some things important in the experience of others—in this case, the magic force that seems to unite the couple, their acting out of traditional gender roles, their curious blend of aloofness, dignity, and suggested passion. Repeatedly in section three of the novel, Lily remembers or creates scenes "that had survived, ringed round, lit up, visible to the last detail," like paintings (p. 254), and meditates on these scenes to increased understanding.

Lily's pictures may seem trivial or—as my students will sometimes have it—"nice, but corny." And yet two factors prevent us from dismissing them. First, the novel seems quite serious in suggesting that visual imagination indicates general sensibility and sensitivity to others. The priggish Charles Tansley, for example, devoid of imagination and of interests beyond the self "would go to picture galleries ... and ... ask one, did one like his tie?" (p. 16.) Second, the characters' breakthroughs in the last sections of the novel are frequently prodded by imaginary, yet "seen," objects: Mrs. Ramsay "in her perfect goodness" sitting on the step for Lily years after her death; James "watching" a perambulator bloody a foot as he approaches understanding of his father. The visual imagination and the pictorial moment thus figure prominently in the novel.

Even more significant in *To the Lighthouse* is what we might call its drama of abstract shapes. Lily's concerns as an artist are explicitly those of a painter working in the abstract mode. In the paintings she attempts in Parts I and III of the novel, "The question being one of the relations of masses, of lights and shadows," becomes the question of "how to connect this mass on the right hand with that on the left" while avoiding "the danger ... that by doing that the unity of the whole might be broken" (pp. 82-83). Note that Lily conceives of Mrs. Ramsay sitting with James (human components in her picture) not as a representational artist or portrait-maker might, but simply as one of the "masses" with which she must work. Her concerns are abstract—the achievement of a general principle of balance and harmony—rather than the preservation of specific, "historical" figures or moments.

In *The Seen and Unseen in "To the Lighthouse,"* Lisa Ruddick offers a plausible reading of the novel in which seeing and combining close-up and distant perspectives form a key to its themes. We might expand her conception to say that combining representational and abstract perceptions is equally a key to the meaning of *To the Lighthouse*. At the famous moment when James appreciates the lighthouse as seen by his mother and by his father, he combines impressionist and realist renderings; his mother's lighthouse "was then a silvery, misty-looking tower with a yellow eye, that opened suddenly, and softly," his father's a photographically perceived "stark and straight" tower (p. 276). Similarly, Lily at the end of the novel unites with both Mr. and Mrs. Ramsay as human beings and with their representations in the forms of abstract art: she "sees" them both in their human bodies and in the abstract elements of her painting.[14]

As is appropriate to the idiom of abstract art, a geometric shape dominates the novel—the triangle, or variations on that three-cornered form. Lily's painting must balance a mass on the left with another on the right with a third mass in the center. The novel is similarly a triptych, with all three parts necessary to complete its form and vision. Frequently in the novel, moreover, Woolf establishes triangular patterns of vision and relation: as Mrs. Ramsay regards Lily and Bankes walking in the garden, for example, they in turn regard her (a pattern of a triangle and a second, but incomplete, triangle). Similarly, when Mrs. Ramsay and Carmichael gaze at Rose's wondrous bowl of fruit, "looking together" unites them in a triangular pattern. When she enters the meditative state often initiated by solitude and the stroke of the lighthouse, moreover, Mrs. Ramsay feels herself shrink to "a wedge-shaped core of darkness" (p. 95). Sensing this of Mrs. Ramsay or at least seeing in the triangle the same principles of stability and balance that painters have classically valued, Lily paints Mrs. Ramsay with James as a "triangular purple shape" (p. 81). As for Bernard in *The Waves*, the classical, quasi-religious subject of mother and child can be reduced "to a purple shadow without irreverence," solid and grounded like a stable triangle. And, as Bernard senses of the Renaissance masters, Lily's venture is not to portray a particular mother and child, but to use their relationship as a symbol of universal balance and harmony. Once again, abstract art provides Woolf with an idiom to express ideas that might sound trite if explicitly stated or if elaborated at great length.

If we accept the rhythm of the final section as the characters' successive attempts to triumph (the triumph being always incomplete, tentative, or at best momentary), we can see that these attempts depend upon each character's internalizing and acting in unison with the others upon his sense of what Mrs. Ramsay "means" in the first section of the novel. And, despite her exaggerations, her sometimes coquetry, her penchant for meddling in the lives of others, and her hesitancy to accept women different from herself (like Lily Briscoe), Mrs. Ramsay finally "means" exactly what Lily tried to paint in the summer spent with the Ramsays: the strong, stable, dark triangle. She is, in the social sphere, the embodiment of familial love, maternity, and warm-hearted concern for others; in the private, mystical sphere, she is the "core of darkness," that religious sense that takes in the imagination the shape of a triangle or of a dome, that being able to feel at one with "trees, streams, flowers." As Lily "knew [,] knowledge and wisdom were stored up in Mrs. Ramsay's heart" (p. 79).

Lily's achievement in Part III of the novel greatly depends on "decoding" the meaning of the purple triangle she originally saw as the inevitable and right way to paint Mrs. Ramsay. When she unpacks the meaning of her earlier visual conception in words (the process of meditating on Mrs. Ramsay that occupies most of section three), "an odd shaped triangular shadow" falls on the step and initiates the final movement of the novel, in which Lily forms a community with those arriving at the lighthouse, James and Cam realize their love for their father, and Lily finishes her painting at last. A series of harmonious triangles prevails also in this last movement of the novel: Lily "having" both Mr. and Mrs. Ramsay, James and Cam at peace with their father, Lily and Carmichael at one with the group on the boat.

As she works to complete her painting, Lily thinks, "One might say, even of this scrawl, not of that actual picture, perhaps, but of what it attempted, that it 'remained forever'" (p. 267). The thoughts, "nice but corny," refer to a crucial attribute of the act of painting, as Woolf saw it. Like meditation, painting is a solitary act in which impersonality prevails and a blending with things similar to Mrs. Ramsay's can properly unfold. As Lily paints, "Certainly she was losing consciousness of outer things. And as she lost consciousness of outer things, and her name and her personality and her appearance, and whether Mr. Carmichael was there or not, her mind kept throwing up from its depths, scenes, names, and sayings, and memories and ideas, like a fountain spurting over that glaring, hideously difficult white space, while she modelled it with greens and blues" (p. 238). In a device favored by Woolf and used also in *The Waves*, the movement into the impersonal, mystic state of mind evokes in one character's mind images found elsewhere in the novel. Here, the fountain image associated with Mrs. Ramsay by the narrator and by James occurs also to Lily, and the colors green and blue in themselves suggest the mystic, "oceanic" sense. Important too for Lily's venture at the end of *To the Lighthouse* is the sense in which "tunnelling her way into her picture" simultaneously becomes tunnelling her way "into the past" (p. 258). For, while Lily is "screwing up her eyes and standing back as if to look at her picture," she has "all her faculties in a trance, frozen over superficially but moving underneath with extreme speed" (p. 298). Woolf's portrayal of Lily when painting accords well with Bernard's sense of the power of nonrepresentational art: painting takes her out of the "sequence" and puts her in touch with the "sublime" "fish-world" of art.[15] Although a visual form, abstract art could, Woolf believed, lead us to "something unvisual beneath," and it thus provided Woolf with the idiom for describing one of the things she valued most—insight into the mystical "essence of reality."[16] As a foreign medium, one more obviously and immediately stylized than literature, abstract art gave Woolf a vocabulary and images for expressing unconventional states of mind.

V

Critics addressing the topic of D. H. Lawrence and the visual arts tend to assume that Lawrence's interest in painting must lend each of his novels a pictorial quality, must prompt in each of his novel's the author's use of his visual imagination. In actuality, however, of his novels, *Women in Love* most consistently and regularly uses pictorial effects, and even it counterpoints passages intensely pictorial with passages intensely linguistic. Its complex uses of the visual arts and of pictorialism form the subject of Chapter Six and will, therefore, be largely omitted from the discussion in this chapter. In two other of Lawrence's major novels, however—*The Rainbow* and *Lady Chatterley's Lover*—Lawrence's use of the visual arts and his movements *away* from pictorialism in important passages reflect ideological uses analogous to those we have seen in Woolf's novels and sometimes similarly based on the idioms of Modern art.

In *The Visual Imagination of D. H. Lawrence*, Keith Alldritt identifies with great care the historical works of art alluded to in *The Rainbow* and notes how characters' tastes in the visual arts tend to define them. As Alldritt says, "the evolving consciousness of main characters is rendered in significant part through the presence or discovery of certain art images," a device similar to what I call perceptual uses of the visual arts.[17] Will Brangwen's early passion for Gothic churches and for Carpaccio's painting of St. Ursula mark him, for example, as a Ruskinite, one whose combination of aestheticism and sexual disorder limits his achievement of individuality.[18] Will's mature fondness for Della Robbia (especially following his earlier love for the more brilliant Fra Angelico) similarly suggests the limitations of his aesthetic capacities.[19] Other characters also reveal themselves by the aspects of art they chose as mental icons. Shown Fra Angelico's *The Last Judgment* by her husband, Anna curiously sees only one part of the triptych—the "heavenly" third in which "the Blessed held each other by the hand as they moved towards the radiance."[20] Conversely, her daughter Ursula "liked the demons and enjoyed the hell" in Fra Angelico's triptych, but finds herself bored by the portions that interested her mother. Her difference from her mother in artistic tastes coincides entirely with her rejection of the Brangwens' family life (p. 277). Art works and contrasting reactions to them form, then, an important aspect of *The Rainbow*. Other examples include Anna's refusal to be swept away by the cathedral that Will shows her early in their marriage and her focussing on the tiny gargoyles to hold herself back, and Ursula's employment of imagery from the Fra Angelico painting to chart her great expectations and greater disillusionment during her relationship with Skrebensky (see pp. 436 and 438).[21]

Although the author of a book like mine must find so many

references to the visual arts gratifying, such references are ultimately less significant than the ways in which the novel withdraws from the visual and the pictorial and less significant than its borrowings of imagery from Futurist art to express negative aspects of Lawrence's ideology. Here I disagree with Keith Alldritt, who apparently finds moments in *The Rainbow* as pictorial as moments in *Women in Love* and largely connects art in the novel with nineteenth-century movements. Alldritt sees five crucial "icons" (his term) in the novel, in which kinesis gradually accelerates. The first "icon" portrays Tom Brangwen looking through a window and seeing Lydia Lensky with her child:

> Looking through the window, he saw her seated in the rocking-chair with the child, already in its nightdress, sitting on her knee. The fair head with its wild, fierce hair was drooping towards the fire warmth, which reflected on the bright cheeks and clear skin of the child. ... The mother's face was dark and still, and he saw, with a pang, that she was away back in the life that had been. The child's hair gleamed like spun glass, her face was illuminated till it seemed like wax lit up from the inside. The wind boomed strongly. (p. 37)

Thus far the sequence shows marked pictorialism. The scene is doubly "framed," by Tom's controlling eye and by the window. Its source of light is repeatedly stressed as the fire that illuminates Anna's hair and skin, creating effects like those in Caravaggio or in La Tour. And Lawrence provides (both here and in sentences, omitted for brevity, that follow) enough visual detail for the scene to be imagined as a painting. Two elements minor in the selection as thus far quoted, however, qualify its pictorialism: the strong subjectivity of "he saw, with a pang," pointing to Tom's emotions more than to anything one can visualize, and the sound recorded in the last sentence.

The sequence continues:

> The mother began to rock, he heard the slight crunch of the rockers of the chair. Then he heard the low, monotonous murmur

of a song in a foreign language. Then a great burst of wind, the mother seemed to have drifted away, the child's eyes were black and dilated. Brangwen looked up at the clouds which packed in great, alarming haste across the dark sky. (p. 38)

Much of the "picture's" point now rests in the contrast between the quiet and stillness of the scene inside the window and the turbulence of the scene outside it—the "frame" has now broadened to include not just Tom outside the window but the awareness of nature "framed" by his consciousness. Aural stimuli assume, moreover, an importance equal to that of visual stimuli—the noise of the chair rocking, of the mother singing, of the wind blowing. Tom perceives these things heard as strongly as he perceives things seen and *not* as mere functions of what he sees (which would be the case, say, if Tom implied the noise of the rocker from seeing it move). The passage has settled, moreover, strongly in Tom's consciousness, in his subjective and emotional interpretation of objective visual stimuli, and that interpretation gradually emerges as its real point: "Brangwen waited outside, suspended, looking at the wild waving of the trees in the wind and the gathering darkness. He had his fate to follow, he lingered there at the threshold" (p. 38). What Tom sees is the adjunct, not solely the stimulus, for what Tom feels. And Lawrence's phrases to describe Tom's feelings have an abstractness that blocks full pictorialism.

Another passage, describing an encounter between Ursula and Skrebensky, will clarify my point. It will also suggest some ways in which Lawrence typically *does* use images drawn from Post-Impressionist and Modern art in his novels. Once again, Alldritt cites the passage as one high in appeal to the visual imagination, largely on the basis of its interplay of light and dark. But such general uses of the terms "visual" and "pictorial" vitiate their usefulness. After a dance, Ursula and Anton

went towards the stackyard. There he saw, with something like terror, the great new stacks of corn glistening and gleaming transfigured, silvery and present under the night-blue sky, throwing dark, substantial shadows, but themselves majestic and dimly present. She, like glimmering gossamer, seemed to burn among them, as they rose like cold fires to the silvery-bluish air. All was intangible, a burning of cold, glimmering, whitish-steely fires. He was afraid of the great moon-conflagration of the cornstacks rising above him. His heart grew smaller, it began to fuse like a bead. He knew he would die.

   She stood for some moments out in the overwhelming luminosity of the moon. She seemed a beam of gleaming power. She was afraid of what she was. Looking at him, at his shadowy, unreal, wavering presence a sudden lust seized her, to lay hold of him and tear him and make him into nothing. Her hands and wrists felt immeasurably hard and strong, like blades. He waited there beside her like a shadow she wanted to dissipate, destroy as the moonlight destroys a darkness, annihilate, have done with. She looked at him and her face gleamed bright and inspired. She tempted him. (p. 319)

As in the first and simpler passage from *The Rainbow*, elements of pictorialism certainly exist in this passage: light and dark do have prominence in the scene (though sometimes, especially near the end, as abstract symbols and not as elements that might be found in a painting), and the setting amid the haystacks recalls the earlier encounter of Will and Anna among the sheaves and tempts an analogy based upon the visual memory of setting and place.[22] Visualization of the passage is not at all possible, however, in any traditionally realistic style, a factor which Alldritt overlooks and one to which I will return shortly. In this passage, moreover, far more than in that concerning Tom and Lydia, the most important features of the characters' emotions have no pictorial equivalents. For example, the first paragraph quoted, though imaginable in an impressionist, post-impressionist, or expressionist style, leads to the last sentence, which summarizes a state of mind in a linguistic, unpictorial phrase: "His heart grew smaller, it began to fuse like a bead. He knew he would die."

The sequence climaxes in a paragraph strongly subjective and emotional, filled with unpictorial phrases:

> But hard and fierce she had fastened upon him, cold as the moon and burning as a fierce salt. Till gradually his warm, soft iron yielded, yielded, and she was there fierce, corrosive, seething with his destruction, seething like some cruel, corrosive salt around the last substance of his being, destroying him, destroying him in the kiss. And her soul crystallized with triumph, and his soul was dissolved with agony and annihilation. So she held him there, the victim, consumed, annihilated. She had triumphed: he was not any more. (p. 320)

This paragraph develops, not visual stimuli or pictorial images, but Ursula's highly irrational and highly abstract feelings. One might argue that the hallucinatory setting enables the characters' aberrant emotions, that visual stimuli influence emotional perception. But after the first paragraph quoted from this sequence, the characters seem far more affected by each other and by tactile stimuli than by the scenery or visual stimuli around them.

With its contrasts of light and dark and its qualified pictorialism, elements in the first "icon," that of Tom and Lydia, are imaginable in a realistic style, especially in a style that, like La Tour's, uses dramatically localized sources of light. Even those portions of the Ursula and Skrebensky "icon" that I see as derived from the visual arts, however, could not be related to any style of painting before the Impressionists. Lawrence alludes in portions of the passage to qualities of Impressionist and later art that we know, from his fictional and nonfictional writings, he intensely disliked. Thus, his description of the setting does not really attempt to render the tactile reality of the cornstacks, but portrays "great new stacks of corn glistening and gleaming transfigured, silvery ... and dimly present." Objects in nature dematerialize under light as in much Impressionist and later art; they are eerie and almost metallic. Similarly, the figures dematerialize. Ursula, "like gleaming gossamer, seemed to burn among them [the haystacks] as they rose like cold fires." We have here a nonrealistic, expressionist rendering of setting and figure; when we notice similarities between the setting and painting, we probably have in mind something much closer to Boccioni or Munch than to Constable or Millais.

The transition in style from realistic to expressionist or futurist underscores a central theme in *The Rainbow*. For all its problems, the union of Tom and Lydia assumes a numinosity as the novel proceeds; the couple comes to represent the "angelic" union of male and female of which Tom tipsily speaks at Anna's wedding. Appropriately, the grandparents' generation is depicted in what Lawrence saw as a less debased style than that used for the comparable scene between Ursula and Anton.

The second and later paragraphs I have quoted from this sequence elaborate and expand the passage's initial references to metal. Like metal, Ursula's "face gleamed bright" and "Her hands and wrists felt immeasurably hard and strong, like blades." Similarly, Anton's body becomes "soft iron." If we knew nothing of Modern art, we would probably find such images unpictorial, linking them, perhaps, with industry, but clearly reading them as negative comments on the love scene being enacted. Repeatedly in Cubist and Futurist art, however, bodies appear (as Lawrence himself saw it) as "the phenomena of the science of physics" (like power, fire, or force) or as "huge lumps, tubes, planes, volumes, spheres, cones, cylinders."[23] Think, for example, of Boccioni's *The Laugh* (1911, plate 16) or of Leger's *Three Women (Le Grand Déjeuner, 1921)*, or of many other works of Cubist and Futurist art.

Although I do not find in the Stackyards scene a high degree of actual pictorialism based on such art, many facts combine to suggest that Lawrence discovered in the Futurists the source for many of his characteristic images in *The Rainbow* and *Women in Love*. Even before he knew their art, Lawrence shared with the Futurists a fondness for certain symbolic objects, like the locomotive or horse. But the special quality of language in the Stackyards scene bears great similarities to Futurist images, as

5. *Dance Sketch*, D. H. Lawrence, 1928
(Saki Karavas, Taos, New Mexico)

6. *Red Willow Trees*, D. H. Lawrence, 1927
(Saki Karavas, Taos, New Mexico)

7. *The Rape of the Sabine Women*, D. H. Lawrence, 1928
(Saki Karavas, Taos, New Mexico)

8. *Flight Back into Paradise*, D. H. Lawrence, 1927
(Saki Karavas, Taos, New Mexico)

9. "Mr. Peggotty's Dream Comes True," H. Hablot Browne, 1849-1850 (from *David Copperfield*, by Charles Dickens)

10. "I am Hospitably Received by Mr. Peggotty," H. Hablot Browne, 1849-1850 (from *David Copperfield*, by Charles Dickens)

11. Alec Surprising Tess as She Farms by Night, Hubert Herkomer,
1891 (from *Tess of the D'Urbervilles*, by Thomas Hardy;
The Graphic, 1 December 1891)

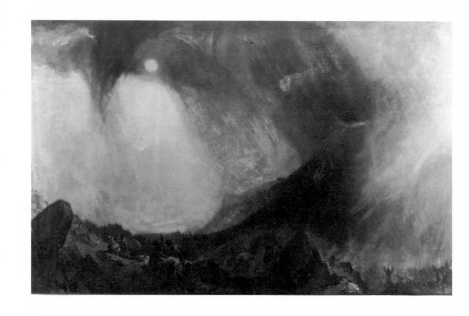

12. *Snow Storm: Hannibal and His Army Crossing the Alps*,
J.M.W. Turner, 1812 (The Tate Gallery, London)

13. *Abstract Painting*, Vanessa Bell, 1914
(The Tate Gallery, London)

14. *Adrian and Virginia Stephen on the Lawn*, Vanessa Bell,
c. 1909-1910 (Private Collection)

expressed in their art, in the initial Futurist manifesto, and in the "Technical Manifesto of Futurism."

In the *Le Figaro* column that introduced the Futurists to the world, Marinetti announced his mission in this way:

> We will sing of great crowds excited by work, by pleasure, and by riot. We will sing of the multicolored, polyphonic tides of revolution in the modern capitals; we will sing of the vibrant nightly fervor of arsenals and shipyards blazing with violent electric moons; greedy railway stations that devour smoke-plumed serpents; factories hung on clouds by crooked lines of their smoke; bridges that stride the rivers like giant gymnasts, flashing in the sun with a glitter of knives; adventurous steamers that sniff the horizon; deep-chested locomotives whose wheels paw the tracks like the hooves of enormous steel horses, bridled by tubing; and the sleek flight of planes whose propellers chatter in the wind like banners and seem to cheer like an enthusiastic crowd.[24]

The Futurists' use of crowds made frenzied by motion, of locomotives conflated with horses, of propellers compared to crowds, crystallized for Lawrence his long-developing sense of the fearful identity arising between inorganic and organic things. In the "Technical Manifesto" (which Lawrence read in 1914), Marinetti in fact proposed that every noun for human beings have a linked nonorganic noun (like "Man-torpedo boat" or woman-gulf ").[25] The imminent violence of the Futurists' "violent electric moons," bridges like "giant gymnasts, flashing in the sun with the glitter of knives" probably inspired directly the imagery of the scenes between Ursula and Anton. We know, at any rate, from Lawrence's letters that he read the Futurists as he finished the novel and was strongly moved by them; we also know that he revised the novel to add its metallic imagery after 1914, when he did the very last revisions.[26]

In this passage from *The Rainbow*, then, Lawrence uses images almost definitely derived from the Futurist manifestoes and Futurist art to signify the sexual corruption that engulfs Ursula and Skrebensky. The idioms of Modern art provide, not the vehicle for expressing Lawrence's ideals (as they had expressed Woolf's ideals), but the idiom for expressing much that he found most frightening and most distasteful in modern relations between men and women. That idiom continued, moreover, to inform the imagery of *Women in Love*. In *The Rainbow*, Ursula is the lost Modern woman; her sexuality represents a decline from that of Lydia or even from that of Anna. Insofar as it is described in images from the visual arts, therefore, her lovemaking fits the idioms of Modern art that Lawrence loathed, not the older idioms of art he could sometimes admire.

If some of *The Rainbow*'s least ideal moments portray men and women making love, so too, certainly, do some of its most ideal moments. And while the least ideal moments (like that between Anton and Ursula) frequently contain images derived from Modern art, the most ideal moments do not. When Tom and Lydia quarrel and then achieve a deeper, more lasting harmony, for example, the passage describing their lovemaking reads like this:

> His blood beat up in waves of desire. He wanted to come to her, to meet her. She was there, if he could reach her. The reality of her who was just beyond him absorbed him. Blind and destroyed, he pressed forward, nearer, nearer to receive the consummation of himself. . . .
>
> They had passed through the doorway into the further space, where movement was so big, that it contained bonds and constraints, and labours, and still was complete liberty. She was the doorway to him, he to her. At last they had thrown open the doors, each to the other, and had stood in the doorways facing each other, whilst the light flooded out from behind on to each of their faces, it was transfiguration, glorification, the admission. (pp. 90-91)

The passage's imagery of dark and light, doorways, liberty within constraint, and transfiguration suggests religious art, but the passage as a whole is highly unpictorial. As so often in *The Rainbow*, it emphasizes emotional states of mind and vague, subjective feelings based upon no objective, visual data. Its use of the door image is, moreover, doubly metaphorical. A painting which tried, in fact, to capture the passage's essence would look plain silly—with lovers and doorways hopelessly entangled— and would badly need the verbal gloss of title or subtitle to indicate its reference to triumphant sexuality.

Other ideal moments in *The Rainbow* and *Women in Love* have to an even greater extent the same abstract, linguistic, unpictorial quality. One of the best examples occurs in *Women in Love*, a novel whose use of Modern art and of pictorialism based upon such art to embody Lawrence's ideologies about modern society is, as we shall see, pronounced indeed. As Birkin and Ursula cross by boat to the continent, they cuddle outdoors with the kind of intimate but not particularly sexual feeling that Lawrence valued so highly. Lawrence renders this ideal moment as follows:

> they sat down, folded together, folded round with the same rug, creeping in nearer and ever nearer to one another, till it seemed they had crept right into each other, and become one substance. It was very cold, and the darkness was palpable.[27]

The initial description might be visualized, but it immediately yields to the subjective, not visually translatable impression of the two creeping into one body. The last sentence emphasizes the withdrawal from the visual: sensations of cold and darkness prevail, yet the darkness is not "seen" but "palpable."

A sailor comes upon the two, but "he withdrew like a phantom." As the interruption fades, the moment's true ideality unfolds:

> They seemed to fall away into the profound darkness. There was no sky, no earth, only one unbroken darkness, into which, with a soft, sleeping motion, they seemed to fall like one closed seed of life falling through dark, fathomless space. (p. 479)

The passage continues at some length, repeatedly emphasizing the couple's abstraction from their setting and the dark, "unrealised" quality of their intensely emotional state.

Another passage in the novel further illustrates my point. In "Excurse," after blissful lovemaking, Ursula and Birkin are to each other the "immemorial magnificence of mystic, palpable, real otherness," a state which cannot be "seen" or "known" (p. 403). Highly linguistic and unpictorial, the language dissociates the highest achievements of the characters from the seen and, consequently, from both pictorialism and the idiom of the visual arts. Lawrence thus quite reverses Woolf's idiom for the mystical and the sublime, and uses the idiom of Modern art to embody negative rather than positive aspects of his ideology.

VI

If *The Rainbow* experiments tentatively with ideological uses of the visual arts and *Women in Love* employs such uses extensively (as shall be discussed in a later chapter), *Lady Chatterley's Lover* involves an almost thorough abandonment of effects based upon the visual arts and pictorialism. *Lady Chatterley's Lover* is a talky novel, one in which virtually every aspect of ideology must be spelled out, again and again, with a too overt didacticism that uses of the visual arts and pictorialism help avoid in better novels, like *The Rainbow* and *Women in Love.*

Symptomatic of *Lady Chatterley's* distance from the visual arts is its portrait of the artist. In the novel, the painter Duncan Forbes appears most unattractive. Long drawn to Connie, his desires extend only to proximity, not to sexual union. When Connie seeks a faux-correspondent for her divorce from Clifford, Duncan Forbes seems just the man—potentially attractive to women, but not attractive to a woman like Connie, knowing a "real man" like Mellors. His fashionable art, moreover, "all tubes and valves and spirals and strange colors, ultra modern," has "a certain power, even a certain purity of form and tone," but "murders all the bowels of compassion in a man" (p. 356).[28]

Despite the novel's general lack of pictorialism and dislike of Modern art, however, it stresses an element important in Lawrence's theories about the visual arts, an element also present in

Women in Love, but present less complexly and more clearly in *Lady Chatterley* and hence useful here as an introduction. For Lawrence, the cultivation of visionary awareness is a vital first step to the rejection of a culture that takes as its art the tubes and spirals of a Duncan Forbes.

Connie Chatterley exists in a dead society, one whose deadness has two hallmarks in the novel: a language that masks reality through abstraction and cliché, and a dampened visual awareness to both the ugliness of the industrial world and the beauty of nature and the human body. The novel frequently reiterates its theme of language as corrupt, sometimes implicitly by using that corrupt language as the only one possible to describe the characters and their situation, sometimes explicitly, as in the following passage:

> Connie went slowly home to Wragby. "Home!" ... it was a warm word to use for that great, weary warren. But then it was a word that had had its day. It was somehow cancelled. All the great words, it seemed to Connie, were cancelled for her generation: love, joy, happiness, home, mother, father, husband, all these great dynamic words were half dead now, and dying from day to day.
> ... As for sex, the last of the great words, it was just a cocktail term for an excitement that bucked you up for a while, then left you more raggy than ever. (p. 102)

Governed by third person subjective or *erlebte Rede*, the passage displays Connie's awareness that words in her culture blanket realities rather than name them. Language, then, provides no way to salvation for Connie, but the questioning of language and the ability to use her eyes do. They enable her to get beyond the dead words of her culture and prepare her for the greater, nonverbal world of Mellors. Connie's growing awareness of the cliché, like the tour she takes of Teversall (when we see the hideous place through her eyes), prepares her for Mellors and confirms the rightness of her alliance with him.

Mellors lives amid nature and rejects corrupt normative English for dialect and for "taboo" words used as incantation, not

small talk. The potential for intimacy with Mellors opens to
Connie first by using her eyes. Shortly after the passage quoted
above, when Connie's disgust with language crystallizes, she sees
Mellors and begins to sense his alternative world. Walking
through the forest, Connie comes upon the gamekeeper's cottage
and

> went around the side of the house. At the back of the cottage the
> land rose steeply, so the back yard was sunken, and enclosed by
> a low stone wall. She turned the corner of the house and stopped.
> In the little yard two paces beyond her, the man was washing
> himself, utterly unaware. He was naked to the hips, his velveteen
> breeches slipping down over his slender loins. And his white slim
> back was curved over a big bowl of soapy water, in which he
> ducked his head, shaking his head with a queer, quick little
> motion, lifting his slender white arms, and pressing the soapy
> water from his ears, quick, subtle as a weasel playing with water,
> and utterly alone. (pp. 106-07)

Connie leaves the scene and tries to dismiss what she has seen
from her mind. But "in some curious way it was a visionary
experience: it had hit her in the middle of the body. She saw
the clumsy breeches slipping down over the pure, delicate, white
loins, the bones showing a little, and the sense of aloneness, of
a creature purely alone, overwhelmed her" (p. 107). "Framed"
by the stone wall and by Connie's eyes, Mellors is experienced
in a "visionary" way—in a way that uses all Connie's faculties.
Later, in the second quotation, she dwells on her visual impression and arrives through it at the revelation of singleness. The
moment accords well with Lawrence's theories (discussed in
Chapter One) of the need to cultivate visionary awareness as a
way to achieve a more general "vision" or insight, here insight
into the quality of Mellor's integrity.

Visual appreciation is thus a crucial step for Connie toward
the reawakening of her being, but it is a step that the novel
leaves rather quickly behind. Once lovers, Connie and Mellors
rely on tactile sensation, not visual sensation, and the novel's

scenes of lovemaking have the same abstract, emotional, non-visual quality of similar scenes in *The Rainbow* and *Women in Love*. Perhaps because he rarely found contemporary works that lived up to his high expectations for the potential of painting to integrate the faculties and illuminate the being, Lawrence rarely expressed ideal values in his novels through references to the visual arts or through pictorialism. But the characters' awareness of the truth about their culture is often piqued by the visual arts or by scenes pictorially rendered. We shall see this pattern emerge more strongly and complexly in *Women in Love*, as Birkin and Ursula clarify, through visual awareness, their ideas about modern culture and relations between men and women, and thereby move closer to the unvisual, but ideal, "immemorial magnificence of real palpable otherness."

VII

Central to the ideologies of both Woolf and Lawrence are states of mind difficult to render in language because their essence is to transcend language. Woolf's theorizing about art led her, I believe, to conclude that art either overtly abstract or capable of being perceived as abstract could initiate meditation and facilitate the oceanic sense. She used this belief in her novels, employing the idioms of abstract art for describing mystic states of mind and transcendent ideals in her novels. Lawrence's theorizing led him to condemn the very aspects of the visual arts that Woolf admired. Thus, though Lawrence often uses objects or scenes based upon the visual arts, or more generally pictorial, to trigger his characters' perceptions, he alludes to the visual arts more often negatively than not. His assault upon the transcendent rests in the emphatic use of unvisual, unpictorial language and in questioning the ability of either language or the seen to capture the transcendent. Lawrence believed, as Woolf did, in the importance of the eye as the threshold of knowledge. But he also believed that the degeneracy of Western art as he saw it made elements borrowed from the visual arts more likely to encode the negative and the corrupt than the positive and the ideal. For Lawrence, unless and until the visual conveyed tactile and emotional truths, as it did, say, in Cézanne, the visual belied transcendent experience.

I noted in the Introduction to this study that we can neither conceive nor create works of art in styles that are unknown to us. Accordingly, Woolf and Lawrence tend to use the visual arts ideologically in their novels in ways indicated by their personal contact with art: their ideological uses of the visual arts and of pictorialism suit their habits of mind and recorded thoughts on art. Although grounded in the documentary mode, however, the uses of the visual arts and pictorialism described in this chapter move us far down the continuum described in the Introduction to this study. They move us beyond the verbal surface of the novel and its grossest aspects of plot and characterization—decorative uses—and also beyond the lives and idiosyncracies of the authors themselves—biographical uses. They take us, in fact, into the central metaphors and concerns of each novel, thus illustrating what I call ideological uses of the visual arts and of pictorialism. Because both Lawrence and Woolf tend to communicate their ideologies through the perceptions of their characters, the chapter has also touched, in several instances, on interpretive uses of the visual arts or of pictorialism, uses which will be discussed more specifically in the next two chapters.

════════════

FIVE

PERCEPTION, IMPRESSION, AND
KNOWLEDGE IN
THE PORTRAIT OF A LADY, THE AMBASSADORS,
AND *THE GOLDEN BOWL*

James's *The Portrait of a Lady* seems, at first, no more deeply involved with the visual arts or pictorialism than *Roderick Hudson* or *The Tragic Muse*, whose decorative uses are the subject of Chapter Two. The visual arts are abundantly present in the novel's early sections (those before the introduction of Osmond), but their use seems static. The characters live amid art, and their galleries form prime locations for relaxation and the entertainment of guests. But the pictures beheld seem more a mark of the characters' social class and level of culture than a vital element in their consciousness or a prompter of moral or intellectual growth.

Noticeable from the first, however, are differences in the characters' capacities to appreciate the arts. Evaluating their responses to the visual arts thus becomes one way to group and understand the characters. Shallow figures like the Misses Molyneux find pictures "so very pleasant when it rains"—mere diversion and pastime. Smart but pragmatic characters, like Henrietta, reveal themselves suspicious of things like "charming Constable[s]." Shown such a painting by Ralph Touchett, Henrietta can only exclaim "Do you always spend your time like this?" and we may freely read "waste" for "spend."[1] She remarks to Isabel at the National Gallery, "I've not a true sympathy with inanimate objects," although by the end of the novel she has developed some liking for them (III, p. 198). Caspar Goodwood too has no proper appreciation for art and can never remember paintings. And Ned Rosier favors "comparatively frivolous periods," like the Rococo (IV, p. 90). Isabel, on the other hand, vibrates thrillingly to the art she beholds, especially to that of Florence and Rome, a difference from the others that marks both her superior sensibility and her vulnerability to Gilbert Osmond. Significantly, as I will discuss shortly, Isabel's enthusiasm for the visual arts diminishes as she comes to know Osmond better; she moves, in fact, much closer to the pragmatic stance of Henrietta and Caspar.

Once Gilbert Osmond enters the novel, its uses of the visual arts assume greater, more ideological, dimensions, and the novel begins its movement up the continuum of uses of the visual arts and pictorialism. In fact, James experiments in *The Portrait of a Lady* with a distinction based on his experience of the visual arts between impressions and knowledge, a distinction that finds fruition in later novels like *The Ambassadors* and *The Golden Bowl*.

II

Osmond and his family not only live amid art; they have in a sense taken works of art as their models. It is not so much—as F. O. Matthiessen puts it—that James "interrelates Osmond's character with his surroundings" as that Osmond's character has absorbed utterly the nature of the art it prefers.[2] We first meet Osmond as "part of a small group that might have been described by a painter as composing well" (III, p. 325). Hardly the most spontaneous of men, Osmond probably calculated and adopted the posture that would make the group "compose well." James's famous, frequently commented upon, description of Osmond's home—one of the places so significant in *Portrait*—immediately follows;[3] its chief feature is a facade that ominously seems a "mask" rather than a "face" (III, p. 325). Osmond collects art and also himself paints; in fact, his painting is mentioned the first and the last time we see him (when Isabel announces that she must be at Gardencourt for Ralph's death). Similarly, when we first meet Pansy "she was looking at the [Osmond's] picture in silence," and we almost immediately learn that she draws "very—very carefully" (III, p. 329).

This much reference to the visual arts in the introduction of Osmond's family might be merely neutral, might signify simply its relatively high level of culture. James's details quickly point, however, to the characters' unwholesome assimilation of qualities appropriate to the visual arts but inappropriate for men and women. Pansy, for example, wears a "painted" smile and has a "glaze" of prudence (III, p. 329; both words added in revision for the New York Edition).[4] When she tries to hide her unhappiness, James marks Isabel's dissimulation as similarly static like the visual arts. He notes of her face "something fixed and mechanical in the serenity painted on it" (IV, p. 142). All these references to the visual arts share negative connotations, to which I will return shortly.

The greatest affinities between art and character cluster around Gilbert Osmond. He probably, in fact, chose his coiffeur and beard by his preferences in art: "He was a man of forty, with a high but well-shaped head, on which the hair, still dense, but prematurely grizzled, had been cropped close. He had a fine, narrow, extremely modelled and composed face, of which the only fault was its running a trifle too much to points; an appearance to which the shape of the beard contributed not a little. This beard, cut in the manner of the portraits of the sixteenth century and surmounted by a fair moustache, of which the ends had a romantic upward flourish, gave its wearer a foreign, traditionary look and suggested that he was a gentleman who studied style" (III, p. 328). Similarly, "he was fine, as fine as one of the drawings in the long gallery above the bridge of the Uffizi" (III, p. 356). In the first quotation, James manages to pack an extraordinary number of terms applicable to the visual arts into his description of the man. Osmond has a "modelled and composed face," a beard reminiscent of sixteenth-century portraits (one not becoming but expressive of personality), a "look," and a "style" that is "studied." Like Browning's Duke,

Osmond admires the high art and the style of the Renaissance—
its civilized elegance and its stark authoritarianism. Such descriptions perhaps prepare us for Osmond's own choice "never
to stoop" and for his authoritarian treatment of wife and daughter. They also reinforce the sense that used as Osmond uses
them—as models for his own conduct—the fine arts can be a
dangerous thing.

As a connoisseur of the arts, Osmond has suitably formed the
habit of thinking in pictures. Thus, when he cooly sketches for
his wife the details of Pansy's sequestration in the convent after
Warburton leaves Rome, we are told: "His tone . . . was that of
a man not so much offering an explanation as putting a thing
into words—almost into pictures—to see, himself, how it would
look" (iv, p. 348). Similarly, as Isabel falls under Osmond's spell,
she too (but in her case uncharacteristically) thinks in pictures:
she carried "the image of a quiet, clever, sensitive, distinguished
man, strolling on a moss-grown terrace above the sweet Val
d'Arno and holding by the hand a little girl whose bell-like
clearness gave a new grace to childhood. The picture had no
flourishes, but she liked its lowness of tone and the atmosphere
of summer twilight that pervaded it" (iii, p. 399). Here again,
the visual arts and the act of thinking in pictures have sinister
or at least delusory qualities that we would not have expected,
given James's admiration for painting and sculpture.

James's most remarkable allying of Osmond with art comes
in one of his most significant revisions for the New York Edition.
The revision substitutes the following passage for an account of
Osmond's thoughts perhaps eight times as long. The revised
passage refers to Osmond's dawning awareness of what the
marriageable Isabel might do for him, how she might bring him
success without any need for him to assert himself vulgarly:

> If an anonymous drawing on a museum wall had been conscious
> and watchful it might have known this peculiar pleasure of being
> at last and all of a sudden identified—as from the hand of a great
> master—by the so high and so unnoticed fact of style. His "style"

was what the girl had discovered with a little help; and now, besides herself enjoying it, she should publish it to the world without his having any of the trouble. She should do the thing *for* him, and he would not have waited in vain. (IV, p. 12)

The revision underscores the alliance between Osmond's aestheticism and works of art by identifying him with "an anonymous drawing on a museum wall," the "anonymous" perhaps pointing to the man's lack of heritage and lack of achievement. The idea of a drawing merely hung beautifully captures the passivity and static quality of Osmond's life; but then James chillingly complicates the image by attributing a "watchful" and "conscious" air to Osmond that would be most uncanny in a drawing. The marvelous conceit of a sudden discovery by merit of style nicely accords with what would be, for Osmond, the best, indeed the only, form recognition could take, recognition like that accorded a work of art. And such recognition would be Isabel's "do[ing] the thing for him," not his having done anything for himself (IV, p. 12).

James's pithy image summarizes much that needed far more explicit explanation in the 1881 first American edition: "Osmond had felt that any enterprise in which the chance of failure was at all considerable would never have an attraction for him; to fail would have been unspeakably odious, and would have left an ineffable stain upon his life. Success was to seem in advance definitely certain—certain, that is, on this one condition, that the effort should be an agreeable one to make."[5] Or again: "Certain it is that Osmond's desire to marry had been deep and distinct. It had not been notorious; he had not gone around asking people whether they knew a nice little girl with a little money. ... He was a failure, of course; that was an old story. ... But there were degrees of ineffectiveness, and there was no need of taking one of the highest. ... When at last the best did present itself Osmond recognized it like a gentleman."[6] The revision, moreover, avoids the original passage's disclosure that Osmond considered Isabel's defiance possible, a discovery more appropriately reserved, in the New York Edition, for later in their relationship. It thus strengthens the book by underscoring what Isabel herself realizes: that Osmond too has been victimized by their marriage; that he expected a patron but got instead a critic. Finally, the original version somewhat distorts the essence of Osmond by attributing to him these thoughts before his marriage: "If she were only willful and high tempered, the defect might be managed with comparative ease; for had one not a will of one's own . . . as pure and keen as a sword in its sheath."[7] Such a passage attributes Goodwoodian masculine vigor to Osmond, while the image of the drawing emphasizes his asexuality and his ability to wound, seemingly without effort.

Isabel's seduction by Osmond is simultaneously a seduction by art. Other men in the novel court by pressing their physical attractiveness, their general competence, their material splendor, or all three. Osmond courts by offering the accumulated beauties of the visual arts. As "the kindest of ciceroni," he guides Isabel about his home, and around Florence and Rome, until "she was oppressed at last with the accumulation of beauty and knowledge to which she found herself introduced," but nonetheless strains to "appear as intelligent as she believed Madame Merle had described her" and fears exposing "her possible grossness of perception" (111, p. 379). Their courtship proceeds amid discussions of Correggio, rare sixteenth-century plates, and other splendors from the Italian heritage, always with Isabel as pupil and Osmond as guide. In marrying Osmond, Isabel no doubt believes herself to be marrying as well the achievements of the great masters. In a sense, she anticipates Osmond's image of himself as a rare but as yet unappreciated drawing. In her naïveté and in her desire for initiation into the world of culture, she mistakes Osmond for the real thing. As Mrs. Touchett jokingly and yet not so wrongly puts it, Isabel might well be marrying Osmond because he owns an autograph of Michelangelo!

During Isabel's courtship by Osmond, James declines "to report in its fullness our young woman's response to the deep appeal of Rome, to analyse her feelings as she trod the pavement of the Forum or to number her pulsations as she crossed the threshold of Saint Peter's. It is enough to say that her impression was such as might have been expected of a person of her freshness and eagerness" (III, p. 413). In its use of "impression" to signify initial but not final perceptions, the description suggests a distinction based on the historical visual arts to which James would often return. And we should be aware that the word "impression" with regard to specifically visual perception was still something of a novelty when James wrote. According to the *Oxford English Dictionary*, uses of "impression" in this sense were uncommon before Impressionism achieved notoriety.

The description hints at qualities in Rome, as in Osmond, that Isabel cannot yet perceive, but that she will perceive at leisure, once she knows better and has lost her "freshness and eagerness." When she returns to Gardencourt at the end of the novel, in fact, "she thought with a kind of spiritual shudder of Rome" (IV, p. 421)—a change indeed—and a reaction not just against Osmond but against a city which, in a sense, made possible her acceptance of him. James thus moves Isabel very far from her initial enthusiasm not only for her husband but also for the beauty he seems to represent. We must examine the reasons for Isabel's change to understand what kinds of ideological uses James makes of the visual arts in *The Portrait of a Lady*. For while it is frequently noted that connoisseurship can be morally suspect in James, the basis of that suspicion has not been sufficiently elucidated for *Portrait*.

Part of Isabel's change results, quite naturally, from her growing distaste for her husband and from the principle that guides their unhappy married life: whatever you like or wish, that shall I not like or wish. Thus, although she furnishes Osmond with the cash to richly decorate the Palazzo Roccanera, Mrs. Osmond, as Pansy tells Rosier, exerts her considerable taste not on art or decoration but on "literature" and "conversation" (IV, p. 110). But part of her revulsion comes, I believe, from her sense that the values inherent in the visual arts—highlighted in their grotesque absorption by Osmond—are dangerous to morally aware individuals. James does not greatly elaborate Isabel's conclusions, but those conclusions seem comparable to Keats's in "Ode on a Grecian Urn," one of James's favorite poems and one alluded to on occasion in his novels. As Isabel tours Gardencourt while Ralph lies dying, she naturally enough comes upon his gallery of paintings. It prompts these reflections:

> She envied the security of valuable "pieces" which change by no hair's breadth, only grow in value, while their owners lose inch by inch youth, happiness, beauty; and she became aware that she was walking about as her aunt had done on the day she had come to see her in Albany. She was changed enough since then—that had been the beginning. It suddenly struck her that if her Aunt Lydia had not come that day in just that way and found her alone, everything might have been different. She might have had another life and she might have been a woman more blest. She stopped in the gallery in front of a small picture—a charming and precious Bonington—upon which her eyes rested a long time. But she was not looking at the picture: she was wondering whether if her aunt had not come that day in Albany she would have married Caspar Goodwood. (IV, pp. 403-04)

Note here how Isabel reacts more like Henrietta than like her younger self as she stands before the paintings but thinks of other things, thinks especially of romantic happiness that she had once disdained as too banal and unaesthetic. More important, however, is Isabel's realization that works of art derive value from their static quality—their inability to feel and change—a quality immensely different from the central facts of human experience. Appreciation of the arts—carried so far as Osmond carries it—confuses categories aesthetic and vital. In revulsion from Osmond, Isabel also withdraws from the visual arts. She wishes to renounce all static masks of life and the life of Osmond, so intimately bound with the fine arts.

James's ideological use of the visual arts is, admittedly, only tentative in this novel. As we saw repeatedly in Chapter One, James himself believed that paintings can foster the sensitive observer's psychological awareness and teach him much about human life. It is thus unclear whether James intends to show that Isabel *twice* misinterprets the visual arts (once valuing them too blindly, once devaluing them too extremely), or whether he shares her sense that the visual arts have, finally, too little to do with human experience. Since he wrote few pieces of art criticism after completing *Portrait*, his nonfiction writing provides few clues, and the evidence from the fictions is ambiguous. But it remains true, even as James composed his prefaces for the New York Edition, that he repeatedly compared the novelist's to the painter's art; and James certainly did not believe literature irrelevant to human experience.

A possible answer to the question of how we are to regard Isabel's withdrawal from the visual arts may be found in her reluctance to link picture and idea and hence her tendency to perceive things superficially (a reluctance and a tendency to which I will return shortly). James himself, as his travel literature and art criticism suggest, always looked for the idea *behind* the picture, and tried to overcome the "will-to-meaning, which would transform the 'seen' into a rhetoric of defences."[8] Even that "charming and precious Bonington" is not just a mimetic representation of landscape, but also "a *sign* which is supposed to mediate some suprapersonal *meaning* . . . a certain attitude on the part of man toward the *entire* reality which surrounds him, not only towards that reality which is directly represented in the given case,"[9] a sign Isabel could read if she wished to read it. Indeed, James's characteristic comparison of the novelist to the visual artist (as in the preface to *Roderick Hudson*) rests on the association—one of the oldest of visual and verbal puns— of seeing and knowing. Thus, for all her attractiveness, Isabel adds to her collection of flaws the unwillingness to fully read works of art in a way separate from her preconceptions and prejudices and thereby comprehend their relevance to the human situation.

Still, James's distancing of Isabel from the visual arts seems quite consistent in the revisions of *The Portrait of a Lady*. The usual direction of changes for the New York Edition was the *addition* of references to the visual arts, especially for Osmond, Madame Merle, and Pansy. In only a handful of instances does James *remove* references to the visual arts, and in most of these instances the deletions serve to distance the heroine from paintings and to suggest that her insights derive not from art but from experience.[10] Thus, in her confrontation with Madame Merle after she has learned Pansy's parentage, Isabel fathoms the depths of the deep Serena, but she sees the truth "reflected in a large clear glass," not as clearly as if in a "picture on the wall," as in the original version.[11] Near the novel's end, pictures do not provide models of illumination; they have been contaminated by their association with Osmond and by their status as "silent forms."

III

James's distancing of Isabel from the visual arts complicates the interpretation of a crucial moment in the novel: Isabel's seeing Madame Merle and Gilbert Osmond casually and unexpectedly posed, and her subsequent meditation on the nature of her marriage. The scene promises a high degree of pictorialism and a strong perceptual use of that pictorialism, insofar as Isabel's visual impression prompts (along with Osmond's suggestion that Isabel persuade Warburton to marry Pansy) her night-long meditation on and new awareness of her union. But claims for the scene's pictorialism must be made tentatively, especially in light of some revisions that seem designed to minimize the scene's pictorial qualities.

Everyone who has read the novel will recall the moment when Isabel sees Serena Merle and Gilbert Osmond without their, at first, seeing her:

> Just beyond the threshold of the drawing-room she stopped short, the reason for her doing so being that she had received an impression. The impression had, in strictness, nothing unprecedented;

but she felt it as something new, and the soundlessness of her step gave her time to take in the scene before she interrupted it. Madame Merle was there in her bonnet, and Gilbert Osmond was there talking to her; for a minute they were unaware she had come in. Isabel had often seen that before, certainly; but what she had not seen, or at least not noticed, was that their colloquy had for the moment converted itself into a sort of familiar silence, from which she instantly perceived that her entrance would startle them. Madame Merle was standing on the rug, a little from the fire; Osmond was in a deep chair, leaning back and looking at her. Her head was erect, as usual, but her eyes were bent on his. What struck Isabel first was that he was sitting while Madame Merle stood; there was an anomaly in this that arrested her. Then she perceived that they had arrived at a desultory pause in their exchange of ideas and were musing, face to face, with the freedom of old friends who sometimes exchange ideas without uttering them. There was nothing to shock in this; they were old friends in fact. But the thing made an image, lasting only a moment, like a sudden flicker of light. Their relative positions, their absorbed mutual gaze, struck her as something detected. But it was all over by the time she had fairly seen it. Madame Merle had seen her and had welcomed her without moving; her husband, on the other hand, had instantly jumped up. He presently murmured something about wanting a walk and, after having asked their visitor to excuse him, left the room. (IV, pp. 164-65)

Aspects of the passage recommend that we treat it pictorially as well as dramatically. Paramount throughout is the presence of Isabel's eye, which frames and controls the material presented. The scene beheld, moreover, allows the reader to imagine a painting in the narrative tradition so popular in the nineteenth century. It is true that a greater amount of detail would facilitate visualization: What did the principals wear, for example? How did they look, and from what angle did they regard each other? What was the appearance of the room? James provides, however, much of this information earlier in the novel. And too much of such information might have obscured the central features of the scene: the relative positions of Osmond and Merle, and the extraordinary gaze that links them. These details provide the key to interpreting what Isabel beholds and would surely strike us more forcefully than details of dress or decor in a painting of the scene.

Although somewhat ambiguous (referring to drama as well as painting), the vocabulary of the passage also points toward pictorialism. Isabel has received an "impression," a word James uses twice, and a word that surely comes to him because of exposure to the artistic movement of that name and his sense that the Impressionists' work had more immediacy, but less finish, than that of older art. Much stress falls on verbs of perception, verbs frequently used for visual perception: "Isabel had seen," "what struck Isabel first," "she perceived." Finally, she remains arrested by "an image." None of these phrases necessarily indicates pictorialism, but each has a place in the vocabulary of the visual arts and, cumulatively, they incline us to regard the passage as pictorial. Perhaps most strikingly, the passage renders Isabel's gradual "reading" of what she sees, a process very like that which controls the perception and interpretation of the visual arts.[12] I should stress, however, a point to which I will return that modifies any simple notion of pictorialism in the passage: the moment ends before "she had fairly seen it," before she can "read" its meaning. In this incompletion of the "picture" and frustration of the perceptual process lies, I believe, much of the scene's importance for my study.

In the chapters that follow, Isabel's partial "picture" returns several times, but always without the specificity and completion available in a real painting of the narrative, dramatic kind that James preferred. At the end of her long meditation, for example, Isabel "stopped again in the middle of the room and stood there gazing at a remembered vision—that of her husband and Madame Merle unconsciously and familiarly associated" (IV, p. 205). In the original version of the novel, James wrote "unconsciously and familiarly grouped," the last word more specifically suggestive of pictorialism.[13] This revision constitutes one reason to qualify identification of the scene as pictorial. Congruently with his distancing of Isabel from the visual arts, James may have wished to mute this scene's pictorial elements. He may, however—and this seems more likely—have acted to stress the difference between a finished painting and the incomplete visual impression Isabel takes from this encounter.

Although the magnificent chapter in which Isabel meditates on Osmond and Mme. Merle and on the nature of her marriage (Chapter Forty-Two) contains many characteristic Jamesian images, it is an intensely linguistic sequence without any elements of pictorialism besides the visual impression that helps initiate it and to which it returns at the end. If you try, for example, to imagine the two following extended images as "pictures," you will see why they should be called linguistic and not pictorial:

> She could live it over again, the incredulous terror with which she had taken the measure of her dwelling. Between those four walls she had lived ever since; they were to surround her for the rest of her life. It was the house of darkness, the house of dumbness, the house of suffocation. Osmond's beautiful mind gave it neither light nor air; Osmond's beautiful mind indeed seemed to peep down from a small high window and mock at her. (IV, p. 196)

> Her mind was to be his—attached to his own like a small garden-plot to a deer-park. He would rake the soil gently and water the flowers; he would weed the beds and gather an occasional nosegay. (IV, p. 200)

Although both passages develop architectural metaphors, the metaphors link such heterogeneous elements that no "picture" could adequately capture their meaning. How to imagine a large park with an adjacent small garden in which a proprietorial looking man gardens while his wife looks on so as to render the sense of the second passage? No way, I believe. Again, how could one portray in a painting Osmond as center and circumference as he appears in the first quotation? If we imagine him looking down at his wife "from a small high window" (accepting "his mind" as synedoche), would that not vitiate the sense of Isabel as irretrievably enclosed within Osmond's mind that forms the central burden of the image? Some dadaist or surrealist rendering might begin to approximate the first image; but it is not altogether helpful to bring to bear an image from artistic styles that follow the novel by several decades.

If we return now to the scene when Isabel beholds Madame Merle and Osmond and try to imagine it as a painting in the nineteenth-century narrative style, we shall see that the "painting" produced would point fairly accurately to the meaning of the scene as the two "translations into painting" just attempted did not. First, however, we must make a choice: do we include Isabel in the "painting" or do we omit her, presenting just the two individuals she beholds? Either option has its merits. The first captures a necessary component of the passage—Isabel's puzzlement, her not-quite-there realization about her husband and their best friend—and accounts for all the words in the passage, including those which recount Isabel's thoughts rather than what she sees. The second more purely preserves one of the scene's chief claims to pictorialism—its control by Isabel's eye. But it limits the "painting" to only the descriptive portion of the passage. I prefer the first option, but will handle both in my "translation."

The second option would be easier to imagine as a painting and easier to interpret. In a nineteenth-century painting (perhaps in the style of Egg, or Millais, or Calderon), a man and woman in such a posture and costume, entangled in such a glance, would suggest an intimate relationship, one in which sexual intimacy would be strongly implied by their overall positions and by the detail of the fire. Quite skillful in suggesting marital status, the anecdotal master in paint could easily display that the lady is not married to the gentleman (perhaps by the absence of a ring on a carefully positioned, well-shaped hand, or by an iconographic object or a painting in the decor). Good examples of the use of gesture, pose, iconography, and background to help to tell the story of love triangles are Augustus Leopold Egg's *Past*

and Present, No. 1 (1858, plate 17) and Philip Hermogenes Calderon's *Broken Vows* (1856).[14]

Egg's *Past and Present, No. 1* is part of a trilogy chronicling
the consequences of a woman's infidelity. In the initial painting
(initial as to scene presented but hung *between* the other two),
the husband has just confronted the wife with her guilt; the
other paintings show the two daughters of the family, now young
women, staring at a moon after their father's death and the
mother, seated in a disreputable part of the city and nursing an
illegitimate baby, regarding the same moon. In the initial painting (plate 17), the wife's prostrate position testifies to the guilt
revealed in the letter her husband holds. Her outstretched arms
feature bracelets rendered so as to resemble a criminal's man-
acles. In the background, to each side of the now empty hearth,
hang paintings: above a miniature of the wife hangs a rendering
of Adam and Eve's expulsion from Paradise; above a miniature
of the husband hangs a rendering of a shipwreck, Clarkson
Stanfield's *The Abandoned*. The Adam and Eve motif repeats in
the cut-up apple, part of which (pierced by a knife that points
toward the despairing husband) rests on the table, half of which
has dropped to the floor. As in the story of Adam and Eve, the
male has been betrayed into sorrow by the female. Additional
sexual props—many suggestive of the disorder that has entered
the household—are the scissors on the table, the partly rendered
umbrella on the floor, and the litter of torn envelope and dis-
carded needlework.

To the left and in the middle ground, the couple's daughters
build a house of cards (symbolic of the state of this marriage).
The older child glances over her shoulder, aware of a crisis and
showing a face that is an innocent and ironic reflection of her
mother's guilty, hidden face. Above the mantle is an ornate
mirror which reflects an open door, through which the husband
(one presumes) has just entered and which prefigures the wife's
exit. The mirror also reflects a lamp which in the main picture
appears to have two globes but, in the mirror, distinctly has
three. All the elements of the painting thus combine to tell its

story, a story barely hinted at in the fairly neutral title (given the painting after its exhibition in 1858).

In the hypothetical painting of the scene from *The Portrait of a Lady*, a narrative painter could also easily demonstrate that the gentleman treats the lady with a surprising casualness and familiarity, since the woman's standing position and her wearing a bonnet would indicate that she is a guest, or a relative about to depart or just arrived; in either case, the man should be standing as well. If Osmond's posture and facial expression were painted right, the viewer could further identify his attitude as careless, or even disdainful. The woman's erect head but entangled glance would suggest her pride and yet her dependence on the man over whom she stands but who, clearly, controls the conversation and situation.

In the second option (a "painting" that includes Isabel), all these factors would remain the same, but we would add, to the far left of the canvas, a spectator, Isabel, who would be identified as the lady of the house—perhaps by a beringed hand or by her being bareheaded while Madame Merle is not. The position of the hands and the facial expression should suggest thoughtfulness and uneasiness about the conjunction she sees before her. In this imaginary "painting," Isabel (perhaps in three-quarter view) would see both Madame Merle and Osmond in profile, but the "viewer" of the "painting" would see Madame Merle frontally and Osmond in sharp profile or one-quarter view. The sharp profile or quarter view would still allow us to see his posture and the position of his head, but allow him to face Madame Merle, as he must from the description. Madame Merle would stand slightly off-center (a little higher than center and a bit to the right), the fire would be to the far right, and Osmond would be closer to the foreground, at the third corner of a triangle of which Madame Merle occupied the major angle (of about sixty degrees).

The viewer of this painting would no doubt interpret the piece as showing a wife in the unpleasant process of discovering her husband intimately associated with an older, less attractive, but still threatening woman. Based upon the relative positions of the man and older woman, that association would be irregular, and probably (note the fire and the wife's troubled look), sexual. The viewer might think the affair between the two still ongoing, but this would be an insignificant difference. Interestingly, although she notices all the significant details, Isabel fails to "read" the scene as the beholder of a Victorian narrative painting almost certainly would. Her failure has, I think, several explanations. First, as has already been suggested, the "painting" does not have time to fully compose itself in Isabel's mind before it is disrupted by Madame Merle's greeting and Osmond's hasty exit. Second, Isabel does not really want to know the "truth," as a banal Victorian lady in such a painting might. Third, Isabel continues her reluctance to link picture and idea—to read what she sees without the preconceptions she brings to it (in this case, her belief that her marriage to Osmond was a free act, performed in good faith by both parties). She fails to memorize the scene before her in part because that memory might force her to confront the nature of Osmond's relationship to Serena Merle and to recognize a powerful and unexpected motive for her having brought Isabel and Osmond together. Initially, she prefers to leave her impressions unexamined, to avoid moving from the impression to certain knowledge, and this is consistent with other ways that Isabel acts in the novel. Still, even to the limited degree to which Isabel "reads" the scene as one would "read" a painting, it prepares her for the Countess Gemini's information, for her giving of names and facts to explain the feelings that have grown in Isabel since the day she found her husband and friend in the drawing room. Although incomplete and abortive, we have here still a significant perceptual use of pictorialism, as I defined such uses in the Introduction.

Earlier, I stressed that Isabel comes to perceive differences between art and life that cause her to recoil in favor of life: art is static but life dynamic; art is neat and framed, and knowable, while life involves change and ambiguity. James's approaches to and withdrawals from pictorialism in the sequence concerning

Madame Merle and Osmond in the drawing room nicely capture the difference between art and life as Isabel defines it. The sequence involves a moment perceived and operating in Isabel's consciousness like a work of art and yet less lasting, less available for repeated consultations, and therefore more ambiguous, like life. James refines the distinction between impression and knowledge and expands the perceptual uses implicit in *The Portrait of a Lady* in *The Ambassadors*, the novel of James's canon most complexly dependent upon its references to the visual arts.

IV

Like many characters in the later novels of Henry James, Lewis Lambert Strether is a keen observer and a discriminating man about what he chooses to see. His fullest experiences depend absolutely on the faculties of sight and thought. Virtually each detail with which James introduces Strether heightens our awareness of his visual, cerebral orientation. The first significant glimpse we have of him, for example, reveals a man scrupulously arranging what he shall or shall not see as his first sight of Europe. Strether avoids notifying Waymarsh of the precise time and place of his arrival, lest the American's "countenance . . . present itself to the nearing steamer as the first 'note,' of Europe."[15] Later, in Waymarsh's room, Strether realizes why that note would have been discordant. Waymarsh's "personal type . . . of the American statesman, the statesman trained in 'Congressional halls,' of an elder day" just simply refuses to feel comfortable abroad, refuses to "float" (xxi, p. 25). Indeed, "nothing so little resembled floating as the rigour with which, on the edge of his bed, he hugged his posture of prolonged impermanence. It suggested to his comrade something that always, when kept up, worried him—a person established in a railway-coach with a forward inclination. It represented the angle at which poor Waymarsh was to sit through the ordeal of Europe" (xxi, p. 26). Even here, though in joking fashion, Strether shows his inclination to "read" facial expressions and postures as one "reads" a painting.

Similar visual acuity and a similar anchoring in Strether's eye controls the introduction of Maria Gostrey. Confronted with this amiable woman, Strether relies more on facial expression than on conversation to understand her. At their first London encounter, for example, he is struck by "the play of something more in her face" than the usual and expected (xxx, p. 6). In his openness to visual impressions and in his incipient willingness to "arrange" such impressions, Strether begins to reveal sides of himself sympathetic to the European experience. Consummate arrangers, the Europeanized Americans Strether meets, like Strether himself, have eyes for ordinary experience like those usually reserved for drama and painting: analyzing eyes, remembering eyes, eyes able to appreciate aesthetic qualities even above moral qualities. Strether's devious note to Waymarsh prefigures more of the novel than we might expect of so small an incident.[16]

As the novel develops, Strether continues to arrange the sights he shall see in Europe, as though his consciousness is to be a consummate tour-book. When, for example, he finds himself possessed of an important letter from Mrs. Newsome, he seeks out the appropriate spot in which to read it, finding one in the lovely Luxembourg gardens. James presents the setting with Strether as the observing eye and with a vocabulary that several times alludes to the visual arts: "on a penny chair from which terraces, alleys, vistas, fountains, little trees in green tubs, little women in white caps and shrill little girls at play all sunnily 'composed' together, he passed an hour in which the cup of his impressions seemed truly to overflow" (xxi, p. 80). Charles Anderson in *Person, Place, and Thing in the Novels of Henry James* is surely right to see the scene as "the first of a half-dozen major scenes in *The Ambassadors* that are described in language that increasingly suggests the mode of the Impressionist painters."[17] He even advances a particular model for the description in Pisarro's *Les Tuileries* (1899-1900), though we need not be so

particular in identifying sources, I think, given James's ambivalence about Impressionist art (see Chapter One), and given the
appropriateness of Impressionist inspirations in so very Parisian
a novel. We should note, however, that the setting in the gardens,
perhaps because of its several associations with art, seems to
Strether the appropriate place for the first of his long meditations
in the novel on experiences past, present, and to come.

Strether's sojourn in the gardens immediately precedes and
directly prepares for his introduction to arrangers and arrange-
ments more sophisticated than his own in the circle of Chad
and Marie de Vionnet. From the moment Strether sees Chad's
balcony on the Boulevard Malesherbes, he is, in American par-
lance, a "goner." He stands across the street staring at the lovely
thing for a full five minutes and then recognizes (already with
treachery to Mrs. Newsome's cause) that "the balcony in question
didn't somehow show as a convenience easy to surrender" (xxi,
p. 96). Of a "quality produced by measure and balance, the fine
relation of part to part and space to space," the balcony prompts
Strether to realize that "wherever one paused in Paris the imagination reacted before one could stop it" (xxi, p. 96). The entire
city offers visual impressions that "pile up consequences" by
stimulating the imagination and urging impetuous conduct on
those, like Lewis Lambert Strether, with a developing aesthetic
sense.

Penetrating Chad's household also offers acute visual impressions, impressions of "a charming place; full of beautiful and
valuable things" that speak volumes about the quality of Chad's
new life (xxi, p. 108). The entire sequence of the visit to the
Boulevard Malesherbes serves as a good example of a feature
Charles Anderson observes as typically Jamesian: the association
of objects with characters, objects through which another character comes to understand the first.[18] A similar association of
objects with personality marks Strether's experience of Marie de
Vionnet's home. Her lovely things form a "large and high and
clear ... picture" that comes for Strether to be associated with

her and to be evoked by her presence or her name (xxii, p. 271).

Both uses of objects also illustrate a feature of the novel noted by David Lodge in *The Language of Fiction* and important to my argument here: Strether's "customary mood of sensitive but indulgent and idealizing appreciation . . . with his 'vaguely' feeling something."[19] Grounded in Strether's consciousness, the novel often mimics the vagueness of his thoughts and perceptions. Typically, although Strether finds himself impressed by the objects in Chad's rooms, the novel (like Strether himself) does not pause to observe the rooms in detail. The novel's pictorialism thus stops short, in most cases, from including the reader in the pictorial process, although Strether frequently encodes and remembers what he sees as pictures. Early in the novel, moreover, Strether almost always stops short of moving beyond his "impressions." He tends to experience Europe and things European with the superficiality of the moment only. That course will prove dangerous in time, as Strether transmutes impressions into knowledge.

Despite the higher percentage of pages devoted to conversation or to rumination in *The Ambassadors*, despite the limited pictorialism typical of most sections of the novel, and despite the gap between impression and knowledge, the novel's motif of visual impressions as educative is both consistent and important. In company with Maria Gostrey and Little Bilham at the Louvre, for example, moved by the art that he sees, Strether finds himself understanding Maria's cryptic dictum that the young man is "all right—he's one of us!" and thus moves closer to the Parisian moral sense (xxi, p. 125). Similarly, Strether confirms that Chad's lovely objects do not belie him when he takes in the young man's splendidly altered, sterling appearance at the theatre. Strether was "to go over . . . afterwards again and again" the fact of Chad's new appearance, marked by "a cleaner line . . . a form and a surface, almost a design" (xxi, pp. 135 and 152). Once again, the novel associates vivid visual impressions with the process of thinking matters through. And Strether's description of Chad suggests through its vocabulary ("line, form, design") the visual arts. Instances of visually acute or pictorial impressions in *The Ambassadors* used perceptually, then, are many. In this discussion, however, which does not attempt to be a complete explication of the novel, I will focus only on two of the most important instances as a way of defining the uses and limitations of James's references to the visual arts and pictorialism and the relationship of impressions to knowledge: the garden party at which Strether first meets Marie de Vionnet and the famous incident of Strether by the river, the second more overtly pictorial than the first.

V

Strether arrives at Gloriani's party conscious of feeling "rather smothered in flowers [sensations in first edition], though he made in his other moments the almost angry inference that this was only because of his odious ascetic suspicion of any form of beauty" (xxi, pp. 193-94). Like Isabel Archer touring Rome with Osmond, Strether feels overwhelmed and yet blames himself for the feeling, striving to please Chad as Isabel strove to please Osmond. At the garden party, several more sensations have been arranged for Strether by Chad: first, the meeting with Gloriani, noted sculptor; second, the meeting with Madame de Vionnet; third, a brief glimpse of her daughter, Jeanne. The terms James uses for the series of meetings suggest, I think deliberately, a show at a museum or gallery: Strether, for example, "had known beforehand that Madame de Vionnet and her daughter would probably be on view" (xxi, p. 194); Chad presents Jeanne with "consummate calculation of effect" (xxi, p. 220); Strether also notes that "The whole exhibition" of Jeanne is deliberately brief (xxi, p. 223). If Strether began the novel choosing for himself what he would see, at this point in the novel *others* choose the sights that will create his vivid impressions. Their "plot," while not sinister like Osmond's, nonetheless counts upon Strether as a man able to be influenced by what he sees, even manipulated by what he sees; to some extent it uses Strether's visual sensitivity to exploit his naïveté.

James repeatedly uses the word "impression" in this episode of the garden party, leading some critics to identify—too strongly—a new sympathy between James and the Impressionists or an analogy between the Impressionist method and the ambiguity of perception typical of Strether's moral education.[20] Surely, the repeated use of "impression" indicates that James, consolidating the motifs we saw in *The Portrait*, now associated with the artistic movement certain distinct qualities: an emphasis on the perceiving subject; the fleeting, "unfinished" quality of the perceptions involved; a relative view of reality implicit in the emphasis on the dynamic relationship of perceiving subject and perceived object. Yet the identification of James's method in *The Ambassadors* and other novels too closely with the Impressionists or the frequent notion that "impressions" reflect a modern perception of reality and are, therefore, "good," can be misleading. As we saw in Chapter One, James remained skeptical of the Impressionists and always maintained that the value of any "impression" depended entirely on the quality of the mind registering it. And in this scene it is rather clear that Strether's "impressions"—like Isabel's of Osmond and of Rome—are partial or naive.[21] He values, for instance, Gloriani's "medal-like Italian face" enough "to remember [it] repeatedly" and to think of the sculptor's mien and manner "as the source of the deepest intellectual sounding to which he had ever been exposed" (xxi, p. 197). The reaction seems extreme, even infatuated, especially when we remember Gloriani's rather uninspired artistry in *Roderick Hudson* and note the brevity and impersonality of their encounter at the party. Similarly, Strether's "impression" of Jeanne—"A young girl in a white dress and a softly plumed white hat"—makes him erroneously (though understandably) assume that daughter, not mother, forms the object of Chad's interest (xxi, p. 220). Strether's visual impressions certainly move him at the garden party. He urges Little Bilham to "Live all you can" directly as a result of "This place and these impressions" (xxi, p. 217). But we do the study of the visual arts and pictorialism in literature no service by sliding too easily between Impressionism as an artistic movement and impressionism as a general literary phenomenon concerned with perception through seeing and especially with ambiguities of perception. And we misread the text if we see "impressions" as a final or necessarily admirable form of consciousness.

A striking metaphor used later in the novel indicates that each experience in Europe enters Strether's mind pictorially, even when it is not presented pictorially in the text for the reader's visual imagination. He notes that he moves "these days, as in a gallery, from clever canvas to clever canvas" (xxii, p. 273). The garden party is surely among the cleverest of these canvases, with the word "clever" suggesting some of the novel's moral ambiguities. To use the term "pictorialism" accurately with regard to this scene, however, we should stress that while Strether carries away from it a number of "pictures" to fuel meditation, the reader emerges with far fewer. For, despite the sequence's ample references to the visual arts, descriptions are vague, dialogue prevails, and the garden party is not experienced visually by the reader. Hence the usefulness of the term "perceptual," as opposed to "hermeneutic," to describe this use of the visual arts.

The scene of Strether by the river is more explicitly ruled by references to the visual arts than is the garden party and contains more emphatically pictorial moments. It crystallizes James's distinction between impressions and knowledge, just as it crystallizes Strether's relationship to Chad and Marie de Vionnet. Structured around the memory of "a certain small Lambinet that had charmed him, long years before, at a Boston dealer's and that he had quite absurdly never forgotten," Strether's journey into the French countryside attempts to recapture the open sense offered him in the past—but denied through lack of funds—by the Lambinet, "the only adventure of his life in connexion with the purchase of a work of art ... the picture he *would* have bought" (xxii, pp. 245-46). Perhaps typical of Strether is the sense that the one painting he *would have* bought was a painting he *could not* afford. The first American edition makes Strether's sense of loss in connection with the Lambinet even more explicit, calling it "the material acquisition that, in all his time, he had most sharply failed of."²² The result of impulse, the journey seeks to actually experience "that French ruralism, with its cool special green, into which he had hitherto looked only through the little oblong window of the picture-frame. It had been as yet for the most part but a land of fancy for him— the background of fiction, the medium of art, the nursery of letters; practically as distant as Greece, but practically also well-nigh as consecrated" (xxii, p. 245). Through its association with the Lambinet, the journey becomes implicated with other things that Strether has missed—especially with the things regretted when he urges Little Bilham to "live." It thus nicely prepares us for the unexpected irruption of Madame de Vionnet and Chad into the tranquil, aesthetic communion with nature and art that Strether anticipates on his journey.

Several aspects of Strether's state of mind must be noted if we are to understand the impact of his encounter with Chad and Mme. de Vionnet. First, the journey commemorates Sarah Pocock's departure and celebrates his sense of being at last "safe." Second, that sense of safety is largely delusory, since, although Strether feels that "his appointment was only with a superseded Boston fashion" on the trip, he is really destined to take the true measure of Chad and Marie's situation and consequently of his own (xxii, pp. 246-47). As though to urge a gently ironic view of Strether, James inserts several phrases at the beginning of the sequence that indicate his naïveté and childishness, despite his age: "Romance could weave itself, for Strether's sense, out of elements mild enough"; "It will be felt of him that he could amuse himself, at his age, with very small things"; and, with regard to the Lambinet (like Isabel Archer never looking out into the Albany street) "he never found himself wishing that the wheel of time would turn it up again" (xxii, pp. 245 and 246). Finally, and third, we need to stress the way that Strether perceives his adventure as bounded by the Lambinet and as safe because of this boundary. The Lambinet utterly controls his perceptions of the countryside and forms his expectations for what the day will bring. And he expects his experience to be framed, knowable, predictable, like the remembered painting.

As James's repeated references to Strether's experience as "framed"—a metaphor drawn from art for controllable—implies, the trick at first works. As Strether walks along in the countryside,

> The oblong gilt frame disposed its enclosing lines; the poplars and willows, the reeds and river—a river of which he didn't know, and didn't want to know, the name—fell into a composition, full of felicity, within them; the sky was silver and turquoise and varnish; the village on the left was white and the church on the right was gray; it was all there, in short—it was what he wanted: it was Tremont Street, it was France, it was Lambinet. (XXII, p. 247)

Here, once more, we see a certain contented vagueness in Strether's perceptions: he "didn't want to know" the name of the river before him and he illogically experiences the landscape as the equivalent of three different locales: Boston, France in general, and the setting of the painting (XXI, p. 247). Again with too smug a contentment, Strether turns from thought as he "lost himself anew in Lambinet" (XXII, p. 249). Yet again, James stresses Strether's vulnerability to the unnerving experience to follow: "He really continued in the picture—that being for himself his situation—all the rest of this rambling day . . . [he had] not once overstepped the oblong gilt frame. The frame had drawn itself out for him, as much as you please; but that was just his luck" (XXII, pp. 251-52). Implicit in James's and Strether's use of references to the visual arts and art metaphors is a view of art analogous to Keats's in "Ode on a Grecian Urn," alluded to earlier when I discussed *The Portrait of a Lady*: the view that art is static and knowable and safe, while life is dynamic, and unknowable, and, therefore, dangerous. When the frame of the

Lambinet ceases to expand, Strether's consciousness must itself grow to encompass less tidy views of experience than it has hitherto allowed. And this process is infinitely more painful than dwelling in a pleasant aesthetic memory.

Several critics have noted that, despite the reference to Lambinet, what Strether sees in the countryside suggests Impressionist art.[23] Many of the descriptions surely do have the vividness of color, and the blurred, rapid quality associated with Impressionist landscape. Thus, "the biggest village . . . affected him as a thing of whiteness, blueness, and crookedness, set in coppery green," almost like an abstract painting with an interest in color rather than representation (xxii, p. 252). Similarly, "The valley on the further side was all copper-green level and glazed pearly sky, a sky hatched across with screens of trimmed trees, which looked flat, like espaliers; and, though the rest of the village straggled away in the near quarter, the view had an emptiness that made one of the boats suggestive" (xxii, p. 255). As at the garden party, the use of the word "impression" and the terms of the description definitely evoke the artistic movement. These pictorial descriptions certainly raise "pictures" like the Impressionists' in the reader's imagination. Impressionist colors, textures, and lines dominate: the "copper green" valley, the "glazed pearly sky," and the phrase "hatched across," for example, all might be transcriptions in words of elements in typical Impressionist paintings. And yet, as I suggested earlier, the references probably do not indicate any wholehearted belief by James that impressions are the truest perceptions of experience. For while Strether's "impressions" are uniformly pleasant, they quickly yield to less facile and less comfortable thoughts once Strether begins to "read" the picture before him as that "suggestive" boat comes into view.

Into the remembered picture by Lambinet floats an unexpected element which seems, at first, "exactly the right thing" (xxii, p. 256), but proves more complicated than that, proves, in fact, the most important of the "clever canvases" Strether encounters in the European gallery. The "picture," of course, shows two people, obviously lovers, spending some days and nights together in the country, lovers who prove to be Chad and Madame de Vionnet. Strether "reads" the picture before him by noticing first its central focus, then the overall subject, then telltale matters of posture and expression:

> What he saw was exactly the right thing—a boat advancing round the bend and containing a man who held the paddles and a lady, at the stern, with a pink parasol. It was suddenly as if these figures, or something like them, had been wanted in the picture, had been wanted more or less all day, and had now drifted into sight, with the slow current, on purpose to fill up the measure. ... For two very happy persons he found himself straightway taking them—a young man in shirt-sleeves, a young woman easy and fair, who had pulled pleasantly up from some other place and, being acquainted with the neighborhood, had known what this particular retreat could offer them. The air quite thickened, at their approach, with further intimations; the intimation that they were expert, familiar, frequent—that this wouldn't at all events, be the first time. They knew how to do it, he vaguely felt—and it made them but the more idyllic; though at the very moment of the impression, as happened, their boat seemed to have begun to drift wide, the oarsman letting it go. It had by this time none the less come much nearer—near enough for Strether to dream the lady in the stern had for some reason taken account of his being there to watch them. She had remarked on it sharply, yet her companion hadn't turned round. ... She had taken in something as a result of which their course had wavered, and it continued to waver while they just stood off. ... He too had within the minute taken in something, taken in that he knew the lady whose parasol, shifting as if to hide her face, made so fine a pink point in the shining scene. (xxii, pp. 256-57)

James's handling of the moment splendidly captures both the process of "reading" what we see (described in the Introduction) and the very instant at which "impression" yields to knowledge, the instant for Strether at which the predictability and form of art yields to the messier categories of life. As the boat unexpectedly drifts wide, Strether's "impression"—all pleasant and admiring—yields to knowledge. And the lovers' relationship that had seemed so simply admirable and enviable in the "painting," becomes awkward, embarrassing, and complex. The pink parasol nicely indicates the change. At first merely an object to focus and compose the picture, it ends by being an instrument of deception that fails in its purpose: "he knew the lady whose parasol, shifting as if to hide her face, made so fine a pink point in the shining scene."[24] Upon its failure, moreover, Strether must instantly not only accommodate his new vision of Chad and Madame de Vionnet, but also must excuse his prior blindness and explain the contradiction between his admiration for the unknown lovers but uneasiness over the known ones.

Strether takes from this encounter a variety of information. Some information is visual (like the pregnant pause of the two figures on the boat before greeting him and the incongruity of Marie's dress with the title she gives the "picture," "A Day Trip"); some, not visual (like Marie's atypical chattering in French to cover her confusion). Like Isabel Archer in the perceptual use of the visual arts discussed earlier, Strether meditates through the night on remembered "pictures" from the encounter (as well as on other, nonvisual facts). He thereby arrives not just at the truth about the couple, but also at the truth about himself—that he has failed to view things properly largely because he did not choose to and also because he himself has never experienced intimacy with a woman. Masterfully, James intercuts allusions forward to Strether's meditation with the unrolling of the dinner at the inn:

When he reached home that night, however, he knew he had been, at bottom, neither prepared nor proof [against the knowledge of the couple's adultery]; and since we have spoken of what he was, after his return, to recall and interpret, it may as well immediately be said that his real experience of these few hours put on, in that belated vision—for he scarce went to bed until morning—the aspect that is most to our purpose. (xxii, pp. 261-62)

It was the quantity of make-believe involved [in covering their affair] and so vividly exemplified that most disagreed with his spiritual stomach. . . . That was what, in his vain vigil, he oftenest reverted to: intimacy, at such a point, was *like* that—and what in the world else would one have wished it to be like? (xxii, pp. 265-66)

A good deal of what makes Strether a likeable character in this novel is surely his ability to accept the displacement of the safe, historical Lambinet and to enter more fully into life and self-awareness. In the after-shock of the encounter by the river, Strether makes the inevitable connection between picture and idea, and accepts the fact that the idea communicated by the "picture" he has seen differs from the idea of a platonic friendship between Chad and Marie that he had previously cherished. The education of Strether's eye allows for spiritual and moral education as well, and in his remaining encounters in the novel—with Marie, with Chad, and with Maria Gostrey—his actions and words have a self-irony and a surer basis than earlier in the novel: the "impressions" of the apprentice have yielded to the knowledge of the mature man. And the climax of the process comes, as I have shown, in one of James's purest and most sustained perceptual uses of the visual arts and pictorialism.

VI

In *The Golden Bowl*, as in *The Ambassadors*, the visual arts and the visual appreciation of lovely things figure prominently in the background. All the novel's main characters are people of high culture and strong aesthetic sense. Moreover, the typically Jamesian themes of connoisseurship and the relation of the aesthetic to the moral sense haunt the novel and have been frequently handled by critics, especially those interested most in evaluating Maggie.[25] In an earlier study of the novel, I focussed

on gestural patterns as a key to interpreting its action and especially its ending. Such "reading" normally occurs in the arts
of drama and of narrative painting like that James tended to
admire.[26]

In *The Golden Bowl*, however, there are relatively few actual
references to the visual arts and very, very little pictorialism. To
be sure, characters in the novel often have their perceptions
quickened by what they see or by moments referred to as "pictures." Yet *The Golden Bowl* is, overwhelmingly, a novel of
characters' ruminations and feelings and of narrative analysis of
those thoughts and feelings. And, although the characters experience moments as "pictures," even more strikingly than in
The Ambassadors, James omits pictorial details which might enable the reader to imagine these "pictures" as well. There is,
then, no scene or sequence in the novel with as acute and specific
a relationship to the visual arts or pictorialism as that of Strether
by the river. A remarkable sequence near the beginning of
Maggie's section of the novel involves, however, a perceptual
use of references to art works worthy of examination as another
step toward defining the nature of perceptual uses of the visual
arts, among the most important in novels.

In *The Golden Bowl*, most references to the visual arts or
instances of characters thinking pictorially cluster in Maggie's
portions of the novel, perhaps reflecting her training and gifts
as the daughter of a great collector. And, while Maggie's impressions are not, as I have said, experienced pictorially by the reader,
the text explicitly refers to Maggie's dwelling on memories she
encodes pictorially. The most interesting sequence in connection
with the visual arts in this novel occurs as Maggie gropes her
way toward the truth about her husband and stepmother following the pair's fateful trip to Gloucester. Some critics have
identified Maggie's observing the bridge game at Fawns as the
more relevant to the topic of Henry James and the visual arts.[27]
But a careful reading shows that, in the Fawns sequence, dramatic metaphors (always very close for James to metaphors
drawn from the visual arts, but not identical) overwhelmingly

prevail. In the sequence I have chosen, which initiates the entire action of Part Two, however, art metaphors are key.

When Charlotte and Amerigo return late from Gloucester, Maggie arranges an unexpected surprise for her husband to signal her trouble by returning to Portland Place instead of remaining at Eaton Square for dinner. She gets more than she bargains for from the encounter with Amerigo that follows and finds herself with a situation more painful and difficult than Strether's to interpret. James and Maggie express in art metaphors her return (again and again) to the encounter in an effort to understand it: "It [her return home] had been a poor thing, but it had been all her own, and the whole passage was backwardly there, a great picture hung on the wall of her daily life for her to make what she would of. It fell for retrospect into a succession of moments that were *watchable* still" (xxiv, pp. 10-11). Here, as so often in James, art and dramatic metaphors slide inexorably together, but the particularity of the moments Maggie remembers suggests, not an ongoing drama, but a moment from a drama frozen in the memory. And, as we saw in Chapter One, a dramatic moment frozen on canvas was essentially James's definition of a fine painting.

The first of these moments occurs when the door opens and Amerigo enters. Maggie scrutinizes his face and demeanor much as she might the subtlest of portraits: "he had come back, had followed her from the other house, *visibly* uncertain—this was written in the face he for the first minute showed her" (xxiv, p. 15). As for Isabel confronting Madame Merle and Gilbert Osmond, however, the moment does not last. For the Prince, also a reader of faces, after "harbouring the impression of something unusually prepared and pointed in her attitude and array ... had advanced upon her smiling and smiling, and thus, without hesitation at the last, had taken her into his arms" (xxiv, pp. 16-17). But the visual impression of Amerigo irritates Maggie's mind and stimulates it to return again and again to the visual memory in search of knowledge: "Such things, as I say, were to come back to her—they played through her full after-sense like lights on the whole impression" (xxiv, p. 20). Note that, as in *The Portrait of a Lady* and in *The Ambassadors*, James uses the word "impression" only while the character struggles toward a not yet available knowledge. Also as in *The Ambassadors*, James emphasizes that the visual impression, although striking at the time, does not make full sense to the character until retrospective analysis, until the "after-sense" has had time to operate.

Needing more information, Maggie the next day visits Charlotte. And Charlotte's portrait too becomes one of the pictures for analysis in Maggie's gallery. Maggie sees "Charlotte, at the window" and "in the light, strange and coloured, like that of a painted picture, which fixed the impression for her, objects took on values not hitherto so fully shown. It was the effect of her quickened sensibility; she knew herself again in presence of a problem, in need of a solution for which she must intensely work" (xxiv, pp. 30-31). Her work—coming to understand the Prince's and Charlotte's true relationship—prospers from fixing their similar facial expressions in her memory as "pictures" and then dwelling upon them. Her process of interpretation explicitly involves comparing the expressions of her husband's face and her stepmother's, remembered as she would remember paintings in a locket around her neck: "The miniatures were back to back, but she saw them for ever face to face" (xxiv, p. 36). Moreover, "To make the comparison at all was, for Maggie, to return to it often, to brood upon it, to extract from it the last dregs of its interest" (xxiv, p. 35). And the process bears fruit. For Maggie, as for Isabel and Strether, when the crucial piece of information comes (for Maggie, the information about the excursion to buy the golden bowl), impressions deepen and metamorphose into knowledge.

In *The Golden Bowl* as in *The Ambassadors*, then, the perceptual process based upon things seen and referred to as pictures develops more fully and less ambiguously than we saw it develop in *The Portrait of a Lady*. While James's references to the visual arts, pictorialism, or both are rarely separate from his references to drama, and moments are most frequently experienced pictorially by *characters* rather than *readers* in the two late novels, James clearly uses the visual arts, pictorialism, or both perceptually in the examples I have given. And the distinctions between moral and aesthetic categories, impressions and knowledge, operate with more certainty and self-consciousness than in the earlier great work. James moves—in limited aspects but important aspects of his novels—well up the continuum that guides this study. In fact, this discussion of *The Portrait of a Lady*, *The Ambassadors*, and *The Golden Bowl*, along with the material in Chapter Four, now enables us to make a stronger definition of perceptual uses than has been given previously.

VII

In the examples I examined in Chapter Four from *To the Lighthouse*, Lily uses both her painting and her vivid, "framed" recollections of the Ramsays in ways comparable to the ways that Isabel, Strether, and Maggie use pictures actual and figurative. Cumulatively, these instances of perceptual uses of the visual arts and pictorialism in James and in *To the Lighthouse* enable us to define more fully some special qualities of the Modern novel's perceptual uses of the visual arts and pictorialism. Through her visual memory and imagination, Lily achieves a greater understanding of Mrs. Ramsay's meaning as a symbolic figure, of her own mission as a painter, and of the broader potentials for human community. When Lily Briscoe "coaxes into meaning" moments partially rendered in paint (like Mrs. Ramsay seated on the step with her son and Mr. Ramsay arriving at the lighthouse) or held pictorially in the memory for years (like Mrs. Ramsay presiding over Lily's game of ducks and drakes with Tansley), she illustrates perceptual uses of the visual arts or pictorialism as surely as do Isabel, Strether, and Maggie— less equivocally Strether and Maggie—in the instances that I have examined from *The Portrait of a Lady*, *The Ambassadors*, and *The Golden Bowl*.

In *To the Lighthouse*, as in the novels by James, three aspects of perceptual uses emerge as paramount, aspects we shall see again in the next chapter, on *Women in Love*. First, such uses unfold over time, with the process of understanding (of glossing the meaning of the art object or pictorial scene) taking a number of hours (as for Strether), or days, weeks, and months (as for Maggie), or even years (as for Lily). Second, such uses involve the characters' "piecing together" data from various points in the novel, so that the characters, though inevitably caught in the ongoing time of the novel, freeze various objects or moments as "pictures" in the visual imagination and can, at will, have all the "pictures" simultaneously present. Third (and this is the least invariable aspect of perceptual uses and one I will discuss more fully in the next chapter), the knowledge reached through the art object or visual impression frequently causes the perceiver discomfort or pain. I will return to these novels briefly in the next chapter to expand my definition of perceptual uses, after examining some larger sequences in *Women in Love* also involving perceptual uses of the visual arts, pictorialism, or both.

SIX

ENCODING THE TABOO IN
WOMEN IN LOVE

Early in the novel, when Birkin and Gerald stay at Halliday's
flat, they see the African statue of a woman in labor. When the
statue is first presented, it is described in the third person, yet
apparently from Gerald's point of view, as "strange and dis-
turbing" like a "foetus," conveying a suggestion of "the extreme
of physical sensation, beyond the limits of mental consciousness."¹ Though secretly fascinated by the piece, Gerald dismisses
the statue as "rather obscene" in a conversation with one of
Halliday's friends. Present at this conversation, Birkin comments
on the statue only the next morning, and only in response to
Gerald's direct, insistent questions. "Strangely elated" and yet
"shocked" by the statue, Gerald asks Birkin: " 'Why is it [the
statue] art?' " Birkin replies: " 'It contains the whole truth of
that state, whatever you feel about it' " (p. 133). To Gerald's
accusation that such a statue cannot be considered "*high*" art,"
Birkin replies: " 'High! There are centuries and hundreds of
centuries of development in a straight line, behind that carving;
it is an awful pitch of culture, of a definite sort' " (p. 133).² His
comments are muted—even rather vague. Like Gerald, Birkin
has a curious attraction to and repulsion from the statue that he
is reluctant to admit, even to himself.

Ostensibly, the men's discussion of the statue involves aesthetic
issues, issues of some importance. Broadly tolerant, Birkin's remarks epitomize Lawrence's belief that good art reveals "the
relation between man and his circumambient universe, at the
living moment."³ To Lawrence and to Birkin, good art is moral
art, though not moralistic art or even art expressive of values

Lawrence approved. The African artist's statue reveals forever the state *in extremis* of his culture. Similarly, Lawrence believed that the chaotic motion favored by Loerke and the Futurists aptly expressed the forms chosen in his own civilization's love affair with death. Thus, both primitive art and Modern art were good—even great—art for Lawrence, though he personally disliked most of it and preferred other values and other forms. Instructive in this regard are Lawrence's comments to his friend, Mark Gertler, on *The Merry go Round* (1916, plate 4), the model for Loerke's factory frieze in *Women in Love* and like that frieze "good" art in Lawrence's judgment.

In Gertler's work, the figures are geometrically rendered in simple ovaloid shapes and have mouths uniformly open, in unison (presumably) with the music of the carousel or the thrill of mechanical motion. Loerke's factory frieze includes similar details:

> It was a representation of a fair, with peasants and artizans in an orgy of enjoyment, drunk and absurd in their modern dress, whirling ridiculously in roundabouts, gaping at shows, kissing and staggering and rolling in knots, swinging in swing-boats, and firing down shooting galleries, a frenzy of chaotic motion. (p. 517)

Although it presents more than just a carousel, Loerke's frieze shares Gertler's emphasis on the peasant or artisan absurdly dressed up and on whirling, "roundabout" motion. More crucially, the works share a principle that Loerke articulates as central to both work and leisure in an industrialized system: "it is nothing but this, serving a machine or enjoying the motion of a machine—motion, that is all" (p. 519).

When Gertler sent Lawrence a photograph of *The Merry go Round*, Lawrence replied, in a letter to the painter, that the painting was "great, and true" and "the best *modern* picture I have seen," but he also found it "horrifying and terrifying" in its revelation of the direction of contemporary society. The work, moreover, made Lawrence want to "howl in self-lacerating de-

spair,"[4] with the self-lacerating howl a key difference in Lawrence's reaction to the state of his culture from those of the
African sculptor and good artists—but villainous characters—
like Gudrun and Loerke, who willingly advance cultural dissolution. Lawrence warned Gertler that the painting would be
called obscene and that the charge would be true. He added,
however, that "since obscenity is the truth of our passion today,
it is the only stuff of art." In the same vein, Lawrence commented: "in this combination of blaze, and violent mechanized
rotation and complete involution, and ghastly, utterly mindless
intensity of sensational extremity, you have made a real and
ultimate revelation."[5] Art that expresses questionable values can
thus still be "good" if those values are truly those of the artist,
his society, or both. The point, while simple, needs emphasis
because it is essential in understanding the roles that art and
artists—the African statue and sculptor as well as Loerke's frieze
and Loerke himself—play in the novel. And it governs Birkin's
comments about the African piece.

The exchange between Birkin and Gerald has, however, implications more personal and more taboo in ordinary conversation than the aesthetic theory they agree to discuss. In fact,
the discussion of what constitutes "good" and "high" art effec-
tively displaces the real interest of the statue for the two men.
As is often the case when characters contemplate art objects in
this novel, the African statue is indirectly used to explore attitudes which neither the characters nor the novel is as yet ready
to confront directly and frankly. The discussion of the art object
provides the occasion for a preliminary skirmish between characters—an indirect skirmish about issues more wideranging and
more sensitive than those immediately suggested by the object
at hand. As we shall see, in this scene Birkin and Gerald approach, but do not discuss, extremes of "physical sensation": they
are interested in a complex of attitudes toward sado-masochistic,
homosexual, and other unconventional sexual practices, and toward cultures whose art and mores could encompass such practices. An analogy between the woman in the statue and the

"slavelike" pregnant Pussum (Minette) he has just slept with especially piques Gerald's interest, for example; but he refrains from making the comparison aloud, even though he thinks of it several times. Cool, distant, and quickly finished, the discussion of the statue provides a relatively safe, neutral approach to these emotionally charged issues. Similar skirmishes occur between Birkin and Hermione when they discuss the Chinese paintings at Breadalby and between Loerke, Gudrun, and Ursula when they discuss the bronze statue of a young girl on a stallion. In Chapter One, we saw that Lawrence connected the aesthetic doctrines of Bloomsbury, as articulated by Fry and Bell, with onanism and the sexual involution of the group. His use of aesthetic discussions and art objects to encode complexes of attitudes about taboo sexual subjects in *Women in Love* is, I believe, one product of that connection.

II

After the conversation between Gerald and Birkin, there is no mention of the African statues for several hundred pages. But, at the beginning of the "Moony" chapter, when Birkin is estranged from everyone, it becomes clear that he has thought often about the African statues and is now ready to articulate his impressions of them more fully. Birkin

remembered the African fetishes he had seen at Halliday's so often. There came back to him one, a statuette about two feet high, a tall, slim, elegant figure from West Africa, in dark wood, glossy and suave. It was a woman, with hair dressed high, like a melon-shaped dome. He remembered her vividly; she was one of his soul's intimates. Her body was long and elegant, her face was crushed tiny like a beetle's, she had rows of round heavy collars, like a column of quoits, on her neck. He remembered her: her astonishing cultured elegance; her diminished, beetle face, the astounding long elegant body, on short, ugly legs, with such protuberant buttocks, so weighty and unexpected below her slim long loins. She knew what he himself did not know. She had thousands of years of purely sensual, purely unspiritual knowledge behind her. It must have been thousands of years since her race had died, mystically: that is, since the relation between the senses and the outspoken mind had broken, leaving the experience all in one sort, mystically sensual (p. 330).[6]

Birkin's meditation begins by recreating the visual stimulus; he recalls the statue in considerable detail and with special emphasis on the contrast between the figure's slim body and "protuberant buttocks," an emphasis suggesting anal intercourse.[7] As has frequently been noted, the beetle imagery also links the statue with Lawrence's stated dislike for homosexuality, which (in association with Bloomsbury) made him think of beetles. The statue he remembers here, like that observed with Gerald, is described as emphasizing "the extreme of physical sensation," an extreme including cruelty and subjection.

Birkin clearly "sees" the statue as his meditation continues, and the text imitates the statue's effect on him through the hypnotic incantation of "he remembered her." More important, Birkin moves directly from the visual memory of the art object to a series of statements about mores and attitudes. In fact, the statue, when its meaning has been fully glossed, reveals the fate of whole cultures. Birkin's ability to generalize from the art object to the culture once again reflects Lawrence's view of art as able to express the moral condition of the men and society producing it. His meditation leads, in fact, to the important discussion of the African and Arctic ways to cultural disaster, ways both present in the idioms of Modern art: the African in the primitive statues newly in vogue and assimilated in some Cubist paintings (like Picasso's *Les Demoiselles d'Avignon*), in the work of other historical artists or movements, and in Gudrun's art (which resembles the primitive); the Arctic, in the blazing metallic triangles so typical of both the Cubist and Futurist styles.

Of the African way, Birkin ponders that "Thousands of years ago, that which was imminent in himself must have taken place in these Africans: the goodness, the holiness, the desire for creation and productive happiness must have lapsed, leaving the

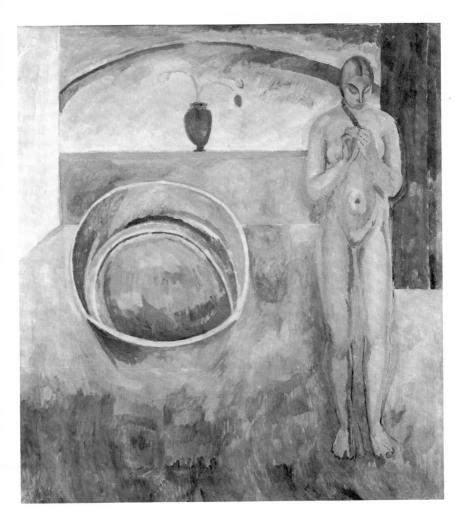

15. *The Tub*, Vanessa Bell, 1917 (The Tate Gallery, London)

16. *The Laugh*, Umberto Boccioni, 1911 (The Museum of Modern Art, New York; Gift of Herbert and Nennette Rothschild)

17. *Past and Present, No. 1*, Augustus Leopold Egg, 1858
(The Tate Gallery, London)

18. *The City Rises*, Umberto Boccioni, 1910 (The Museum of Modern Art, New York; Mrs. Simon Guggenheim Fund)

single impulse for knowledge in one sort, mindless, progressive knowledge through the senses, knowledge arrested and ending in the senses, mystic knowledge in disintegration and dissolution" (p. 330). His solution for avoiding the sensual debauch "imminent in himself," paradisal love with Ursula, fails of sustained realization in the novel. Sometimes it becomes entangled in sexual demands that trouble Birkin; sometimes it stumbles over earthly issues like jealousy and power. Birkin fully understands the nature of the African way and has consciously abandoned it. But he fears that his understanding of the cultural and personal issues raised by the African statue may help him no more than it helped the African sculptor or, for that matter, no more than having "touched the whole pulse" of Modern society helps Gudrun and Loerke to avoid the contamination rife in their society (p. 511).[8] In a sense, the African sculpture encodes a cautionary tale that Birkin both needs and yet fears to tell himself. At Halliday's apartment, the fear wins out, and Birkin forestalls realization; the gap between picture and idea remains intact. In "Moony," however, the meaning of the statue and its implications for himself erupt into Birkin's consciousness.

The visual image of the African statue known and articulated, Birkin is now ready to gloss the meaning of Gerald's hidden interest in African art:

> There remained this way, this awful African process, to be fulfilled. It would be done differently by the white races. The white races, having the arctic north behind them, the vast abstraction of ice and snow, would fulfil a mystery of ice-destructive knowledge, snow-abstract annihilation. . . .
>
> Birkin thought of Gerald. He was one of these strange white wonderful demons from the north, fulfilled in the destructive frost mystery. . . .
>
> Birkin was frightened. He was tired too, when he had reached this length of speculation. (p. 331)

Part of what frightens Birkin is his continuing fascination for Gerald, whom he believes "a messenger, an omen of the universal dissolution into whiteness and snow." That fascination suggests that while Birkin has resolved to abandon the African way, something in him yearns for the coming apocalypse of ice as surely as do Gerald, Gudrun, and Loerke. As is true for his escape from the African way through love with Ursula, Birkin's escape from the Arctic way depends upon fiercely held theories that may or may not be realizable about a brotherhood with Gerald that will turn the latter from the Arctic way.

The long sequence (much abbreviated here) in which Birkin meditates on cultural dissolution and on Gerald's symbolic "meaning" is intensely linguistic. But the meditation arises from a prolonged, often only half-conscious, contemplation of the African statue as a remembered visual image, as a "soul's intimate." The passage not only illuminates the meaning of the African statues but also elaborates how Gerald represents the "destructive frost mystery," a concept visually fulfilled in the Alpine setting of the novel's climactic action.

I I I

The perceptual use to which Lawrence puts the art object in this sequence from *Women in Love* has affinities with those in *The Portrait of a Lady, The Ambassadors, The Golden Bowl,* and *To the Lighthouse.* In each case, the meaning of the art object or pictorial scene unfolds gradually, after a long process of retrospective meditation. Also in each case, that meaning arises from a character's holding in his mind several different art objects or pictorial moments. Finally, in each instance, the art object or pictorial moment provokes a line of thought that leads the character to pain or discomfort, or provokes an awareness of facts that the character has tried not to notice or perhaps even repressed. Lily's meditations fit this definition least, and yet her vivid recollection of Mrs. Ramsay sitting on a rock watching the game of ducks and drakes "wrung the heart and wrung it again and again! Oh, Mrs. Ramsay! she called out silently, to that essence which sat by the boat, that abstract one made of her, that woman in grey" (p. 266). In, moreover, all instances but

Lily's, meditation on the art object leads the character to taboo, often sexual, issues. Even Lily's meditation may be seen as approaching taboo issues, if we accept Mark Spilka's identification of this moment as one in which Woolf imaginatively relives and revises her own aberrant reactions to her mother's death.[9] Such perceptual uses seem sufficiently distinct as to deserve a special name, the name "insinuation," a term introduced earlier, but needing now further explication.

Insinuation refers to a character's conscious or unconscious dwelling on an art object or pictorial image over a period of time, with a gradual clarification of meaning. One can usefully appropriate Lawrence's own words to define the process: insinuation is the life of "the image as it lives in the consciousness, alive like a vision, but unknown."[10] At the moment when the visual image becomes "known," its meaning crystallizes and is rendered in words or otherwise expressed: Lily "getting" the meaning of Mrs. Ramsay and finishing her painting; Strether dotting his i's at last in his conception of Chad's relation to Marie; Maggie knowing—directly she hears about the trip to buy the golden bowl—of her husband and stepmother's adultery; Birkin glossing the meaning of the statue. Paradoxically, we readers often know that insinuation has occurred when the process is essentially over. In its essence, then, insinuation is a form of visual memory or visual contemplation and, as such, is often absent in the words of the novel. Insinuation enters the novel directly only as the visual memory yields to the verbal articulation of its meaning, though the presence of insinuation may be assumed as occurring behind the lines of the novel. The technique allows novels to allude to whole processes of thought and feeling—sometimes unconscious ones—without tracing each step in those processes. The technique thereby enriches the psychological scope of the novel and its ability to transcend its verbal medium without inordinately increasing its length or abstractness.

Readers of *Women in Love* also undergo the process of insinuation. They too dwell on certain art objects or certain highly visual moments until the image is "known" and its meaning can be rendered in words. When a pictorial image insinuates itself into the mind of a reader, however, the yielding of the image in words usually occurs outside the text—in the mind of the reader or, alternately, in a critical essay. Actually, that yielding to words need not take place at all, though the insinuated elements will undoubtedly resonate in the interpreter's mind. A good example is the fashion show in *Women in Love*: Lawrence's persistent emphasis upon what women wear and particularly upon the colors of their clothing. The scene in which Ursula and Gudrun walk with their parents to the water-party at the Criches' is particularly vivid:

> The sisters both wore dresses of white crepe, and hats of soft grass. But Gudrun had a sash of brilliant black and pink and yellow colour wound broadly round her waist, and she had pink silk stockings, and black and pink and yellow decoration on the brim of her hat, weighing it down a little. She carried also a yellow silk coat over her arm, so that she looked remarkable, like a painting from the Salon. (pp. 219-20)

> Ursula was all snowy white, save that her hat was pink, and entirely without trimming, and her shoes were dark red, and she carried an orange-coloured coat. (p. 220)

In noting that Gudrun looks like a painting, Lawrence urges his reader to visualize the scene and to let it sink into his imagination. We may note that of the two sisters, Gudrun wears the more intense colors and the more striking, flamboyant color combinations. In this, she is very like Hermione—a helpful identification. Ursula also wears bright, contrasting colors, but her color combinations are always quieter than Gudrun's or Hermione's. Moreover, Ursula's propensity to bright dress diminishes as the book progresses, an objective correlative to her movement away from Gudrun and Hermione and toward Birkin. Gudrun and Hermione also share a fondness for a color that Ursula never wears—bronze green, like the sheen of an insect, the same color, not accidentally, of Loerke's Lady Godiva. Nowhere in the novel does Lawrence state what the colors worn by the women "mean," nor must the reader decisively articulate that meaning. Yet he uses color as a painter might to group and characterize figures for the reader.

The passage just examined is only one of many similar passages which gradually insinuate themselves into the reader's mind. The interpretive process is often encouraged for both characters and readers by the repetition of visual images that recall, expand, and enrich one another. As noted in the Introduction, I call this procedure "visual rhyme."[11] Insinuation and visual rhyme sometimes work separately in the novel, but more often they work so closely together that it is difficult to declare exactly where insinuation leaves off and visual rhyme begins. A few distinctions between the two processes (beyond those implicit in their definitions) can, however, be made. Insinuation proper is largely absent from the novel, generally revealing itself only when the image has become "known" to a character or to a reader and when the process of insinuation has reached some level of completion. Visual rhyme, on the other hand, is very much present in the novel and is one of the distinguishing features of *Women in Love*. Because visual rhyme involves the perception and nonverbal comparison of similar pictorial images, visual rhyme presses even less insistently than insinuation toward a verbal translation of meaning. The question raised by visual rhyme is not so much "what does this image mean?" as "what other pictorial images in the novel is this image like?" The perception of the image in visual rhyme is analogous to perceiving the history of a given image (the nude, the guitar) when viewing a painting. The important issue is not the "meaning" of the image itself, but the perception of the similarities and differences between the object's use in a given picture and its uses in other pictures. Each rhyme presses toward meaning, but the essence of the technique is to repeat and give resonance without any privileged revelation of meaning.

Before turning to larger units of the novel that depend significantly on insinuation and visual rhyme, I would like to explore one more relatively simple example to clarify its nature. Early in the novel, before they enter love relationships with the male characters, Ursula and Gudrun go to Willey Water to sketch. In a sequence that initially looks rather innocent, Lawrence gives us the following pictorial description:

> Gudrun had waded out to a gravelly shoal, and was seated like a Buddhist, staring fixedly at the water-plants that rose succulent from the mud of the low shores. What she could see was mud, soft, oozy, watery mud, and from its festering chill, water-plants rose up, thick and cool and fleshy, very straight and turgid, thrusting out their leaves at right angles, and having dark, lurid colours, dark green and blotches of black-purple and bronze. But she could feel their turgid fleshy structure as in a sensuous vision, she *knew* how they rose out of the mud, she *knew* how they thrust out from themselves, how they stood stiff and succulent against the air.
>
> Ursula was watching the butterflies, of which there were dozens near the water, little blue ones suddenly snapping out of nothingness into a jewel-life, a large black-and-red one standing upon a flower and breathing with his soft wings, intoxicatingly, breathing pure, ethereal sunshine; two white ones wrestling in the low air; there was a halo round them; ah, when they came tumbling nearer they were orange-tips, and it was the orange that had made the halo. Ursula rose and drifted away, unconscious like the butterflies. (p. 178)

The entire future of both women and of their relationships with men is predicted here, did we but know it on a first reading. To imagine the scene in paint would be relatively easy since Lawrence displays a rich sense of detail and color. The painting might be called "The Two Sisters" or "A Summer's Day," and it would recall the narrative paintings so popular in the nineteenth century, paintings like those of Millais, or one of Lawrence's early favorites, Greiffenhagen's *The Idyll*. Locale and action would pictorially reveal the radically different natures of the women: Gudrun's, with her unwholesome fascination for mud and mud-flowers and especially for such objects as phallic; Ursula's with her spiritualized interest in the butterflies. Reversing the sister's hair colors as recorded in *The Rainbow*, Lawrence would also "use" in this "painting" a device popular in literary and painterly iconography: the "good," more spiritual sister, Ursula, has the lighter hair in *Women in Love* (see p. 150), although, in *The Rainbow*, Ursula's hair is quite dark and Gudrun's lighter.

We make sense of this pictorial rendering in part by retrospectively bringing to it a series of linguistic and pictorial clues. As the novel develops, Lawrence includes brief phrases that gradually suggest broader meanings for this early scene. Pussum, for example, is described as a "flower of mud" by Halliday (p. 475); Loerke is described as a "wizard [sewer] rat" by Birkin, and as a "mud child" by the narrator (pp. 523, 521). In the chapter "Death and Love," Gerald enters Gudrun's room wearing shoes encrusted with graveyard mud. The drowned Diana and the young doctor she has killed rest in mud at the bottom of the lake. Although in literary terminology these phrases and motifs could be called images, they differ from the pictorial images that form at least one unit in visual rhyme. When Pussum is called a "flower of mud," she is compared to an object that may or may not be visualized by the reader. But the image is essentially verbal and is understood as words, not as a picture. The phrase does not vividly create a picture in the reader's mind, nor is it remembered as a nonverbal "picture" alive in the mind of characters and readers. The phrases and motifs do, however, expand the pictorial significance of Gudrun's fascination with mud as she sits near Willey Water. Gudrun, Loerke, Pussum, and Gerald all have in common something corrupt and sinister— something connected with the dissolution of culture of which Birkin speaks, and with corrupt sexual practices and attitudes. I deliberately use the vague word "something," because it points to the absence of paraphrasable meaning that forms the essence of visual rhyme.

To cultivate "visionary awareness" and to acknowledge the complex effects of the novel, we must, then, use both linguistic clues and pictorial ones. Lawrence demands that the interpretive process draw upon a variety of the reader's faculties and both press toward and resist any simple translation into words of the meaning of the visual elements. Thus, the process of visual rhyme has some similarities to more familiar practices in the interpretation of literature, like that used to understand expanding symbols. It may be distinguished, however, by at least one unit in the series' being a painting, a sculpture, or pictorial in one or more of the ways defined in the Introduction of this study.

IV

The most ambitious and compelling interpretive use of the processes of insinuation and visual rhyme occurs in the large and vivid symbolic scenes so characteristic of *Women in Love*. I call these scenes "tableaux" for two reasons: first, because they markedly slow down the tempo of the novel, sometimes almost freezing the action; second, because these scenes are presented pictorially and linger in readers' and characters' minds as distinct, framed images.[12] Each scene could be imagined as a painting or paintings composed of a variety of compelling details, including such apparently nonstatic details as sound and action. Significant tableaux include that of Gerald on the mare at the railroad crossing, Gudrun and Gerald with the rabbit, Birkin stoning the image of the moon, Gudrun dancing before the cattle, the two men collapsed after their wrestling match, and many others. Each of these tableaux is highly pictorial and assumes even greater significance than is at first apparent through the processes of insinuation and visual rhyme.

Let us take the scene of Gerald on the mare as a convenient example. It is a long scene, but worth quoting at length, since I want to comment on it in some detail:

> Going home from school in the afternoon, the Brangwen girls
> descended the hill between the picturesque cottages of Willey

Green till they came to the railway crossing. There they found the gate shut, because the colliery train was rumbling nearer. They could hear the small locomotive panting hoarsely as it advanced with caution between the embankments. The one-legged man in the little signal-hut by the road stared out from his security, like a crab from a snail-shell.

Whilst the two girls waited, Gerald Crich trotted up on a red Arab mare. He rode well and softly, pleased with the delicate quivering of the creature between his knees. And he was very picturesque, at least in Gudrun's eyes, sitting soft and close on the slender red mare, whose long tail flowed on the air. He saluted the two girls, and drew up at the crossing to wait for the gate, looking down the railway for the approaching train. . . .

The locomotive chuffed slowly between the banks, hidden. The mare did not like it. She began to wince away, as if hurt by the unknown noise. But Gerald pulled her back and held her head to the gate. . . . The repeated sharp blows of unknown, terrifying noise struck through her till she was rocking with terror. She recoiled like a spring let go. But a glistening, half-smiling look came into Gerald's face. He brought her back again, inevitably.

The noise was released. . . . The mare rebounded like a drop of water from hot iron. Ursula and Gudrun pressed back into the hedge, in fear. But Gerald was heavy on the mare, and forced her back. It seemed as if he sank into her magnetically, and could thrust her back, against herself. . . . He sat glistening and obstinate, forcing the wheeling mare, which spun and swerved like a wind, and yet could not get out of the grasp of his will. . . . [S]he spun round and round, on two legs, as if she were in the centre of some whirlwind. It made Gudrun faint with poignant dizziness, which seemed to penetrate her heart.

"No—! No—! Let her go! Let her go, you fool, you *fool*—!" cried Ursula. . . . And Gudrun hated her bitterly. . . . (pp. 168-69)

Immediately, in the first paragraph, Lawrence establishes as in a painting precise, significant spatial relationships. The scene is a railway crossing, with its junction of straight lines; the gate is shut. The passage combines visual and aural appeal, as the sounds of the locomotive "register" in the movements of the horse. At the end of the first paragraph, like the troubling detail often found on the periphery of a painting by Breughel, is the one-legged motorman.

Spatial relationships continue to be important in the following paragraphs. At first, Gerald glances away from the women, down the distance of the railroad tracks. Later, in a more significant alignment, he concentrates on the mare, just as Gudrun and Ursula's line of vision focuses directly on Gerald. Rhythmically, with the balancing, diagonal movements so often found in art, the passage includes directions such as "forward" and "back," "rose" and "sank," "out" and "back," in reference both to Gerald and the horse and to the women in relation to the riding couple. Recurring, patterned action unifies the scene.[13] Lawrence provides an indication of the scene's pictorial quality by having Gudrun describe Gerald as "picturesque." Indeed, many elements in the second paragraph sound like verbal transcriptions of a painted subject: "He rode well and softly," "the delicate quivering of the creature between his knees," "the slender, red mare," "whose long tail flowed on the air."

In a sense, the passage successively yields two different imaginary "paintings," in dramatically different styles. The first "painting" is in a realistic, nineteenth-century style, and features Gerald as the "picturesque" master horseman, bringing his horse to a stop at the railway and saluting the two handsome women. Fairly static, the picture accords well with traditionally realistic styles and subjects and is calm in mood, coloration, and tone. With the struggle of the mare and Gerald's exertion of will over it, the style and mood of the passage and its pictorial suggestions alter. Now motion—chaotic, fierce, violent—dominates, and "wheeling," "whirlwind" forces like those favored by the Futurists prevail. In imagining the struggle, diagonal lines of force and flashes of vivid color like those typical of the Futurists seem wholly appropriate.[14]

The red mare in itself suggests a favorite subject of Modern artists, especially the Expressionists, like Franz Marc, and the Futurists, like Boccioni. Moreover, several of the verbs and visual motifs used explicitly recall the mechanical, physics-based images and motifs of the Futurists and were written shortly after Lawrence's exposure to them.[15] Gerald presses the mare "magnetically" and is "glistening" like metal; the mare "rebounded like a drop of water from hot iron." The mare, moreover, "recoiled like a spring let go" and "spun and swerved like a wind." These last images "rhyme" with earlier descriptions of Bismarck, Winifred's rabbit, in the striking tableau in which Gerald and Gudrun recognize their mutual attraction to chaos and cruelty by their reactions to the rabbit. In this tableau, the rabbit "was in mid-air, lunging wildly, its body flying like a spring coiled and released, as it lashed out, suspended from the ears" (p. 315). Visual equivalents of Lawrence's images in the art of the Futurists come readily to mind. Balla's *Dynamism of a Dog on a Leash* (1912, and among the tamest of Futurist works) renders, for example, motion as a spring or coil. Boccioni's *The City Rises* (1910, plate 18) features powerful horses rendered as whirlwinds and diagonal lines of force in strong reds and blues. Through using images reminiscent of the work of the Futurists, Lawrence communicates the terror he felt at the corruption of organic life by mechanism, a joining the Futurists cheered in their manifestoes and encouraged in their art. Machine, mare, and man uneasily meet and cross in this tableau. Gerald's actions are as repetitive and programmed as the locomotive's, but man exceeds machine in willful and deliberate cruelty. Gerald wishes the mare to perform like a machine, with no natural fear of the locomotive; his will is to subsume nature to the machine.

V

As in the earlier example of visual rhyme, the implications of this pictorial scene are elaborated both linguistically and by uses of the visual arts and pictorialism. Shortly after the incident at the railway crossing, as Birkin and Ursula begin to recognize their attraction to each other, they participate in a conversation about the exercise of will. The conversation makes explicit the implicit content of the earlier visual tableau, its reference not just to horsemanship but to male domination over females and the general will to power. The conversation begins with a reference to Gerald's mistreatment of the horse but quickly moves to a more abstract and pointed discussion of the imposition of man's will on nature and the imposition of a lover's will on the beloved. Birkin maintains:

> "And woman is the same as horses; two wills act in opposition inside her. With one will, she wants to subject herself utterly. With the other she wants to bolt, and pitch her rider to perdition."
> "Then I'm a bolter," said Ursula, with a burst of laughter.
> "It's a dangerous thing to domesticate even horses, let alone women," said Birkin. "The dominant principle has some rare antagonists."
> "Good thing too," said Ursula.
> "Quite," said Gerald, with a faint smile. "There's more fun."
> (pp. 202-03)

Each character reacts typically in this scene: Ursula strikes out against male domination; Birkin waffles on the issue but ultimately agrees that any domination is dangerous; Gerald smiles at the idea of "antagonism" as "more fun." The earlier pictorial rendering thus encapsulated issues neither the characters nor the novel was as yet ready to explore head-on. The examination of male-female relationships and of the will to power is not complete at this point of the conversation about horses, nor has the "translation" of the visual tableau into words been thoroughly made. But this conversation begins to illuminate the earlier tableau and, more important, it emphasizes the importance of that tableau and its meanings.

A striking instance of an art object that "rhymes" with the pictorial scene of Gerald with the mare further enhances the importance of the tableau at the railway crossing and helps us to make sense of it. When Loerke shows Ursula and Gudrun a drawing of his green bronze statuette of a young girl on a horse, we immediately recall Gerald on the mare:

The statuette was of a naked girl, small, finely made, sitting on
a great naked horse. The girl was young and tender, a mere bud.
She was sitting sideways on the horse, her face in her hands, as
if in shame and grief, in a little abandon. Her hair, which was
short and must be flaxen, fell forward, divided, half covering her
hands.
   Her limbs were young and tender. Her legs, scarcely formed
yet, the legs of a maiden just passing towards cruel womanhood,
dangled childishly over the side of the powerful horse, pathetically,
the small feet folded one over the other, as if to hide. But there
was no hiding. . . .
   The horse stood stock still, stretched in a kind of start. It was
a massive, magnificent stallion, rigid with pent-up power. Its neck
was arched and terrible, like a sickle, its flanks were pressed back,
rigid with power. (pp. 523-24)

   In this statuette, the situation of Gerald with the mare seems
to be reversed: the girl rides the stallion. But she "sits" the horse
passively, her legs dangling "childishly, pathetically." There is
no will to power in the girl's attitude toward the horse—not
even the sense that power and control could be exercised over
it. All power resides in the stallion; as in the earlier scene of
horse and rider, the female member of the couple is dominated
and abused by the male. As if to dramatize the sexual politics
reflected in the statue, Lawrence deliberately withholds information concerning the gender of the horse until the end of the
description of the statue. He then emphasizes the "rigid. . . .
pent-up power" of the stallion and adds a note of sadism with
the description of the neck as "like a sickle."
   More consciously than in the earlier scenes, Gudrun and Ursula perceive the symbolic significance of the statue and react
characteristically to the idea of male domination. As was true
in the instance of the African statue, however, a discussion about
the nature of art displaces the more personal and taboo level of
the controversy. Like Loerke a professional artist, Gudrun begins
by asking details of size and medium. The information given,
Gudrun appreciatively murmurs, "Yes, beautiful; . . . looking

up at him [Loerke] with a certain dark homage," "with a certain supplication, almost slave-like" (p. 524). Ursula, however, challenges Loerke's "triumphant" look with an objection reminiscent of Sissy's in *Hard Times* when confronted with a definition of the horse different from ordinary experience: " 'Why,' said Ursula, 'did you make the horse so stiff? . . . *Look* how stock and stupid and brutal it is. Horses are sensitive, quite delicate and sensitive, really' " (p. 524). Loerke responds with a theory of art straight from Bloomsbury: " 'that horse is a certain *form*, part of a whole form. It is part of a work of art, a piece of form. It is not a picture of a friendly horse to which you give a lump of sugar, do you see—it is part of a work of art, it has no relation to anything outside the work of art' " (p. 525). Gudrun supports Loerke's position, saying that Loerke's idea of a horse may well differ from Ursula's. Ursula struggles for words and then rebuts: " 'But why does he have this idea of a horse! . . . I know it is his idea. I know it is a picture of himself, really—' " (p. 525).

Goaded by this insult, Loerke still more grandly declares the separation of art and life:

"Wissen sie, gnädige Frau, that is a Kunstwerk, a work of art. It is a work of art, it is a picture of nothing, of absolutely nothing. It has nothing to do with anything but itself, it has no relation with the everyday world of this and other, there is no connection between them, absolutely none, they are two different and distinct planes of existence, and to translate one into the other is worse than foolish, it is a darkening of all counsel, a making of confusion everywhere. Do you see, you *must not* confuse the relative work of action with the absolute world of art. That you *must not* do." (p. 525)

Loerke's views once again echo Bloomsbury's and also those of the Futurists, whose *Technical Manifesto of Cubism* (1912), known to Lawrence, urged the abolition of the artist's personality as the motive force of art. Furious and violent, Ursula first accuses Loerke of having abused the girl-model for the statue and then, "white and trembling," maintains that " 'The world of art is only the truth about the real world, that's all—but you are too far gone to see it'" (p. 526).

Various critics have had their say about which voice in the dialogue speaks for Lawrence, with the majority opinion being that Ursula's does.[16] In the context developed in this chapter, however, none of the participants speaks for Lawrence, because none is able to separate aesthetic judgment and personal taste, as we saw Birkin and Lawrence do earlier, with regard to the African statues. Gudrun and Loerke use the notion of form to remove art from reality, ignoring one of Lawrence's main points about Modern art: an art which detaches form from reality reveals a serious disorder in the artist's relationship to the cosmos; its connection to the "circumambient universe" will be one of denial, a denial that reveals its spiritual emptiness. Ursula's insistence on simple realism, on the other hand, is too much a reaction and too naive. She ignores an obvious prerogative of the artist: the right to use objects and creatures symbolically, a right often exercised through the distortion of photographic realism. While right about all art's revelation of the artist, she too narrowly and moralistically defines the boundaries of the acceptable, revealed self. No one in this debate about the Godiva entirely speaks, then, for Lawrence. As his comments about Gertler's painting, the nature of art, and the qualities of Modern art indicate, Lawrence's reactions to Loerke's statue would be mixed: he could recognize simultaneously its form and power *and* its deathly origins and implications.

The debate about the nature of art precipitated by Loerke's statue has an obvious weight and importance in the novel and in itself. But, like the earlier conversation between Gerald and Birkin about the African statue, it is, in a sense, a cover, a way of approaching issues more taboo and explosive. The clarity and ease with which the women move between aesthetic and sexual issues suggests that they too, using psychological methods equivalent to the devices I am calling "insinuation" and "visual rhyme," have arrived at a full understanding of the sexual and moral issues posed by the two pictorial images of horse and rider. Gudrun has, clearly, thrown in her lot with the forces of dissolution. Ursula has committed herself to fighting those forces through her alliance with Birkin. Significantly, the discussion of the statue proves a vital turning-point in the plot of the novel. As the sequence unfolds, Gerald joins Loerke and Gudrun in ridiculing Ursula for her views on art. She immediately decides to leave the Tyrol and departs shortly thereafter with Birkin for Italy. That departure leaves Gudrun and Gerald free to work out their deathly struggle.

Just as Lawrence's uses of the visual arts and of pictorialism in these instances help the characters to interpret the action, they help the reader to interpret the novel. Lawrence could have communicated all that insinuation and visual rhyme convey in the novel without using these processes. But it would have taken him many more words to do so—most of them rather preachy and obvious as compared to what we actually find in the novel. In the scene just examined, for example, without having prepared the reader through insinuation and visual rhyme to understand what occurs between Loerke, Gudrun, and Ursula as they look at the statue, Lawrence would have had to state the relevance of the statue and of its subject (girl on horse) to male-female relationships and to point out the similarity of Gudrun to the girl-model and to Minette, whose hair, like the model's, is short and flaxen, and whose look is "slavelike" as is Gudrun's. Finally, Lawrence would have had to reiterate Ursula's contrary nature, her rejection of both cruelty and domination. Such a passage would certainly lack the economy and suggestiveness of the passage just examined. The processes of insinuation and visual rhyme help to account, then, for some of what seems most characteristic and most worthy of praise in *Women in Love*. The novel's pictorial images allow themes and issues to resonate in characters' and readers' minds without the kind of explicit verbalizing that might flatten the novel, and does spoil a later novel like *Lady Chatterley's Lover*.

By inviting the reader to participate fully in the processes of insinuation and visual rhyme, Lawrence encourages the full use of the powers of the mind—defined by Lawrence as "instinct, intuition, mind, intellect"—[17] through what I called in the Introduction hermeneutic uses of the visual arts and of pictorialism. For characters (in perceptual uses) and for readers (in hermeneutic ones), references to the visual arts and uses of pictorialism provide vital interpretive clues in *Women in Love*. The novel fulfills Lawrence's ambition to stimulate "visionary awareness" by forcing the reader to know "real vision pictures" by "dwelling on them and, really, dwelling in them."[18] In doing so, it takes us to the end of the continuum for uses of the visual arts and pictorialism defined in the Introduction to this study.

CONCLUSION

At the far end of the continuum, scenes based upon the visual arts or pictorially rendered become miniatures of the novel, initiating a process of repetitions and mirrorings that both illuminate the meanings of the novel and render its structure simultaneously lucid and complex. In a sense, interpretive uses of the visual arts are comparable to the mirrors used in paintings like Jan Van Eyck's *Giovanni Arnolfini and his Bride* (1434) and Velasquez' *Las Meninas* (1656), as they are discussed by Michel Foucault in *Les Mots et les choses* and Lucien Dällenbach in *Le Récit spéculaire*.[1] They import into the frame of the work figures, or things, or ideas, at first and in the formal sense extrinsic—but ultimately essential. The impulse to move beyond the novel's own medium, words, and to appropriate the effects and media of the visual arts ends in not only superimposing the model of another (visual) art on the novel, but also in affirming the very powers and capacities of the original art and medium. We do not "find" the meanings of a novel and appreciate its wonder when we identify the models it uses from the visual arts: that is the essential error of the documentary mode. We find those meanings and appreciate that wonder when we maintain a double vision of the artistic model and the verbal text, with the image of the former deepening our appreciation of the latter.

A novel written after the Modern period—but which uses the heritage of the Moderns like James (and Proust) conspicuously—ranges the continuum described in this study with virtuosity and provides in one of its extended sequences a stunning emblem of how works of art miniaturize and reveal—without oversimplifying or flattening—the meanings of the literary works that use them. It will be worthwhile to end with a brief discussion of that novel, Anthony Powell's *A Dance to the Music of Time*.

Even in its title, Powell's *A Dance to the Music of Time* evokes a number of interdisciplinary comparisons, all apt for his novel, which have caused the interdisciplinary comparison to the visual arts to remain relatively unexamined. One does not read far in this multi-volume text, however, without discovering that art references and instances of pictorialism abound. *Dance* is a first-person narrative, and the narrator's, Nicholas Jenkins', involvement with the visual arts dates from his boyhood. He sees art in his parents' home and at their friends' homes, and a close associate of the family, Edgar Deacon, is a painter in an academic, neo-classical style. Later, Jenkins becomes involved in publishing art books. Thus, references to the visual arts multiply, with the works mentioned sometimes historical and sometimes fictional: Deacon's *Boyhood of Cyrus*, paintings by the Impressionists, the work of Horace Isbister, R. A., Modigliani's head of a woman, Bruegel's *The Return of the Hunters*, Tiepolo's ceiling paintings, and so on are all named in the course of the novel.

If we emphasize the historical works of art brought within the frame of the novel, fiction seems to have appropriated reality. The work of art within the novel seems to certify the novel's mimetic aspirations and to illustrate one way that novels mirror reality. But historical paintings take their place—without a murmur of protest—beside paintings that exist in no real paint, on no real canvases, in no real world; and this is entirely typical of the ways that novels use the visual arts. In this sense, references to the visual arts seem anti-mimetic, deliberately artificial, very much calling attention to the fictiveness of the novel's world. The mimetic mirror becomes the kaleidoscopic mirror of the funhouse. Both effects can, indeed, operate at the same time. For example, the historicity of even the familiar Bruegel and Modigliani is called into question since the paintings exist, within the world of the novel, as titles or attributed works whose concrete existence can be evoked but not reproduced in the text (short of illustrations).

Jenkins' special interest in the dance or interrelationship of the old with the new in art saturates the narrative with theoretical speculations. Jenkins also classifies the quality of his contemporaries' minds by their reactions to art. Some characters—like Eleanor and Widmerpool—are "never very capable of painting word pictures" or "felt no interest whatever in pictures, good or bad."[2] Others, like Jenkins himself, live for art; still others—like Pamela, Stringham, and Duport—suggest hidden depths to their personalities by the value they attach to paintings. Like many first-person narrators from the earliest fiction forward, moreover, Jenkins remembers certain moments as pictures. Widmerpool "first took coherent form in [his] mind," for example, when Nicholas sees him, "Heavily built, [with] thick lips and metal-rimmed spectacles" and "two thin jets of steam drift[ing] out of his nostrils," jogging along the road "stiffly, almost majestically."[3] Jenkins' memory operates implicitly by grouping iconographically certain moments widely separate in time as a museum might group works by subject rather than period. The subject of the stark-naked lady groups, for example, the hysterical maid who disrupts a dinner party in Jenkins' boyhood, Jean Templar during her affair with Jenkins, and Pamela Flitton Widmerpool as she stalks Gwinnet through a darkened house. Some of the novel's key memories even find embodiment in visual form, like the photographs of major characters enacting the seven deadly sins at Donners' mansion. All these uses are, initially, essentially decorative. But the work's massive length gradually reveals them as also biographical, ideological, perceptual, and hermeneutic, with that massive length allowing for especially fine examples of insinuation and visual rhyme.[4]

As time performs its dance, certain works of art come to be associated with broad movements in art and culture. Isbister's works become a fulcrum for socialist–realist theories of art when they are reprinted with a new and political introduction. Deacon's *Boyhood of Cyrus* moves from being an emblem of the Victorian age to revealing the sexual preoccupations of the post-World War II society that revives his art. A reviewer in the

1960's sees the painting and writes of its "strong homosexual basis," "fearless sexual candour," and (in Powell's parody of the idiom of art reviews) of its "sadomasochist broodings in paint that grope towards the psychedelic."[5] *Boyhood of Cyrus*, like Borges' *Don Quixote*, has changed its meaning over time, with that change indicating the vast chasms that separate Victorian and modern mores. Works of art thus participate in the dance of time and mark the newness or the repetitions of its steps.

Many of the novel's visual images encode, moreover, a host of metaphoric or symbolic qualities. Widmerpool's dogged running epitomizes his range of careers as company-man and determined social-climber in business, the military, government, and academia. It also helps Powell to get away with one of the more audacious plot developments in fiction: Widmerpool's last transformation, in the late sixties, into the guru and cohort of Scorp Murtlock's cult, and his death one morning on the determined jog that forms one of the cult's rituals. In the initial visual image of Widmerpool lies his life and his end, a property shared by other visual images of other characters, like those in the photographs of the seven deadly sins. Eminently typical of the narrator's mind (and hence of the work's narrative method) is the interpretation of life and time in terms of art or the remembered visual image. In a sense, all the characters seek in the narrator's mind a visual image that, when properly read, reveals all of what is essential to the character.

Hence, the dancing Faniculí / Faniculá man who weaves through *Temporary Kings* rhymes visually with the dancing Bithel of the war volumes and alludes tacitly to the exuberance within decadence typical of that character as of Venice. Hence too, Scorp Murtlock finally emerges as most of all like the Devil, in the narrator's realization that he is the incarnation of a drawing long ago seen in Bunyan's *The Pilgrim's Progress*. As Jenkins watches Murtlock approach him across a field, he says: "Watching the approaching figure, I was reminded of ... an incident in *The Pilgrim's Progress*. ... From the moment of first hearing that passage read aloud—assisted by a lively portrayal of the fiend in an illustration, realistically depicting his goat's horns, bat's wings, lion's claws, lizard's legs—the terror of that image, bursting out from an otherwise at moments prosy narrative, had embedded itself for all time in the imagination."[6] Murtlock, of course, does not actually resemble Bunyan's devil. But that image of evil incarnate, lodged for many years in Jenkins' mind, finds its contemporary embodiment in the cool, sinister Scorpio. What seems at first decorative merges over the time of *Dance* with the ideological and especially with the perceptual.

Powell's richest interpretive use of the visual arts and pictorialism occurs when a ceiling painting by Tiepolo crystallizes much of the novel's action and many of the novel's themes in the extended sequence in which Jenkins, Pamela, Widmerpool, and a group of scholars behold the ceiling in Venice. Coming in the penultimate volume of the very long work (in *Temporary Kings*, the eleventh of its twelve connected novels), the sequence vividly exemplifies the potential of insinuation and visual rhyme to surprise the reader and to illuminate, with drama and suddenness, the text. The Tiepolo ceiling depicts the story of Gyges and Candaules, in which Candaules, King of Lydia, exhibits for his friend Gyges the naked beauty of his wife, without the Queen's consent or approval. The fresco captures the moment at which the Queen, having perceived the reluctant Gyges slipping from the bedchamber, contemplates what will be her subsequent course of action: to propose that Gyges murder the husband who has betrayed her nakedness and marry her himself, thereby rectifying the fact of his having seen her unclothed body. But the explication of the painting's subject is delayed until after the following very long and highly pictorial description:

> The scene above was enigmatic. A group of three main figures occupied respectively foreground, middle distance, background, all linked together by some intensely dramatic situation. These persons stood in a pillared room, spacious, though apparently no more than a bedchamber. ... Meanwhile, an attendant team of intermediate beings—cupids, tritons, sphinxes, chimaeras, the

passing harpy, loitering gorgon—negligently assisted stratospheric support of the whole giddy structure and its occupants. . . .

An unclothed hero, from his appurtenances a king, reclined on the divan or couch that was the focus of the picture. One single tenuous fold of gold-edged damask counterpane, elsewhere slipped away from his haughtily muscular body, undeniably emphasized (rather than concealed) the physical anticipation . . . of pleasure to be enjoyed in a few seconds time; for a lady, also naked, tall and fair-haired, was moving across the room to join him where he lay. To guess what was in the King's mind—if king he were—seemed at first sight easy enough, but closer examination revealed an unforeseen subtlety of expression. Proud, self-satisfied, thoughtful, more than a little amused, he seemed to be experiencing mixed emotions; feelings that went a long way beyond mere expectant sexuality. . . .

The lady—perhaps the Queen, perhaps a mistress—less intent on making love, anxious to augment pending pleasure by delicious delay, suddenly remembering her neglect of some desirable adjunct . . . had paused. Her taut posture, arrested there in the middle of the bed chamber, immediately proposed to the mind these and other possibilities. . . .

The last possibility—that the lady had noticed an untoward happening in the background of the bedchamber—was the explanation. Her eyes were cast on the ground, while she seemed to contemplate looking back over her shoulder to scrutinize further whatever dismayed her. Had she glanced behind, she might, or might not, have been in-time to mark down in the darkness the undoubted source of her uneasiness. A cloaked and helmeted personage was slipping swiftly, unostentatiously, away from the room towards a curtained doorway behind the pillars. . . . At that end of the sky, an ominous storm was plainly blowing up, dark clouds already shot with coruscations of lightening and tongues of flame (as if an air raid were in progress), their glare revealing, in the shadows of the bedchamber, an alcove, where this tall onlooker had undoubtedly lurked a moment beforehand.[7]

In its delayed revelation of subject matter and in Jenkins' multiple speculations on the identity of the figures and their motivations, the handling of the sequence entirely typifies the narrative methods of the novel as a whole which use "uncertainty and imprecision as a narrative aid."[8] Within its narrative context, moreover, the description identifies characters in the painting with characters in the novel, establishing a complex web of repetitions. Pamela wears colors that "might have been expressly designed—by dissonance as much as harmony—for juxtaposition against those pouring down in brilliant rays of light from the Tiepolo: subtle yet penetrating pinks and greys, light blue turning almost to lavendar, rich saffrons and cinnamons melting into bronze and gold. Pamela's own tints hinted that she herself, only a moment before, had floated down out of those cloudy vertical perspectives" (p. 82). As the conversation about the Tiepolo unfolds, Pamela will threaten her husband's political power as the Queen will shortly threaten the King's; she will also reveal more piquant connections between herself and the Queen, Candaules and Widmerpool. The storm about to break in the fresco refers not just to the deposition of Candaules, but also to the deposition of Widmerpool from political power, to the break-up of his marriage, and to Pamela's own dire fate as she devotes herself to Gwinnet (who might be Gyges, except that that would be too obvious and too neat). The grotesques that encircle the central scene, moreover, might well be the attendant scholars and Jenkins himself.

Besides serving as a pivot for the novel's characterization and plot, the painting—in its depiction of an act of voyeurism—opens up what we might (borrowing a phrase from J. Hillis Miller) call a Quaker-Oats-box-effect of voyeuristic act within voyeuristic act, within voyeuristic act, within voyeuristic act, within voyeuristic act.[9] For, with consummate indiscretion, Pamela reveals for anyone who is listening that Widmerpool tolerates her many liaisons from motives essentially voyeuristic and harbors a drawer full of surreptitiously taken photos of Pamela with her most recent lover. Widmerpool thus connects to one of the early patrons in his rise to power—Sir Magnus Donners—and Pamela to Matilda, characters earlier involved in sexual relationships featuring voyeurism, relations which (like Widmerpool and Pamela's) have been the object of much speculation by Nicholas Jenkins. The juxtaposition of Widmerpool and Pamela with the characters in the fresco also renders the mirroring quality of the work of art two-sided: does the work of art "reflect" the narrative situation of *Dance*, or is our perception of the narrative situation shaped by the story communicated by the work of art?

At this point, however, we step through the looking-glass and into Wonderland. For despite the detail with which Powell describes the painting, I have been unable to confirm the existence of a ceiling painting (or any other kind) called "Candaules and Gyges" or on the general subject, painted by Tiepolo, in Venice or anywhere else—and I have consulted the best sources available.[10] The likelihood that the work does not exist is, frankly, a delightful one, for Powell's playful example makes with a vengeance my point that identifying works of art as sources for novels is an inadequate interdisciplinary approach.

Most readers and critics have been content to assume the ceiling's existence, and for several good reasons all connected to Powell's trickily convincing us of its historicity. The ceiling, we are told, adorns a Venetian palazzo belonging to the Bragadin family. According to a scholar in the novel, Dr. Brightman, the painting aroused political controversy when it was unveiled because of the voyeuristic tastes of a prominent noble. The model for the Queen (again according to Dr. Brightman—a suspicious name for a female scholar?) also appears in the famous—and real—paintings of Antony and Cleopatra located (and really located) in Venice. The subject of Candaules and Gyges is also treated—we are told accurately—by André Gide in a play (his *King Candaules* of 1901). This last fact especially teases, since Gide originated the term "la mise en abyme," suggestive of the mirroring functions of a work of art within a work of art.[11]

Regarding both the painting and Pamela with Widmerpool is Jenkins. Suddenly, we recognize more fully than before that Jenkins' interest in and detached observation of life blend imperceptibly into voyeurism. As our narrator, Jenkins (an extreme but certain descendant of Lambert Strether) is an eminent voyeur, particularly fascinated by the romantic dances performed by his friends and acquaintances. His voyeuristic rather than participatory instincts (at least as reflected in the stories he deems worth telling) help to explain a leading peculiarity of *A Dance to the Music of Time*: the oddness of the narrative form, the time (and volumes) it takes for Jenkins to emerge as a clearly defined character and the extent to which his central life experiences (as lover, husband, father, professional) figure only minimally in the novel's action. The subject of the Tiepolo ceiling—voyeurism—and its ambience of speculation, impending action, and suspension become, then, apt metaphors for the central principles of the novel.

But this is not all. For also regarding the painting is a group of visiting scholars, who gape at it with a fascination that threatens to demolish the usual etiquette of a tour. The flustered guide, Jacky Bragadin

> was casting anxious glances round the room. A few members of the Conference had begun to drift into the farther gallery, by far the larger majority continuing to contemplate the Tiepolo. Jacky Bragadin seemed to fear the story of Candaules and Gyges had hypnotized them, caused an aesthetic catalepsy to descend. Their state threatened to turn his home into a sort of Sleeping Beauty's Palace, rows of inert vertical figures of intellectuals, for ever straining sightless eyes upwards towards the ceiling, impossible to eject from where they stood. (p. 112)

The picture of intellectuals gaping at the ceiling suggests a playful metaphor for the open-ended and incapacitating nature of the life of the mind and the process of interpretation. Nor is this all. For regarding the four voyeuristic pageants is the reader, whose very engagement in the act of reading becomes implicated in the voyeuristic circle. Voyeurism, the subject of the seemingly arbitrary Tiepolo ceiling, becomes an inescapable analogue to the process of viewing a work of art, and becomes an apt metaphor, too, for the act of reading novels.[12]

A Dance to the Music of Time ranges the continuum of ways to use the visual arts and pictorialism with stunning virtuosity, coiling and recoiling its uses of the visual arts and pictorialism with effects complex, spiralling, and surely indebted to the uses of the visual arts and pictorialism implicated in the development of Modern fiction. Its uses of the visual arts and pictorialism exemplify the full range of the continuum that has governed my discussion; and its use of the Tiepolo ceiling in which "representation undertakes to represent itself "[13] may serve as a pictorial emblem of the later stages of that continuum. Important works like *Dance* confirm, then, the importance and persistence of the phenomena described in this study. The visual arts and pictorialism (and, though they exceed the boundaries of this study, the modern forms of photography, film, and television) have continued to inspire and provoke novelists and to provide ways of embodying themes, of suggesting models for novelistic form and interpretation, and of stretching the verbal limits of the novel's medium, words.[14] Novelists do indeed want to make us "see," and creative uses of the visual arts and pictorialism encourage the wonder and understanding that accompany seeing well.

NOTES

1. See Charles Rosen and Henri Zerner's discussion of this alliance in "What Is, and Is Not, Realism?" *New York Review of Books*, XXIX:2 (Feb. 18, 1982), pp. 21-26.

2. Quoted in John Rewald, *The History of Impressionism*, fourth, rev. ed. (1946; New York: The Museum of Modern Art, 1973), p. 428.

3. For some excellent essays on these and other relationships between French art and literature in the nineteenth century, see Ulrich Finke, ed., *French Nineteenth-Century Painting and Literature: with special reference to the relevance of literary subject matter to French painting* (Manchester: Manchester Univ. Press, 1972).

4. James's comment occurs in *The Question of Our Speech and The Lesson of Balzac* (Boston: Houghton Mifflin Co., Riverside Press, 1905), p. 109. Cézanne's comment is quoted in H. H. Arnason, *History of Modern Art: Painting, Sculpture, Architecture* (New York: Harry N. Abrams, Inc., and Englewood Cliffs, N.J.: Prentice-Hall, Inc., n.d.), p. 45.

5. Quoted in Rudolph Arnheim, *Visual Thinking* (Berkeley: Univ. of California Press, 1969), p. 56.

6. Virginia Woolf, *Roger Fry: A Biography* (New York: Harcourt, Brace, and Co., 1940), p. 172 and p. 240.

7. Virginia Woolf, "Walter Sickert," rpt. in *Collected Essays*, vol. II (New York: Harcourt, Brace, and World, Inc., 1925), p. 241.

8. George Bluestone discusses the recurrence of this vocabulary in *Novels Into Film* (Baltimore: Johns Hopkins Press, 1957), p. 1. See also Edward Said, *The World, the Text, and the Critic* (Cambridge: Harvard Univ. Press, 1983), pp. 90-101.

9. Wendy Steiner, *The Colors of Rhetoric: Problems in the Relation of Modern Literature and Painting* (Chicago: Univ. of Chicago Press, 1982), p. 18. Ms. Steiner's book appeared after my own manuscript was essentially completed. I was, however, able to incorporate some insights from and comments on her important book in late revisions and hope that the need to absorb her argument into my own has resulted in no distortions in my reading of her book.

10. Mario Praz, *Mnemosyne: the Parallel between Literature and the Visual Arts*, Bollingen Series, XXXV:16 (Princeton: Princeton Univ. Press,

1970), p. 216. I follow the common practice of capitalizing terms that refer to specific movements or periods in art or literary history and not capitalizing terms that refer to general tendencies in the art or literature of any movement or period. Some writers—including Praz and Steiner in this Introduction—do not. Within quotations or when discussing quotations, I will follow the writer's practice, even when, as here, it would be useful to distinguish between Impressionism as a movement and impressionism as a general emphasis on the subjectivity and spontaneity of perception.

11. *New Literary History*, III:3 (Spring 1972), 493.

12. I am thinking here of studies like Jean Hagstrum's *The Sister Arts: The Tradition of Literary Pictorialism and English Poetry from Dryden to Gray* (Chicago: Univ. of Chicago Press, 1958); Ernest B. Gilman's *The Curious Perspective: Literary and Pictorial Wit in the Seventeenth Century* (New Haven: Yale Univ. Press, 1978); and Ronald Paulson's *Emblem and Expression: Meaning in English Art of the Eighteenth Century* (Cambridge: Harvard Univ. Press, 1975).

13. Wylie Sypher, *Rococo to Cubism in Art and Literature* (New York: Random House, 1960), p. 264.

14. See René Wellek, "The Parallelism between Literature and the Arts," *English Institute Annual* (New York: Columbia Univ. Press, 1941).

15. See Wendy Steiner, *Exact Resemblance to Exact Resemblance: The Literary Portraiture of Gertrude Stein* (New Haven and London: Yale Univ. Press, 1978).

16. Steiner, *The Colors of Rhetoric*, p. 179.

17. Jeffrey Meyers, *Painting and the Novel* (New York: Barnes and Noble, 1975); Viola Hopkins Winner, *Henry James and the Visual Arts* (Charlottesville: Univ. of Virginia Press, 1970); Charles Anderson, *Person, Place, and Thing in the Novels of Henry James* (Durham: Duke Univ. Press, 1977); and Keith Alldritt, *The Visual Imagination of D. H. Lawrence* (Evanston: Northwestern Univ. Press, 1971).

18. Richard Shone, *Bloomsbury Portraits: Vanessa Bell, Duncan Grant, and Their Circle* (New York: Dutton, 1976).

19. Meyers, p. 29.

20. See Meyers' discussion in his chapter on *The Rainbow*, p. 54.

21. See Meyers, pp. 73-78; Alldritt, pp. 157-58.

22. Jean Seznec, "Art and Literature: A Plea for Humility," *New Literary History*, III:3 (Spring 1972), 568-74.

23. *Encounters: Essays on Literature and the Visual Arts*, ed. John Dixon Hunt (London: Studio Vista, 1971); *Images of Romanticism: Visual and Verbal Affinities*, eds. Karl Kroeber and William Walling (New Haven: Yale Univ. Press, 1978).

24. In the wake of post-structuralist criticism, notes displaying awareness of post-structuralist principles but maintaining the need to put them aside selectively may prove as prevalent and, ultimately, as unnecessary as notes in the sixties and seventies acknowledging but putting aside the New Critical intentional fallacy. Since that time has not yet come, I here note that despite the argument that any attempt at the description of literature is doomed to the same infinite regresses of meaning as literature itself, I continue to believe that the critic's primary duty is to enhance his reader's appreciation of the texts which motivate the existence of literary criticism and of the historical and aesthetic contexts that motivate those texts. Research, description, and analysis remain the best ways of doing so. My use of a continuum rather than a set of fixed categories will, I hope, render my methodology acceptable to a wide range of critics and critical schools. Some analyses of individual texts reflect, moreover, recent developments in post-structuralist criticism when appropriate, without being written in the idiom of that criticism or replicating its methodologies.

25. Virginia Woolf, "Mr. Bennett and Mrs. Brown," rpt. in *Collected Essays*, vol. I, (New York: Harcourt, Brace, and World, 1925), p. 320.

26. Virginia Woolf, *The Years* (London: Hogarth Press, 1937), p. 206.

27. Reuben A. Brower, "The Novel as Poem: Exploring a Critical Metaphor in Virginia Woolf," in Morton W. Bloomfield, ed., *The Interpretation of Narrative: Theory and Practice*, Harvard English Studies 1 (Cambridge, Mass.: Harvard Univ. Press, 1970), p. 236.

28. Hagstrum, p. xx. An excellent collection of essays developing Hagstrum's ideas in various ways is *Articulate Images: The Sister Arts from Hogarth to Tennyson*, ed. Richard Wendorf (Minneapolis: Univ. of Minnesota Press, 1983).

29. John Russell, "D. H. Lawrence and Painting," in *D. H. Lawrence: Novelist, Poet, Prophet*, ed. Stephen Spender (New York: Harper and Row, 1973), p. 243.

30. Jack Lindsay, "The Impact of Modernism on Lawrence," in *Paintings of D. H. Lawrence*, ed. Mervyn Levy (New York: Viking, 1964), p. 44.

31. D. H. Lawrence, *Sons and Lovers* (1913; Baltimore and London: Penguin, 1976), p. 2. Since no fully satisfactory editions of most of Lawrence's novels are currently available, I have elected in most cases to use the widely available Penguin editions. See subsequent notes.

32. See Svetlana and Paul Alpers, "Ut Pictura Noesis? Criticism in Literary Studies and Art History," *New Literary History*, iii:3 (Spring 1972), 437-58. Svetlana Alpers also stressed this point in a presentation at the 1981 Modern Language Association meeting in New York.

33. Shone, pp. 136 and 162.

34. The only critic who touches on aspects on this matter is Lisa Ruddick in *The Seen and the Unseen: Virginia Woolf's "To the Lighthouse,"* The LeBaron Russell Brigg's Prize Honors Essay in English 1976 (Cambridge: Harvard Univ. Press, 1977), pp. 15-17.

35. Virginia Woolf, *The Waves* (New York: Harcourt Brace Jovanovich, Inc., 1931), p. 189.

36. Alpers, pp. 453-55.

37. See, for example, Georg Lukács, "Narrate or Describe?" in *Writer and Critic, and Other Essays*, trans. and ed. Arthur D. Kahn (New York: Grosse and Dunlap, 1971), and *Towards a Theory of Description*, Yale French Studies, vol. 61 (1981), especially the essays by Phillippe Hamon, Michael Riffaterre, Edward S. Casey, and Michel Beaujour. In a less theoretical (and sometimes old-fashioned) mode, see Michael Irwin, *Picturing: Description and Illusion in the Nineteenth-Century Novel* (London: George Allen and Unwin, 1979).

38. The bibliography of works on metaphor is, of course, vast. A recent volume of interest is *On Metaphor*, ed. Sheldon Sacks (Chicago: Univ. of Chicago Press, 1979).

39. See Mary Ann Caws, *The Eye in the Text: Essays on Perception, Mannerist to Modern* (Princeton: Princeton Univ. Press, 1981). For a discussion of images of perception and mirroring in philosophical discourse (and the consequences of those images for philosophy as a discipline), see Richard Rorty, *Philosophy and the Mirror of Nature* (Princeton: Princeton Univ. Press, 1979).

40. The quotation is from Michel Beaujour, "Some Paradoxes of Description," *Towards a Theory of Description*, p. 32. On this great variety of issues, the bibliography is, once again, virtually endless. See, for example, Edward S. Casey, *Imagining: A Phenomenological Study* (Bloomington: Univ. of Indiana Press, 1976); Jacques Derrida, *Speech and Phenomena and Other Essays on Husserl's Theory of Signs* (Evanston: Northwestern Univ. Press, 1973); Michel Foucault, *This Is Not a Pipe*, trans. and ed. James Harkness (Berkeley: Univ. of California Press, 1983); Jan Mukařovský, *Structure, Sign, and Function*, trans. and eds. John Burbank and Peter Steiner (New Haven: Yale Univ. Press, 1978); and Meyer Schapiro, *Word and Pictures: On the Literal and the Symbolic in the Illustration of the Text* (The Hague: Mouton, 1973). Studies cited elsewhere in these notes also touch on these issues.

41. E. M. Gombrich, *Art and Illusion* (Princeton: Princeton Univ. Press, 1960). Challengers include Rosalind Krauss in a talk at the 1983 Modern Language Association's "Art Criticism at our Centennial"

section and Norman Bryson, *Vision and Painting* (Chicago: Univ. of Chicago Press, 1983).

42. Joyce Cary, *The Horse's Mouth* (1944; New York: Harper, 1950), p. 57.

43. Alan Spiegel's book *Fiction and the Camera Eye* was published by the Univ. of Virginia Press, in Charlottesville in 1976; Richard Pearce's review appeared in *Novel* 13:2 (Winter 1980), 238.

44. A proposal for a paper on Jane Austen from James Thompson of the University of North Carolina at Chapel Hill suggested the connection between Austen and Lawrence described here.

45. Said, p. 101.

46. Michel Foucault, *Les Mots et les choses*, trans. *The Order of Things* (London: Tavistock Publications, 1970), pp. 9-10.

47. Gottfried Lessing, *Laocoön: An Essay on the Limits of Painting and Poetry*, trans. Edward A. McCormick, Library of the Liberal Arts (1766; New York: Bobbs-Merrill, 1962).

48. Paul Kolers, "Reading Pictures and Reading Texts," *The Arts and Cognition*, David Perkins and Barbara Leondar, eds. (Baltimore: Johns Hopkins Univ. Press, 1977), p. 155.

49. Nelson Goodman, *Languages of Art: An Approach to a Theory of Symbols* (Indianapolis and New York: Bobbs-Merrill, 1968).

50. Arnheim, p. 30.

51. Jan Mukařovský, *The Word and Verbal Art: Selected Essays by Jan Mukařovský*, trans. and eds. John Burbank and Peter Steiner (New Haven: Yale Univ. Press, 1977), p. 207.

52. Beaujour, p. 33.

53. Gilman, p. 4.

54. See Joseph Frank, "Spatial Form in Modern Literature," in *The Widening Gyre: Crisis and Mastery in Modern Literature* (New Brunswick: Rutgers Univ. Press, 1963). Frank reiterates this point in the recent anthology *Spatial Form in Narrative*, eds. Jeffrey R. Smitten and Ann Daghistany (Ithaca: Cornell Univ. Press, 1981), pp. 206-07.

55. Joseph Kestner, "Secondary Illusion: The Novel and the Spatial Arts," in *Spatial Form in Narrative*, pp. 100-130.

56. I agree here with W.J.T. Mitchell's view in "Spatial Form in Literature," *Critical Inquiry*, 6 (Spring 1980), 541.

CHAPTER ONE

1. Viola Hopkins Winner, *Henry James and the Visual Arts* (Charlottesville: Univ. of Virginia Press, 1970). James's testimony comes in

A Small Boy and Others (New York: Charles Scribner's Sons, 1913), pp. 53-54.

2. Winner, pp. 1-2.

3. See Leon Edel, *Henry James: The Untried Years*, vol. one of a five-part biography (Philadelphia and New York: Lippincott, 1953), pp. 159-66. In their youth, William excelled at art, and Henry tried to follow in his footsteps.

4. See Edel, pp. 68-76 and Henry James, *A Small Boy and Others*, Chapter Twenty-Five.

5. Winner, p. 10.

6. Roy Strong, *Recreating the Past: British History and Victorian Painting* (Great Britain: Thames and Hudson, 1978). James's exposure to this theme also came via literature, as witness Dickens's Oliver Twist, Little Dorrit, and Jenny Wren.

7. Winner, p. 36. See also *Henry James Letters*, ed. Leon Edel, vols. 1-3 (Cambridge: Harvard Univ. Press, 1974-1980) for references to these and other painters (though fewer than one would expect, given James's references to art in other places). See especially vol. 1, pp. 137-41, 179-81, and 184-85.

In *Literary Architecture* (Berkeley: Univ. of California Press, 1979), Ellen Eve Frank argues that James's ideas about buildings (often derived from Ruskin's) provided him with architectural metaphors that influenced his theory of fiction. Her views supplement the documentary approach I take here and move several steps beyond traditional notations in James's critics that buildings often figure prominently in his novels. See especially pp. 211-15 and p. 218 of Frank's study.

8. Henry James, *Portraits of Places* (Boston: James R. Osgood and Co., 1884), p. 16.

9. Henry James, *The Painter's Eye: Notes and Essays on the Pictorial Arts*, ed. with intro. by John L. Sweeney (London: Rupert Hart-Davis, 1956), pp. 42 and 185.

10. Winner, pp. 45-47.

11. John Rewald, *The History of Impressionism*, fourth rev. ed. (1946; New York: The Museum of Modern Art, 1973), p. 338.

12. Louis Leroi's review of the first Impressionist exhibition is rpt. in *Impressionism and Post-Impressionism 1874-1904*, ed. Linda Nochlin (Englewood Cliffs: Prentice Hall, 1966), p. 12.

13. Sweeney, "Introduction to *Painter's Eye*," p. 28.

14. *Painter's Eye*, p. 114.

15. *Painter's Eye*, p. 114.

16. On Whistler, see Winner, p. 48. For views on Flaubert, see

James's reviews in *Notes on Novelists with Some Other Notes* (1914; New York: Scribner's, 1942), pp. 59-66.

17. Both Winner and Sweeney make this point (pp. 49-52 and pp. 28-29, respectively). And it forms the basis for Peter Stowell's *Literary Impressionism, James and Chekhov* (Athens: Univ. of Georgia Press, 1980).

18. See Leon Edel, *Henry James: The Master*, volume five of the biography (Philadelphia and New York: Lippincott, 1972), pp. 487-89, for the history of this portrait, which included its attempted dismemberment by an irate lady.

19. *Painter's Eye*, p. 217.

20. *Painter's Eye*, p. 35.

21. The quotations are from Henry James, *A Small Boy and Others*, pp. 263-64 and Henry James, *The Art of Fiction and Other Essays* (New York: Oxford Univ. Press, 1948), p. 5. Using James's own (rather too broad) definitions of the pictorial, Christy Morgan Taylor describes the role that the visual arts played in James's theory of fiction in an unpublished dissertation, Stanford, 1955, pp. 40-91.

22. See D. H. Lawrence, "An Introduction to these Paintings," rpt. in *Phoenix: The Posthumous Papers of D. H. Lawrence*, ed. Edward D. McDonald (New York: Viking, 1936), pp. 560-61. The essay originally appeared as the introduction to a privately printed edition of Lawrence's paintings, *The Paintings of D. H. Lawrence* (London: Mandrake Press, 1929), about the accuracy of whose reproductions in terms of coloration he was ambivalent; the original source, which I have consulted, is a rare book, and so interested readers should seek out the *Phoenix* volume. The essay will hereafter be cited as "Introduction." See also Knud Merrild, *A Poet and Two Painters* (New York: Viking, 1939), p. 211. Merrild was a painter with whom Lawrence associated and frequently discussed art. His book contains a great deal of valuable information and interesting quotations, often unidentified as to source but accurate when checked against the original sources.

23. See, for example, F. R. Leavis' *The Great Tradition* (1948; New York: New York Univ. Press, 1967) and *D. H. Lawrence: Novelist* (London: Chatto and Windus, 1955).

24. D. H. Lawrence, "Morality and the Novel," is rpt. in *Phoenix*; this quotation is from pp. 527-28. The second and third quotations are from Lawrence's essay "Making Pictures," rpt. in *Phoenix II: Uncollected, Unpublished, and Other Prose*, eds. Warren Roberts and Harry T. Moore (London: Heinemann, 1968), p. 606. See also Merrild, pp. 216 and 211.

25. Merrild criticizes Lawrence on this basis, p. 213.

26. See Harry T. Moore, *The Priest of Love: A Life of D. H. Lawrence*, rev. ed. (New York: Farrar, Straus and Giroux, 1974), p. 66.

27. E. T. (Jessie Chambers), *D. H. Lawrence: A Personal Record*, 2nd ed. (1935; New York: Barnes and Noble, 1965), p. 62.

28. See Chambers, p. 23. See also *The Letters of D. H. Lawrence*, 1 (1901-1913), ed. James T. Boulton (Cambridge: Cambridge Univ. Press, 1979), p. 491. Hereafter referred to as *Cambridge Letters* to distinguish it clearly from *The Collected Letters of D. H. Lawrence*, 2 vols., ed. Harry T. Moore (New York: Viking, 1962). Moore's edition is destined to be superseded by the Cambridge edition, the first two volumes of which had been published as I completed my manuscript.

29. *Cambridge Letters*, 1, pp. 107 and 113.

30. *Cambridge Letters*, 1, p. 273.

31. *Cambridge Letters*, 1, p. 113.

32. *Cambridge Letters*, 1, p. 124.

33. *Cambridge Letters*, 1, pp. 130 and 266.

34. "Introduction," p. 559.

35. See Jeffrey Meyers, *Painting and the Novel* (New York: Barnes and Noble, 1975). Meyers' chapter on *The White Peacock* discusses Greiffenhagen's influence on that novel. The citation here is to *Cambridge Letters*, 1, p. 103.

36. Emile Delavenay, *D. H. Lawrence: L'Homme et la genèse de son oeuvre (1885-1919)* (Paris: Librairie C. Klincksieck, 1969), p. 36.

37. In *Phoenix*, see "Morality and the Novel," p. 527, and "Introduction," p. 561.

38. Moore, *The Priest of Love*, p. 466, and Delavenay, p. 432.

39. For Lawrence's comments, see *The Letters of D. H. Lawrence*, 2 (1913-1916), eds. George J. Zytaruk and James T. Boulton (Cambridge: Cambridge Univ. Press, 1982), pp. 298-99 and 303. Morrell's comment is rpt. in Edward Nehls, *D. H. Lawrence: A Composite Biography*, vol. 1 (Madison: Univ. of Wisconsin Press, 1957), p. 271.

40. See S. P. Rosenblum, ed., *The Bloomsbury Group* (Toronto: Univ. of Toronto Press, 1975), pp. 363-65.

41. D. H. Lawrence, *Lady Chatterley's Lover* (1928; New York: Grove Press, 1959), p. 356. I use the Grove Press paperback since no satisfactory hardcover of the novel currently is available.

42. See Meyers, pp. 73-78, and Keith Alldritt, *The Visual Imagination of D. H. Lawrence* (Evanston: Northwestern Univ. Press, 1971), pp. 156-59.

43. See Virginia Woolf, "Notes on D. H. Lawrence," *Collected Essays*, vol. 1 (New York: Harcourt, Brace, and World, 1925), pp. 352-55.

44. Roger Fry, *Vision and Design* (New York: Brentano's, n.d.).

45. From Clive Bell, *Art*, rpt. in *Introductory Readings in Aesthetics*, ed. with introduction by John Hospers (New York: Macmillan/The Free Press, 1969), p. 91.

46. *Cambridge Letters*, 2, pp. 180-81.

47. For a discussion of the English reaction to Futurism and of this tendency to group all Modern art under the same heading, see Caroline Tisdall and Angelo Bozzolla, *Futurism* (New York: Oxford, 1978), p. 102.

48. *Cambridge Letters*, 2, pp. 180-81.

49. D. H. Lawrence's "A Study of Thomas Hardy" first appeared in *Phoenix: The Posthumous Papers* (see note 22), pp. 463-64.

50. *Cambridge Letters*, 2, p. 183. Among critics who have explored the relevance of Lawrence's statement to characterization as we find it in his novels are Alan Friedman in *The Turn of the Novel* (New York: Oxford, 1966), and Garrett Stewart in "Lawrence, 'Being,' and Allotropic Style," in *Towards a Poetics of Fiction*, ed. Mark Spilka (Bloomington: Univ. of Indiana Press, 1977).

51. *Cambridge Letters*, 2, p. 60.

52. See Meyers, p. 73.

53. Harry T. Moore, "D. H. Lawrence and his Paintings," in *Paintings of D. H. Lawrence*, ed. Mervyn Levy (New York: Viking, 1964). This volume should not be confused with the very different *The Paintings of D. H. Lawrence* cited above in note 22.

54. Reproductions of the paintings by Lawrence discussed and not included among the plates for this book may be found in *The Paintings of D. H. Lawrence* or *Paintings of D. H. Lawrence*, and often in both. Many of the originals may be seen at the La Fonda Hotel in Taos, New Mexico.

55. A former student, Robert Burge, made the comparison in a very good paper on Lawrence as an artist.

56. For an informative and amusing history of the incident, see Nehls, pp. 328-70. The members of Bloomsbury rallied around Lawrence not from any sense of personal liking (which would have been surprising by 1929), but from a sense that the threat to his art was a threat to all art. The authorities provided fuel for this view by seizing some of Blake's drawings along with Lawrence's, since they too showed pubic hair.

57. See D. H. Lawrence, *Women in Love* (1920; New York: Penguin, 1982), p. 111. The Penguin text is a paperback, but is widely available and—though imperfect, like all current editions—it is the best text of the novel now available, edited and with notes by Charles L. Ross. Another edition is forthcoming from the Cambridge University Press.

58. From Robert Burge's unpublished essay.

59. See *Paintings of D. H. Lawrence*, p. 68.

60. D. H. Lawrence, "Making Pictures," rpt. in *Phoenix II*, p. 606.

61. "Making Pictures," p. 605.

62. John Lehmann, *Virginia Woolf and Her World* (London: Thames and Hudson, 1975).

63. *Notes on Virginia's Childhood: A Memoir by Vanessa Bell*, ed. Richard J. Schaubeck, Jr. (New York: Frank Hallman, 1974), n.p.

64. Richard Shone, *Bloomsbury Portraits: Vanessa Bell, Duncan Grant, and Their Circle* (New York: Dutton, 1976), pp. 21-22.

65. *The Letters of Virginia Woolf: The Question of Things Happening*, II (1912-1922), ed. Nigel Nicolson and asst. ed. Joanne Trautmann (London: Hogarth Press, 1976), pp. 77-78. I will omit the subtitle in subsequent references to this and other volumes of the letters.

66. Fry, p. 12. Woolf's *Roger Fry: A Biography* (New York: Harcourt, Brace, and Co., 1940) was written after Fry's death in tribute to his memory.

67. Bennett's query came in a book called *Books and Persons*, which Virginia Woolf reviewed. The review is rpt. in Virginia Woolf, *Contemporary Writers*, with preface by Jean Guiguet (New York: Harcourt, Brace and World, Inc., 1965), p. 62.

68. Virginia Woolf, "Modern Fiction," *Collected Essays*, vol. II (New York: Harcourt, Brace, and World, Inc., 1925), pp. 105-06.

69. Virginia Woolf, "Roger Fry," *Collected Essays*, vol. IV (New York: Harcourt, Brace, and World, Inc., 1925), pp. 90-91.

70. Virginia Woolf, *Collected Essays*, vol. II, p. 110.

71. *The Letters of Virginia Woolf: A Change of Perspective*, III (1923-1928), ed. Nigel Nicolson and asst. ed. Joanne Trautmann (London: Hogarth, 1977), p. 498.

72. *The Letters of Virginia Woolf: A Reflection of the Other Person*, IV (1929-1931), eds. Nigel Nicolson and Joanne Trautmann (London: Hogarth, 1978), p. 391.

73. Letters of Virginia Woolf, IV, p. 391.

74. *The Letters of Virginia Woolf: Leave the Letters till We're Dead*, VI (1936-1941), eds. Nigel Nicolson and Joanne Trautmann (London: Hogarth, 1980), p. 302.

75. *Letters of Virginia Woolf*, IV, p. 142.

76. Rpt. in *The Bloomsbury Group*, S. P. Rosenbaum, ed., p. 172.

77. *The Diary of Virginia Woolf*, III (1925-1930), ed. Anne Olivier Bell, assisted by Andrew McNeillie (New York: Harcourt Brace Jovanovich, 1980), p. 233.

78. Virginia Woolf, *Diary*, III, p. 321.

79. Virginia Woolf, "Three Pictures," in *Collected Essays*, vol. IV, p. 152.

CHAPTER TWO

1. A study that appeared as my book went to press suggests that new and promising directions in the study of illustrations are now being taken. Martin Meisel's *Realizations: Narrative, Pictorial, and Theatrical Arts in Nineteenth-Century England* discusses how illustrations often inspired theatrical *tableaux-vivants* of novels, thus decisively shaping the popular imagination of the texts (Princeton: Princeton Univ. Press, 1983).

2. Henry James, *Roderick Hudson, The Novels and Tales of Henry James*, vol. I (1874; New York: Charles Scribner's Sons, 1907), pp. 19 and 189. I have chosen to use the New York Edition of each text studied by James since my topic does not demand that I take a developmental approach to the author and the New York Edition received the fullest benefit of James's long exposure to the visual arts. In each case, however, I have also read the novels in their original American editions (my usual preference) and have recorded any significant differences in material quoted between the original American and New York editions. Although a great many of James's tales deal with visual artists, I have not included them in my discussion, largely because their uses of the visual arts would be quite likely different from the extended, developed uses possible in novels.

3. Henry James, "Preface to *Roderick Hudson*," p. xv. Unless otherwise noted, references to the prefaces are to the appropriate volumes of the New York Edition.

4. See "Henry James: The Ideal of Detachment," in Maurice Beebe, *Ivory Towers and Sacred Founts: The Artist as Hero in Fiction from Goethe to Joyce* (New York: New York Univ. Press, 1964), pp. 197-231.

5. Henry James, *The Tragic Muse, The Novels and Tales of Henry James*, vols. VII and VIII (1890; New York: Charles Scribner's Sons, 1908), VII, p. 226.

6. For the sense in which I use the term "linguistic," see the Introduction.

7. Mario Praz, *The Hero in Eclipse in Victorian Literature*, trans. Angus Davidson (London: Oxford Univ. Press, 1956), p. 13.

8. The information about Hazlitt comes from Praz, *Hero*, p. 13. The quotation from Lamb occurs in *Reflector*, II, p. 61. It is quoted in Robert Etheridge Moore, *Hogarth's Literary Relationships* (Minneapolis: Univ. of Minnesota Press, 1948), p. 62.

9. Praz, *Hero*, p. 28.

10. Moore, p. 108.

11. Moore, pp. 124-25.

12. Henry Fielding, *Tom Jones* (1749; Baltimore: Penguin, 1966), p. 79 (I:11).

13. Fielding, p. 494 (x:8). Both quotations from Fielding are discussed by Moore, pp. 124-25.

14. Moore, p. 129.

15. Laurence Sterne, *Tristram Shandy, The Florida Edition of the Works of Laurence Sterne*, vol. 2 (Gainesville: Univ. of Florida Press, 1978), p. 567 (VI:XXXVIII).

16. Mario Praz, "Introduction" to *Three Gothic Novels* (Baltimore: Penguin, 1968), p. 17.

17. William Axton, "Introduction" to *Melmoth the Wanderer* by Charles Maturin (Lincoln: Univ. of Nebraska Press, 1961), p. vii.

18. Ann Radcliffe, *The Mysteries of Udolpho* (1794; London: Oxford Univ. Press, 1970), pp. 42-43.

19. On Charlotte Brontë's interest in the visual arts, see Winifred Gerin, *Charlotte Brontë: The Evolution of Genius* (London and New York: Oxford, 1967), pp. 41-49, and E. C. Gaskell, *The Life of Charlotte Brontë* (London: Smith, Elder, 1857).

20. Charlotte Brontë, *Jane Eyre*, eds. Jane Jack and Margaret Smith (Oxford: Clarendon Press, 1969), p. 112.

21. Alan Spiegel discusses such allusions to type rather than to particular characteristics as typical of pre-nineteenth-century narrative in *Fiction and the Camera Eye* (Charlottesville: Univ. of Virginia Press, 1976), p. 10.

22. J. Hillis Miller, *Fiction and Repetition: Seven English Novels* (Cambridge: Harvard Univ. Press, 1982).

23. The best-known example is Richard Chase in "The Brontës: A Centennial Observance" in *The Brontës: A Collection of Critical Essays*, ed. Ian Gregor (Englewood Cliffs, New Jersey: Prentice-Hall, 1970), pp. 19-33. The essay, originally called "The Brontës, or Myth Domesticated," appeared in *The Kenyon Review* in 1947.

24. Gordon N. Ray, *The Illustrator and the Book in England from 1790 to 1914*, The Pierpont Morgan Library (London: Oxford, n.d.).

25. John Harvey, *Victorian Novelists and Their Illustrators* (London: Sedgwick and Jackson, 1970); Albert Johannsen, *Phiz: Illustrations for the Novels of Charles Dickens* (Chicago: Univ. of Chicago Press, 1965); Edgar Browne, *Phiz and Dickens* (London: Nisbet and Co., 1913); Q. D. Leavis, co-author, F. R. Leavis, *Dickens the Novelist* (London: Chatto and Windus, 1970); Michael Steig, *Dickens and Phiz* (Bloomington:

Univ. of Indiana Press, 1978); J. Hillis Miller, "The Fiction of Realism: *Sketches by Boz, Oliver Twist*, and Cruikshank's Illustrations," in *Dickens Centennial Essays*, eds. Ada Nisbet and Blake Nevius (Berkeley: Univ. of California Press, 1971).

26. Q. D. Leavis, p. 336.

27. Harvey, pp. 105 and 150. I am using The Clarendon Dickens edition of *David Copperfield*, ed. Nina Burgis (Oxford: Clarendon Press, 1981).

28. John Fowles discusses a film's ability to pre-empt our sense of what a character looks like in an article which discusses the filming of *The French Lieutenant's Woman*. See Leslie Garis, "Translating Fowles into Film," *New York Times Sunday Magazine*, August 20, 1981, p. 50.

29. Miller, "Fiction of Realism," p. 129.

30. Edward S. Casey, *Imagining: A Phenomenological Study* (Bloomington: Univ. of Indiana Press, 1976), p. 134

31. Mario Praz discusses the *Beidermeier* ethos as common in genre paintings from the seventeenth through nineteenth centuries and in Victorian fiction in *The Hero in Eclipse in Victorian Fiction*. His thesis is, however, based upon shared subject matter and theme rather than on effects strictly pictorial or actually derived from the visual arts.

32. Q. D. Leavis, p. 360.

33. Generally, I omit from discussion illustrations that were not originally published with the novel or were not used with the novelist's consent. Green's illustrations appear in an edition of *Great Expectations* published after Dickens's death, and thus would ordinarily not be discussed. I justify the exception since it allows me to show how neither stylized nor realistic illustrations suit certain kinds of fiction.

34. I am, of course, aware that *Tess* was published after several of James's novels, including *The Portrait of a Lady*. James, however, published novels into the twentieth century while Hardy did not, and his techniques and forms are widely held (and correctly held) to be more modern than Hardy's.

35. I am indebted for most of the background information on Hardy and illustrations to Arlene M. Jackson, *Illustration and the Novels of Thomas Hardy* (Totowa, New Jersey: Rowan and Little, 1981). See especially pp. 28, 56-58, and 105. More general information on Hardy's relationship to the visual arts can be found in Sir John Betjeman, "Hardy and Architecture," in *The Genius of Thomas Hardy*, ed. Margaret Drabble (New York: Knopf, 1976); Florence Hardy (for Thomas Hardy), *The Early Life of Hardy* (New York: Macmillan, 1928); and

Jane Grundy, *Hardy and the Sister Arts* (London: The Macmillan Press, 1979).

36. All the illustrations discussed below are reproduced in the Jackson book, after p. 80. I have given in parentheses the dates they appeared in *The Graphic*. An alternative location is the Harper edition of Thomas Hardy's works, published in 1904; other editions omit the illustrations or use newer illustrations that are not discussed because they did not figure in the novel's original publication.

37. Jackson, pp. 108-09.

38. The unidentified critic, from an unidentified source, is quoted in Jackson, p. 5.

39. I omit, with reluctance, other wonderful scenes, like Tess on the threshing machine. The text used is the Riverside edition, which follows the definitive Wessex edition; ed. William E. Buckler (Boston: Houghton-Mifflin Company, 1960).

40. For Turner's illustrations of books on English landscape, see Gordon N. Ray, *The Illustrator and the Book in England from 1790 to 1914*. Jane Grundy sees a strong influence of Turner and the Impressionists (largely in terms of atmosphere and color) on Hardy. See *Hardy and the Sister Arts*, pp. 59-64.

41. Hardy was asked to draw a map of Wessex, indicating the locations of the settings for various of his novels. He complied, and the drawing served as frontispiece for the Wessex edition. On the geographical sources for the novel, see Andrew Enstice, *Thomas Hardy: Landscapes of the Mind* (New York: St. Martin's Press, 1978), pp. 111-52.

42. See Evelyn Hardy, "Thomas Hardy and Turner," *London Magazine*, June-July, 1975, pp. 23-25.

43. See Ray, pp. xiii-ix.

44. Stéphane Mallarmé, *Oeuvres complètes*, éd. de la Pleiade (Paris: Gallimard, 1965), p. 878.

45. For information about the New York Edition and illustrations, see Leon Edel, *Henry James: The Master* (Philadelphia and New York: Lippincott, 1972), pp. 333-34. The quotations from *The Golden Bowl*'s preface are on pp. ix-x of the Scribner New York Edition (1909).

46. For discussions of Conrad with regard to the visual, see especially Ian Watt, *Conrad in the Nineteenth Century* (Berkeley: Univ. of California Press, 1970); Edward Said, *The World, the Text, and the Critic*, pp. 44-46; and Geoffrey Galt Harpham, *On the Grotesque: Strategies of Contradiction in Art and Literature* (Princeton: Princeton Univ. Press, 1983), pp. 151-56. Joyce's use of epiphany and his interest in the dynamic relationship between observer and thing observed (like some of what

is found in Conrad and Proust) have affinities with certain aspects of James's, Lawrence's, and Woolf's work that I will discuss, justifying my selection of them as representative Modernists.

47. It is possible to trace many developments in the nineteenth century which contribute to this redefinition and are linked to the visual arts. The art criticism of Ruskin and especially of Pater, for example, emphasized the viewer's emotions and the viewer's contribution to the painting (especially to its implied story). See G. Robert Stange, "Art Criticism as a Prose Genre," *The Art of Victorian Prose*, eds. George Levine and William Madden (New York: Oxford Univ. Press, 1968), and Richard L. Stein, *The Ritual of Interpretation: The Fine Arts as Literature in Ruskin, Rossetti, and Pater* (Cambridge: Harvard Univ. Press, 1975). Both these authors speculate on art criticism's contribution to the Modern novel; this book perhaps provides some examples of how the Modern novel used art criticism.

CHAPTER THREE

1. Virginia Woolf, *Night and Day* (1920; New York: Harcourt Brace Jovanovich, n.d.), p. 58.

2. Identification of Mrs. Ramsay as Julia Stephen has become a critical commonplace. The most innovative use of this identification occurs in Mark Spilka's *Virginia Woolf's Quarrel with Grief* (Lincoln: Univ. of Nebraska Press, 1980).

3. Most of the letters of Vanessa Bell to her sister are available in the Berg Collection of The New York Public Library in their original, handwritten form.

4. Letters of June 2, 1912 and February 2, 1913, quoted (as are all of Vanessa Bell's letters) courtesy of the Berg Collection of The New York Public Library and of Professor Quentin Bell.

5. *The Diary of Virginia Woolf*, III (1925-1930), ed. Anne Olivier Bell, assisted by Andrew McNeillie (New York: Harcourt Brace Jovanovich, 1980), p. 110. Diary references will subsequently be entered in the text, with appropriate volume and page numbers.

6. *The Letters of Virginia Woolf*, III (1923-1928), ed. Nigel Nicolson and asst. ed. Joanne Trautmann (London: Hogarth, 1978), p. 383. As for the diaries, subsequent references to the letters will be entered in the text, with appropriate volume and page numbers.

7. Frances Spalding, *Vanessa Bell* (New Haven and London: Ticknor and Fields, 1983), p. 213. Perhaps because Bell has so long been thought of merely as Virginia's sister, Spalding does not stress the relationship between the two.

8. Several members of Bloomsbury refer to mathematics as a discipline similar in its abstraction to the visual arts, a traditional analogy. Woolf undoubtedly shared this sense of affinity and used it in *Night and Day*. See the selections from *Introductory Readings in Aesthetics* by Fry and Bell cited in Chapter One, note 45.

9. Vanessa Bell's letters to Virginia during this period of early marriage are extremely difficult to read, her handwriting far more illegible than earlier and later, which may reflect the strain between the sisters.

10. Letter of April 1927; also quoted in Volume III of *Letters of Virginia Woolf*.

11. Letter of March 1907.

12. Letters of May 4, 1908 and August 8, 1910, respectively.

13. Letter of January 26, 1913.

14. Letter of April 28, 1924.

15. Vanessa Bell, *Notes on Virginia's Childhood: a Memoir by Vanessa Bell*, ed. Richard J. Schaubeck, Jr. (New York: Frank Hallman, 1974), n.p.

16. Letter of January 13, 1912.

17. Richard Morphet, "The Art of Vanessa Bell," intro. to *Vanessa Bell, Paintings and Drawings* (London: Anthony d'Offay, 1973), p. 8.

18. Morphet, p. 8.

19. *Street Corner Conversation* is reproduced in the Morphet volume.

20. Harry R. Harrington, "The Central Line Down the Middle of *To the Lighthouse*," *Contemporary Literature*, 21:3 (Summer 1980), 363-83. See also Avrom Fleischman, *Virginia Woolf* (Baltimore: Johns Hopkins Univ. Press, 1975), p. 134.

21. These paintings are reproduced in Richard Shone, *Bloomsbury Portraits: Vanessa Bell, Duncan Grant, and Their Circle* (New York: Dutton, 1976).

CHAPTER FOUR

1. See Chapter One, notes 77 and 78.

2. *Kew Gardens* was originally published as a separate volume in 1919; in 1927, Hogarth Press published an unpaginated limited edition decorated by Vanessa Bell. I quote from a more accessible source: Virginia Woolf, "Kew Gardens" in *Monday or Tuesday* (Richmond, Surrey: Hogarth, 1921), p. 68.

3. Lisa Ruddick, *The Seen and the Unseen: Virginia Woolf's "To the Lighthouse,"* The LeBaron Russell Brigg's Prize Honors Essay in English, 1976 (Cambridge: Harvard Univ. Press, 1977), p. 21.

4. I discuss the nature of the oceanic state extensively in the chapter

on *The Waves* in my book *Closure in the Novel* (Princeton: Princeton Univ. Press, 1981).

5. Virginia Woolf, *To the Lighthouse* (New York: Harcourt, Brace, and World, 1927), p. 97.

6. D. H. Lawrence, *The Rainbow* (1915; New York: Penguin, 1979), p. 76. There is no hardcover standard edition of Lawrence's novels and no really good edition of *The Rainbow*, though one is currently being prepared by Cambridge University Press. I have elected to use the widely available Penguin edition in the absence of a true standard edition.

7. For Jack Stewart's comments, see "Lawrence and Gauguin," *Twentieth-Century Literature*, 26:4 (Winter 1980), 385-401. For Lawrence's comments on Van Gogh, see Chapter One, note 39, and "An Introduction to these Paintings," rpt. in *Phoenix: The Posthumous Papers of D. H. Lawrence*, ed. Edward D. McDonald (New York: Viking, 1936). See also Harry T. Moore, *The Priest of Love: A Life of D. H. Lawrence*, rev. ed. (New York: Farrar, Straus and Giroux, 1974), p. 66.

8. *The Letters of D. H. Lawrence*, 2 (1913-1916), eds. George J. Zytaruk and James T. Boulton (Cambridge: Cambridge Univ. Press, 1982), p. 132 (see also p. 82).

9. D. H. Lawrence, "A Study of Thomas Hardy," *Phoenix: The Posthumous Papers of D. H. Lawrence*, ed. Edward D. McDonald (New York: Viking, 1936), p. 458.

10. See *Closure in the Novel*, pp. 176-97.

11. Jean Alexander, *The Venture of Form in the Novels of Virginia Woolf*, National University Publications (New York: Kennikat Press, 1974), pp. 161-73.

12. Joyce Carol Oates, Review of Reynolds Price, *The Source of Light*, *New York Times Book Review*, April 26, 1981, p. 3.

13. In fact, the "picture" may be Lily's visual response to information that she had had earlier from Mrs. Ramsay, who recalls once in the novel getting off a boat aided by her future husband.

14. Many of the standard studies of Woolf's novels develop analogous dichotomies (like fact versus vision), dichotomies helpful as ways into the novels, though the novels quickly complicate the simplicity of the dichotomies. See, for example, Alice Van Buren Kelley, *The Novels of Virginia Woolf* (Chicago: Univ. of Chicago Press, 1971), and Jean O. Love, *Worlds in Consciousness: Mythopoetic Thought in the Novels of Virginia Woolf* (Berkeley: Univ. of California Press, 1970).

15. The phrase is found in *The Letters of Virginia Woolf: A Reflection*

of the Other Person, IV (1929-1931), eds. Nigel Nicolson and Joanne Trautmann (London: Hogarth, 1978), p. 142.

16. The phrase comes from *The Diary of Virginia Woolf*, III (1925-1930), ed. Anne Olivier Bell assisted by Andrew McNeillie (New York: Harcourt Brace Jovanovich, 1980), p. 113. She distinguishes sharply between life in the social sense and "the essence of reality."

17. Keith Alldritt, *The Visual Imagination of D. H. Lawrence* (Evanston: Northwestern Univ. Press, 1971) p. 17.

18. Alldritt, p. 74.

19. Alldritt, pp. 82-83.

20. *The Rainbow*, p. 176.

21. Owing to Lawrence's dialogic style, images from art—especially from the Fra Angelico—sometimes enter the novel through the narrative voice, detached from any character or characters. Thus, after her parents come to terms with one another, the child Anna "was no longer called upon to uphold with her childish might the broken end of the arch" (p. 92). The arch image refers both to the Gothic (pointed) arch and to the rounded arch that echoes the physical shape of Fra Angelico's triptych (shown to grown-up Anna by her husband) and the rainbow from which the novel takes its name.

22. In a study of the revisions of *Women in Love*, Charles L. Ross notes that "scenic echoing is the great and pervasive technical innovation of the novel, binding it together at every level—narrative, thematic, and verbal." We may, I think, add "visual" to the list. Ross also shows how Lawrence's discovery of new imagery patterns when revising his final draft led him to rewrite the scene between Ursula and Skrebensky on the Lincolnshire coast. He then revised the scene between Anna and Will and added that in the stackyard in the new generation to stress their parallelism. See Charles L. Ross, *The Composition of* The Rainbow *and* Women in Love: *A History* (Charlottesville: Univ. of Virginia Press, 1979), p. 83.

23. See Chapter One for a discussion of these quotations from *The Letters of D. H. Lawrence (Cambridge Letters)*, 2, p. 183 and "An Introduction to these Paintings," pp. 564-65.

24. Filippo Tommaso Marinetti, from "The Founding and Manifesto of Futurism," originally in *Le Figaro*, rpt. in *Marinetti: Selected Writings*, ed. R. W. Flint, trans. R. W. Flint and Arthur A. Coppotelli (New York: Farrar, Straus and Giroux, 1971), p. 42.

25. Rpt. in *Marinetti: Selected Writings*, p. 85.

26. See Ross, pp. 32-35 and 83.

27. I am using the Penguin edition of Lawrence's *Women in Love*,

edited by Charles L. Ross and newly published in 1983. See Chapter One, note 57. This quotation is from p. 478.

28. I am using the Grove Press edition of Lawrence's *Lady Chatterley's Lover*. See Chapter One, note 41.

CHAPTER FIVE

1. Henry James, *The Portrait of a Lady, The Novels and Tales of Henry James*, vols. III and IV (1880-1881; New York: Charles Scribner's Sons, 1908), III, p. 124.

2. F. O. Matthiessen, "The Painter's Sponge and Varnish Bottle," rpt. in Henry James, *The Portrait of a Lady* (New York: Norton, 1975), p. 541.

3. Viola Hopkins Winner comments on both the passage and the importance of place in the novel in *Henry James and the Visual Arts* (Charlottesville: Univ. of Virginia Press, 1970), pp. 138-41.

4. All notes for revisions refer to the Norton Critical Edition of the novel, edited by Robert D. Bamberg, which uses the New York Edition text (with different pagination, however) and provides a complete list of significant revisions from the earlier version in a textual appendix (cited hereafter as appendix). This revision is listed on p. 538, in the textual appendix.

5. Appendix, p. 541.

6. Appendix, p. 541.

7. Appendix, p. 541.

8. John Carlos Rowe, "James's Rhetoric of the Eye: Re-marking the Impression," *Criticism*, XXIV:3 (Summer 1982), 237 and 244.

9. Jan Mukařovský, *Structure, Sign, and Function*, trans. and eds. John Burbank and Peter Steiner (New Haven: Yale Univ. Press, 1978), pp. 227-28.

10. Exceptions to this rule are a number of removals of the word "picturesque," overused by James in the original edition, and the substitution of words like "romantic," or "quaint," which James often meant by the word "picturesque."

11. Appendix, p. 571.

12. See the Introduction to this study.

13. Appendix, p. 560.

14. *Broken Vows* is reproduced in Raymond Lister, *Victorian Narrative Paintings* (New York: Clarkson N. Potter, Inc., 1966).

15. Henry James, *The Ambassadors, The Novels and Tales of Henry James*, vols. XXI and XXII (1903; New York: Charles Scribner's Sons, 1909), XXI, p. 3.

16. Ian Watt wrote a classic discussion of the opening paragraph of the novel and its importance. See "The First Paragraph of *The Ambassadors*," *Essays in Criticism*, x (1960), pp. 250-74.

17. Charles Anderson, *Person, Place, and Thing in the Novels of Henry James* (Durham: Duke Univ. Press, 1977), pp. 58-59.

18. In *Person, Place, and Thing in the Novels of Henry James*, p. 4.

19. David Lodge, *The Language of Fiction: Essays in Criticism and Verbal Analysis of the English Novel* (New York: Columbia Univ. Press, 1966), p. 201.

20. The Winner and Anderson books both make this point. See also John L. Sweeney's introduction to Henry James, *The Painter's Eye: Notes and Essays on the Pictorial Arts* (London: Rupert Hart-Davis, 1956) and Peter Stowell, *Literary Impressionism, James and Chekhov* (Athens: Univ. of Georgia Press, 1980).

21. David Lodge makes a similar point in his evaluation of Strether (p. 194), as does Richard Poirier in *A World Elsewhere* (New York: Oxford Univ. Press, 1966) when he notes that "*The Ambassadors* offers remarkably beautiful instances of the hero's efforts to transform things he sees into visions, to detach them from time and from the demands of nature, and to give them the composition of *objets d'art*. The novel is about the cost and profit for such acts of imagination" (p. 124). For other good interpretations of the novel, see Frederick Crews, *The Tragedy of Manners: Moral Drama in the Later Novels of Henry James* (New Haven, Conn.: Yale Univ. Press, 1957); Lawrence Holland, *The Expense of Vision: Essays on the Craft of Henry James* (Princeton: Princeton Univ. Press, 1964); Sallie Sears, *The Negative Imagination: Form and Perception in the Novels of Henry James* (Ithaca: Cornell Univ. Press, 1968); and Philip M. Weinstein, *Henry James and the Requirements of the Imagination* (Cambridge: Harvard Univ. Press, 1971).

22. The Signet version of *The Ambassadors* (New York, 1960) uses the text of the first American edition. This quotation is from pp. 326-27.

23. Once again, the most relevant critics are Winner, Stowell, and Anderson.

24. See Lodge, p. 200.

25. See especially F. R. Leavis, *The Great Tradition* (1937; New York: New York Univ. Press, 1967); F. O. Matthiessen, *Henry James: The Major Phase* (New York: Oxford Univ. Press, 1944); R. P. Blackmur, "Introduction to *The Golden Bowl*," *The Golden Bowl* (New York: Grove Press, 1952); Quentin Anderson, *The Imperial Self* (New York: Knopf, 1971); and Charles Samuels, *The Ambiguity of Henry James* (Urbana: Univ. of Illinois Press, 1971). I am using the New York

Edition of the novel, *The Novels and Tales of Henry James*, XXIII and XXIV (1904; New York: Charles Scribner's Sons, 1909).

26. See *Closure in the Novel* (Princeton: Princeton Univ. Press, 1981), Chapter Seven, pp. 143-56.

27. See Stowell, p. 237.

CHAPTER SIX

1. I am using the Penguin edition edited by Charles L. Ross (1920; New York: Penguin, 1982), the best available text of the novel (see Chapter One, note 57). This quotation is from p. 127.

2. George H. Ford points out that Lawrence had recently read Leo Frobenius' *The Voice of Africa*, which no doubt plays a role in the views expressed by Birkin. See *Double Measure: A Study of the Novels and Stories of D. H. Lawrence* (New York: Holt, Rinehart, and Winston, 1965), p. 192.

3. D. H. Lawrence "Morality and the Novel," rpt. in *Phoenix: The Posthumous Papers of D. H. Lawrence*, ed. Edward D. McDonald (New York: Viking, 1936), pp. 527-28.

4. *The Letters of D. H. Lawrence*, 1 (1901-1913), ed. James T. Boulton (Cambridge: Cambridge Univ. Press, 1979), pp. 133 and 266.

5. *The Letters of D. H. Lawrence*, 2 (1913-1916), eds. George J. Zytaruk and James T. Boulton (Cambridge: Cambridge Univ. Press, 1982), p. 660. The similar vocabulary of this passage and parts of *Women in Love* testifies again to the role the Futurists played in crystallizing Lawrence's ideas.

6. Lawrence's own introduction to African art came via Bloomsbury, after his return to England in 1914. He first saw such art in the composer Philip Heseltine's house, Heseltine being the model for Halliday in the novel. Roger Fry had also written an essay called "Negro Sculpture" which appeared in *Vision and Design* (New York: Brentano's, n.d.). The vogue for primitive art included new attention to Gauguin, and it was reflected in Modern artists like Picasso, Matisse, Brancusi, the Fauves, and others. Late in 1984, a major exhibition at The Museum of Modern Art—"'Primitivism' and 20th-Century Art"—clarified the extent and richness of this influence.

7. George H. Ford explores the novel's references to anal intercourse (including the emphasis here on "protuberant buttocks"), and does so with greater balance than many critics, in *Double Measure*.

8. It is not often enough noted that many of the qualities attributed to Gudrun and Loerke (independence and singleness, personal magnetism, and—in the case of Loerke—a slight build, dark coloring, and

indifference to clothing) are shared with Birkin and Lawrence. These artists are, to some extent, projections of Lawrence himself and of some of the dangers he saw in his artistic role.

9. Mark Spilka, *Virginia Woolf's Quarrel with Grieving* (Lincoln: Univ. of Nebraska Press, 1980).

10. D. H. Lawrence, "Making Pictures," rpt. in *Phoenix II: Uncollected, Unpublished, and Other Prose Works*, eds. Warren Roberts and Harry T. Moore (London: Heinemann, 1968), p. 606. By "consciousness," Lawrence meant something like what we normally call the unconscious mind (a term Lawrence disliked as derogatory) or even a Jungian collective unconscious.

11. I derive the term from the Russian Formalist Victor Shklovsky's idea of "situational rhyme."

12. Keith Alldritt also uses the term "tableau" in *The Visual Imagination of D. H. Lawrence* (Evanston: Northwestern Univ. Press, 1971), though he does not link it to pictorialism in any strict sense. Joseph Kestner also uses the term in "Sculptural Character in Lawrence's *Women in Love*," *Modern Fiction Studies*, 21, 543-53.

13. Even painting in the classical style frequently suggests motion within the static image. A good example is Poussin's *The Rape of the Sabine Women*—which also provides excellent examples of balanced, patterned action.

14. In the Ken Russell film of the novel, Russell attempts to capture this quality of the scene's visual appeal by rapid shifts in camera angle and a blurring of colors. The effect recalls that in paintings like Boccioni's *The City Rises*, described further in the chapter.

15. See the Introduction, and Chapers One and Four for a discussion of Lawrence's reactions to the Futurists and the roles they play in his novels.

16. See Alldritt, pp. 157-58. See also, among sources previously cited in other chapters, Jeffrey Meyers, *Painting and the Novel* (New York: Barnes and Noble, 1975), pp. 77-78; Emile Delavenay, *D. H. Lawrence: L'Homme et la genèse de son oeuvre* (1885-1919) (Paris: Librairie C. Klincksieck, 1969), pp. 354-56; Jack Lindsay, "The Impact of Modernism on Lawrence," in *Paintings of D. H. Lawrence*, ed. Mervyn Levy (New York: Viking, 1964), pp. 52-53. Additional important statements are those in defense of Ursula by F. R. Leavis in *Thought, Words, and Creativity: Art and Thought in Lawrence* (London: Chatto and Windus, 1976), p. 77, and those in appreciation of Loerke by Joyce Carol Oates in "Lawrence's Götterdämmerung: the Tragic Vision of *Women in Love*," *Critical Inquiry*, 4:3 (Spring 1978), 574.

17. D. H. Lawrence, "An Introduction to these Paintings," rpt. in

Phoenix: The Posthumous Papers of D. H. Lawrence, ed. Edward D. McDonald (New York: Viking, 1936), p. 574.

18. D. H. Lawrence. "Making Pictures," p. 605.

CONCLUSION

1. Michel Foucault, *Les Mots et les choses*, English title, *The Order of Things* (London: Tavistock Publications, 1970) and Lucien Dällenbach, *Le Récit speculaire: Essai sur la mise en abyme* (Paris: Seuil, 1977). Dällenbach uses the term "la mise en abyme" to describe the mirroring effect of works of art within works of art. Finding the term too weighted with Existentialist connotations, I have reservations about it and hence use in general alternative formulations.

2. Anthony Powell, *A Dance to the Music of Time* (Fourth Movement: *Hearing Secret Harmonies*) (Boston: Little, Brown and Company, 1971), p. 11. Designating the appropriate reference in Powell's mammoth work is difficult in the text and even in the footnotes. Hence, unless the reference is absolutely clear, I will footnote page references rather than incorporating them in the text. The difficulty arises from the fact that *A Dance to the Music of Time* (itself a novel) is composed of twelve novels originally published separately, which can be read separately, but are intimately connected and gain immensely from being read in sequence. Editions of *Dance* usually exist (as does the Little, Brown edition) in four volumes (each containing three novels), designated the first through fourth movements; some editions use a seasonal division as well, moving from spring through winter. To complicate matters still further, each novel within the composite novel is paginated separately, with the typical length around 250 pages. Thus, *Hearing Secret Harmonies* is the third novel in the fourth movement (Winter) of *Dance*.

3. *Dance* (First Movement: *A Question of Upbringing*), p. 4.

4. I do not deal with the biographical segment of the continuum in the discussion that follows, but refer the reader to the many references to art in Powell's multi-volume autobiography, *To Keep the Ball Rolling*, published in New York by Holt, Rinehart and Winston, 1976-1982.

5. *Dance* (Fourth Movement: *Hearing Secret Harmonies*), p. 245.

6. *Dance* (Fourth Movement: *Hearing Secret Harmonies*), p. 233.

7. *Dance* (Fourth Movement: *Temporary Kings*), pp. 83-85. I have radically edited the quotation to shorten it, but have tried not to distort it.

8. James Tucker, *The Novels of Anthony Powell* (New York: Columbia Univ. Press, 1976), p. 115. Tucker provides a useful census of *Dance* which reflects the highly speculative nature of Powell's narration, fre-

quently following information (rich? at school with Sir John Clarke?) with question marks.

9. J. Hillis Miller, *The Form of Victorian Fiction* (Notre Dame and London: Univ. of Notre Dame Press, 1968), p. 35.

10. The best sources are *Complete Catalogue of the Paintings of Giovanni Battista Tiepolo*, ed. Antonio Morassi (Greenwich, Conn.: Phaidon, 1963) and *L'Opera completa di Giovanni Battista Tiepolo*, Classici dell'arte series, introduction by Guido Piovene, critical apparatus by Anna Pallucchini (Milano: Rizzoli, 1968). Although it seems unlikely that he is the Tiepolo referred to in the novel, I have also checked catalogues of the work of Giovanni Domenico Tiepolo, a lesser artist.

11. Dällenbach credits Gide with originating the term.

12. The theme of voyeurism forms a connection between Powell and the more experimental *nouveau-roman*. Mirroring and its implications in the *nouveau-roman* are discussed in Dällenbach's *Le Récit specularie*. See also Michel Beaujour, "Some Paradoxes of Description," *Towards a Theory of Description*, Yale French Studies, vol. 61 (1981), pp. 57-58.

13. The phrase is Foucault's, p. iv.

14. The uses of Latin American novelists like Julio Cortázar and Manuel Puig are especially rich and suggestive.

BIBLIOGRAPHY

The bibliography includes only those works
actually cited in the text

Alexander, Jean. *The Venture of Form in the Novels of Virginia Woolf.* National University Publications. New York: Kennikat Press, 1974.

Alldritt, Keith. *The Visual Imagination of D. H. Lawrence.* Evanston: Northwestern Univ. Press, 1971.

Alpers, Svetlana and Paul Alpers. "Ut Pictura Noesis? Criticism in Literary Studies and Art History." *New Literary History,* iii:3 (Spring 1972), 437-58.

Anderson, Charles. *Person, Place, and Thing in the Novels of Henry James.* Durham: Duke Univ. Press, 1977.

Arnason, H. H. *History of Modern Art: Painting, Sculpture, Architecture.* New York: Harry N. Abrams, Inc., and Englewood Cliffs, New Jersey: Prentice Hall, Inc., n.d.

Arnheim, Rudolph. *Visual Thinking.* Berkeley: Univ. of California Press, 1969.

Axton, William. "Introduction to *Melmoth the Wanderer.*" *Melmoth the Wanderer,* by Charles Maturin. Lincoln: Univ. of Nebraska Press, 1961.

Beaujour, Michel. "Some Paradoxes of Description." *Towards a Theory of Description.* Yale French Studies, vol. 61 (1981).

Beebe, Maurice. *Ivory Towers and Sacred Founts: The Artist as Hero in Fiction from Goethe to Joyce.* New York: New York Univ. Press, 1964.

Bell, Clive. *Art.* In *Introductory Readings in Aesthetics.* Ed. with introduction by John Hospers. New York: Macmillan/The Free Press, 1969.

Bell, Vanessa. *Notes on Virginia's Childhood: A Memoir by Vanessa Bell.* Ed. Richard J. Schaubeck. New York: Frank Hallman, 1974.

Betjeman, Sir John. "Hardy and Architecture." In *The Genius of Thomas Hardy.* Ed. Margaret Drabble. New York: Knopf, 1976.

Blackmur, R. P. "Introduction" to *The Golden Bowl. The Golden Bowl* by Henry James. New York: Grove Press, 1952.

Bluestone, George. *Novels Into Film.* Baltimore: Johns Hopkins Univ. Press, 1957.

Brontë, Charlotte. *Jane Eyre*. Eds. Jane Jack and Margaret Smith. Oxford: Clarendon Press, 1969.

Browne, Edgar. *Phiz and Dickens*. London: Nisbet and Co., 1913.

Cary, Joyce. *The Horse's Mouth*. 1944; New York: Harper, 1950.

Casey, Edward S. *Imagining: A Phenomenological Study*. Bloomington: Univ. of Indiana Press, 1976.

Caws, Mary Ann. *The Eye in the Text: Essays on Perception, Mannerist to Modern*. Princeton: Princeton Univ. Press, 1981.

Chambers, Jessie (E. T.). *D. H. Lawrence: A Personal Record*. 2nd Edition. 1935; New York: Barnes and Noble, 1965.

Chase, Richard. "The Brontës: A Centennial Observance." In *The Brontës: A Collection of Critical Essays*. Ed. Ian Gregor. Englewood Cliffs, New Jersey: Prentice Hall, 1970.

Crews, Frederick. *The Tragedy of Manners: Moral Drama in the Later Novels of Henry James*. New Haven: Yale Univ. Press, 1957.

Dällenbach, Lucien. *Le Récit speculaire: essai sur la mise en abyme*. Paris: Seuil, 1977.

Delavenay, Emile. *D. H. Lawrence: l'homme et la genèse de son oeuvre*. Paris: Librairie C. Klincksieck, 1969.

Derrida, Jacques. *Speech and Phenomena and Other Essays on Husserl's Theory of Signs*. Evanston: Northwestern Univ. Press, 1973.

Dickens, Charles. *David Copperfield*. Ed. Nina Burgis. Oxford: Clarendon Press, 1971.

Drabble, Margaret, ed. *The Genius of Thomas Hardy*. New York: Knopf, 1976.

Edel, Leon. *Henry James: The Master*. Philadelphia and New York: Lippincott, 1972.

———. *Henry James: The Untried Years*. Philadelphia and New York, 1953.

Enstice, Andrew. *Thomas Hardy: Landscapes of the Mind*. New York: St. Martin's Press, 1978.

Fielding, Henry. *Tom Jones*. 1749; Baltimore: Penguin, 1966.

Finke, Ulrich, ed. *French Nineteenth-Century Painting and Literature: With Special Reference to the Relevance of Literary Subject Matter to French Painting*. Manchester: Manchester Univ. Press, 1972.

Ford, George H. *Double Measure: A Study of the Novels and Stories of D. H. Lawrence*. New York: Holt, Rinehart, and Winston, 1965.

Foucault, Michel. *Les Mots et les choses*. Trans. *The Order of Things*. London: Tavistock Publications, 1970.

———. *This is not a Pipe*. Trans. and ed. James Harkness. Berkeley: Univ. of California Press, 1983.

Frank, Ellen Eve. *Literary Architecture*. Berkeley: Univ. of California Press, 1979.

Frank, Joseph. "Spatial Form in Modern Literature." Rpt. in *The Widening Gyre: Crisis and Mastery in Modern Literature*. New Brunswick: Rutgers Univ. Press, 1963.

Fry, Roger. *Vision and Design*. New York: Brentano's, n.d.

Garis, Leslie. "Translating Fowles into Film." *New York Times Sunday Magazine*, August 20, 1981.

Gaskell, E. C. *The Life of Charlotte Brontë*. London: Smith, Elder, 1857.

Gilman, Ernest B. *The Curious Perspective: Literary and Pictorial Wit in the Seventeenth Century*. New Haven: Yale Univ. Press, 1978.

Gombrich, E. H. *Art and Illusion*. Princeton: Princeton Univ. Press, 1960.

Hagstrum, Jean. *The Sister Arts: The Tradition of Literary Pictorialism from Dryden to Gray*. Chicago: Univ. of Chicago Press, 1958.

Hardy, Evelyn. "Thomas Hardy and Turner." *London Magazine*, June-July 1975, pp. 23-25.

Hardy, Florence (for Thomas Hardy). *The Early Life of Hardy*. New York: Macmillan, 1928.

Hardy, Thomas. *Tess of the D'Urbervilles*. Riverside edition. Ed. William E. Buckler. Boston: Houghton-Mifflin, 1960.

Harpham, Geoffrey Galt. *On the Grotesque: Strategies of Contradiction in Art and Literature*. Princeton: Princeton Univ. Press, 1983.

Harrington, Harry H. "The Central Line Down the Middle of *To the Lighthouse*." *Contemporary Literature*, 21:3 (Summer 1980), 363-83.

Harvey, John. *Victorian Novelists and Their Illustrators*. London: Sedgwick and Jackson, 1970.

Holland, Lawrence. *The Expense of Vision: Essays on the Craft of Henry James*. Princeton: Princeton Univ. Press, 1964.

Hospers, John. *Introductory Readings in Aesthetics*. New York: Macmillan/The Free Press, 1969.

Hunt, John Dixon, ed. *Encounters: Essays on Literature and the Visual Arts*. London: Studio Vista, 1971.

Irwin, Michael. *Picturing: Description and Illusion in the Nineteenth-Century Novel*. London: George Allen and Unwin, 1979.

Jackson, Arlene M. *Illustration and the Novels of Thomas Hardy*. Totowa, New Jersey: Rowan and Little, 1981.

James, Henry. *The Ambassadors. The Novels and Tales of Henry James*. Vols. xxi and xxii. 1903; New York: Charles Scribner's Sons, 1909.

James, Henry. *The Ambassadors*. New York: Signet/New American Library, 1960.

———. *The Art of Fiction and Other Essays*. New York: Oxford Univ. Press, 1948.

———. *The Golden Bowl*. The Novels and Tales of Henry James. Vols. XXIII and XXIV. New York: Charles Scribner's Sons, 1909.

———. *Henry James Letters*. Ed. Leon Edel. 3 vols. Cambridge: Harvard Univ. Press, 1974-1980.

———. *Notes on Novelists with Some Other Notes*. 1914; New York: Scribner's, 1942.

———. *The Question of Our Speech and The Lesson of Balzac*. Boston: Houghton-Mifflin/Riverside, 1905.

———. *The Painter's Eye: Notes and Essays on the Pictorial Arts*. Ed. and introduction by John L. Sweeney. London: Rupert Hart-Davis, 1956.

———. *The Portrait of a Lady*. The Novels and Tales of Henry James. Vols. III and IV. 1880-1881; New York: Charles Scribner's Sons, 1908.

———. *The Portrait of a Lady*. Ed. Robert D. Bamberg. New York: Norton, 1975.

———. *Roderick Hudson*. The Novels and Tales of Henry James. Vol. I. 1874; New York: Charles Scribner's Sons, 1907.

———. *A Small Boy and Others*. New York: Charles Scribner's Sons, 1913.

———. *The Tragic Muse*. The Novels and Tales of Henry James. Vols. VII and VIII. 1890; New York: Charles Scribner's Sons, 1908.

Johannsen, Albert. *Phiz: Illustrations for the Novels of Charles Dickens*. Chicago: Univ. of Chicago Press, 1965.

Kelley, Alice Van Buren. *The Novels of Virginia Woolf*. Chicago: Univ. of Chicago Press, 1971.

Kestner, Joseph. "Sculptural Character in Lawrence's *Women in Love*." *Modern Fiction Studies*, 21, 543-53.

———. "Secondary Illusion: The Novel and the Spatial Arts." In *Spatial Form in Narrative*. Eds. Jeffrey R. Smitten and Ann Daghistany. Ithaca: Cornell Univ. Press, 1981.

Kroeber, Karl, and William Walling. *Images of Romanticism: Visual and Verbal Affinities*. New Haven: Yale Univ. Press, 1978.

Lawrence, D. H. (David Herbert). *The Collected Letters of D. H. Lawrence*. 2 vols. Ed. Harry T. Moore. New York: Viking, 1962.

———. "An Introduction to these Paintings." In *Phoenix: The Posthumous Papers of D. H. Lawrence*. Ed. Edward D. McDonald. New York: Viking, 1936.

————. *Lady Chatterley's Lover.* 1928; New York: Grove Press, 1959.

————. *The Letters of D. H. Lawrence.* Vol. 1. Ed. James T. Boulton. Cambridge: Cambridge Univ. Press, 1979.

————. *The Letters of D. H. Lawrence.* Vol. 2. Eds. George J. Zytaruk and James T. Boulton. Cambridge: Cambridge Univ. Press, 1982.

————. *The Paintings of D. H. Lawrence.* London: Mandrake, 1929.

————. *Phoenix: The Posthumous Papers of D. H. Lawrence.* Ed. Edward D. McDonald. New York: Viking, 1936.

————. *Phoenix II: Uncollected, Unpublished, and Other Prose.* Eds. Warren Roberts and Harry T. Moore. London: Heinemann, 1968.

————. *The Rainbow.* 1915; New York: Penguin, 1979.

————. *Sons and Lovers.* 1913; Baltimore and London: Penguin, 1976.

————. *Women in Love.* Ed. Charles L. Ross. 1920; New York: Penguin, 1982.

Leavis, F. R. *D. H. Lawrence: Novelist.* London: Chatto and Windus, 1955.

————. *The Great Tradition.* 1948; New York: New York Univ. Press, 1967.

Leavis, Q. D., and F. R. Leavis. *Dickens the Novelist.* London: Chatto and Windus, 1970.

Lessing, Gottfried. *Laocoön: An Essay on the Limits of Painting and Poetry.* Ed. Edward A. McCormick. Library of the Liberal Arts. 1766; New York: Bobbs-Merrill, 1962.

Levine, George, and William Madden, eds. *The Art of Victorian Prose.* New York: Oxford, 1968.

Levy, Mervyn, ed. *Paintings of D. H. Lawrence.* New York: Viking, 1964.

Lindsay, Jack. "The Impact of Modernism on Lawrence." In *Paintings of D. H. Lawrence.* Ed. Mervyn Levy. New York: Viking, 1964.

Lister, Raymond. *Victorian Narrative Paintings.* New York: Clarkson N. Potter, Inc., 1966.

Lodge, David. *The Language of Fiction: Essays in Criticism and Verbal Analysis.* New York: Columbia Univ. Press, 1966.

Love, Jean O. *Worlds in Consciousness: Mythopoetic Thought in the Novels of Virginia Woolf.* Berkeley: Univ. of California Press, 1970.

Lukács, Georg. "Narrate or Describe?" *Writer and Critic and Other Essays.* Trans. and ed. Arthur D. Kahn. New York: Grosse and Dunlap, 1971.

Mallarmé, Stéphane. *Oeuvres complètes.* Ed. de la Pléiade. Paris: Gallimard, 1965.

Matthiessen, F. O. *Henry James: The Major Phase.* New York: Oxford Univ. Press, 1944.

Marinetti, Tommaso Filippo. "The Founding and Manifesto of Futurism." Rpt. in *Marinetti: Selected Writings*. Ed. R. W. Flint. Trans. R. W. Flint and Arthur A. Coppotelli. New York: Farrar, Straus and Giroux, 1971.

Merrild, Knud. *A Poet and Two Painters*. New York: Viking, 1939.

Meisel, Martin. *Realizations: Narrative, Pictorial, and Theatrical Arts in Nineteenth-Century England*. Princeton: Princeton Univ. Press, 1983.

Meyers, Jeffrey. *Painting and the Novel*. New York: Barnes and Noble, 1975.

Miller, J. Hillis. *Fiction and Repetition: Seven English Novels*. Cambridge: Harvard Univ. Press, 1982.

———. "The Fiction of Realism: *Sketches by Boz, Oliver Twist*, and Cruikshank's Illustrations." In *Dickens Centennial Essays*. Eds. Ada Nisbet and Blake Nevius. Berkeley: Univ. of California Press, 1971.

Mitchell, W.J.T. "Spatial Form in Literature." *Critical Inquiry*, 6 (Spring 1980), 541.

Moore, Harry T. *The Priest of Love: A Life of D. H. Lawrence*. Rev. ed. New York: Farrar, Straus and Giroux, 1974.

Moore, Robert Etheridge. *Hogarth's Literary Relationships*. Minneapolis: Univ. of Minnesota Press, 1948.

Morassi, Antonio, ed. *Complete Catalogue of the Paintings of Giovanni Battista Tiepolo*. Greenwich, Conn.: Phaidon, 1963.

Morphet, Richard. "The Art of Vanessa Bell." Introduction to *Vanessa Bell, Paintings and Drawings*. London: Anthony d'Offay, 1973.

Mukařovský, Jan. *Structure, Sign, and Function*. Trans. and eds. John Burbank and Peter Steiner. New Haven: Yale Univ. Press, 1978.

Nehls, Edward. *D. H. Lawrence: A Composite Biography*. Vol. 1. Madison: Univ. of Wisconsin Press, 1957.

New Literary History, III:3 (Spring 1972).

Oates, Joyce Carol. "Lawrence's Götterdämmerung: The Tragic Vision of *Women in Love*" *Critical Inquiry*, 4:3 (Spring 1978).

Paulson, Ronald. *Emblem and Expression: Meaning in English Art of the Eighteenth Century*. Cambridge: Harvard Univ. Press, 1975.

Piovene, Guido, ed. *L'Opera completa di Giovanni Battista Tiepolo*. Critical apparatus by Anna Pallucchini. Milano: Rizzoli, 1968.

Poirier, Richard. *A World Elsewhere*. New York: Oxford Univ. Press, 1966.

Powell, Anthony. *A Dance to the Music of Time*. 4 vols. Boston: Little, Brown, and Company, 1971.

————. *To Keep the Ball Rolling: The Memoirs of Anthony Powell.* New York: Holt, Rinehart and Winston, 1976-1982.

Praz, Mario. *The Hero in Eclipse in Victorian Fiction.* Trans. Angus Davidson. London: Oxford Univ. Press, 1956.

————. "Introduction." *Three Gothic Novels.* Baltimore: Penguin, 1968.

————. *Mnemosyne: The Parallel between Literature and the Visual Arts.* Bollingen Series, xxxv:16. Princeton: Princeton Univ. Press, 1970.

Radcliffe, Ann. *The Mysteries of Udolpho.* 1794; London: Oxford Univ. Press, 1970.

Ray, Gordon N. *The Illustrator and the Book in England from 1790 to 1914.* The Pierpont Morgan Library. London: Oxford, n.d.

Rewald, John. *The History of Impressionism.* Fourth, rev. ed. 1946; New York: The Museum of Modern Art, 1973.

Rorty, Richard. *Philosophy and the Mirror of Nature.* Princeton: Princeton Univ. Press, 1979.

Rosen, Charles, and Henri Zerner. "What Is, and Is Not, Realism?" *New York Review of Books.* xxix:2 (February 18, 1982), pp. 21-26.

Rosenbaum, S. P., ed. *The Bloomsbury Group.* Toronto: Univ. of Toronto Press, 1975.

Ross, Charles L. *The Composition of* The Rainbow *and* Women in Love: *A History.* Charlottesville: Univ. of Virginia Press, 1979.

Rowe, John Carlos. "James's Rhetoric of the Eye: Re-marking the Impression." *Criticism,* xxiv:3 (Summer 1982).

Ruddick, Lisa. *The Seen and the Unseen: Virginia Woolf's "To the Lighthouse."* The LeBaron Russell Brigg's Prize Essay in English 1976. Cambridge: Harvard Univ. Press, 1977.

Sacks, Sheldon, ed. *On Metaphor.* Chicago: Univ. of Chicago Press, 1979.

Said, Edward. *The World, the Text, and the Critic.* Cambridge: Harvard Univ. Press, 1983.

Samuels, Charles. *The Ambiguity of Henry James.* Urbana: Univ. of Illinois Press, 1971.

Schapiro, Meyer. *Word and Pictures: On the Literal and the Symbolic in the Illustration of the Text.* The Hague: Mouton, 1973.

Sears, Sallie. *The Negative Imagination: Form and Perception in the Novels of Henry James.* Ithaca: Cornell Univ. Press, 1968.

Shone, Richard. *Bloomsbury Portraits: Vanessa Bell, Duncan Grant and Their Circle.* New York: Dutton, 1976.

Smitten, Jeffrey R., and Ann Daghistany. *Spatial Form in Narrative.* Ithaca: Cornell Univ. Press, 1981.

Spalding, Frances. *Vanessa Bell*. New Haven and London: Ticknor and Fields, 1983.

Spender, Stephen, ed. *D. H. Lawrence: Novelist, Poet, Prophet*. New York: Harper and Row, 1973.

Spiegel, Alan. *Fiction and the Camera Eye*. Charlottesville: Univ. of Virginia Press, 1976.

Spilka, Mark. *Virginia Woolf's Quarrel with Grieving*. Lincoln: Univ. of Nebraska Press, 1980.

Stange, G. Robert. "Art Criticism as a Prose Genre." In *The Art of Victorian Prose*. Eds. George Levine and William Madden. New York: Oxford Univ. Press, 1975.

Steig, Michael. *Dickens and Phiz*. Bloomington: Univ. of Indiana Press, 1978.

Stein, Richard L. *The Ritual of Interpretation: The Fine Arts as Literature in Ruskin, Rossetti, and Pater*. Cambridge: Harvard Univ. Press, 1975.

Steiner, Wendy. *The Colors of Rhetoric: Problems in the Relation of Modern Literature and Painting*. Chicago: Univ. of Chicago Press, 1982.

————. *Exact Resemblance to Exact Resemblance: The Literary Portraiture of Gertrude Stein*. New Haven and London: Yale Univ. Press, 1978.

Sterne, Laurence. *Tristram Shandy*. *The Florida Edition of the Works of Laurence Sterne*. Vol. 2. Gainesville: Univ. of Florida Presses, 1978.

Stewart, Jack. "Lawrence and Gauguin." *Twentieth-Century Literature*, 26:4 (Winter 1980), 385-401.

Stowell, Peter. *Literary Impressionism, James and Chekhov*. Athens: Univ. of Georgia Press, 1980.

Strong, Roy. *Recreating the Past: British History and Victorian Painting*. Great Britain: Thames and Hudson, 1978.

Sweeney, John L. "Introduction." *The Painter's Eye*, by Henry James. London: Rupert Hart-Davis, 1956.

Sypher, Wylie. *Rococo to Cubism in Art and Literature*. New York: Random House, 1960.

Torgovnick, Marianna. *Closure in the Novel*. Princeton: Princeton Univ. Press, 1981.

Towards a Theory of Description. Yale French Studies, Vol. 61 (1981).

Tucker, James. *The Novels of Anthony Powell*. New York: Columbia Univ. Press, 1976.

Watt, Ian. *Conrad in the Nineteenth Century*. Berkeley: Univ. of California Press, 1970.

————. "The First Paragraph of *The Ambassadors.*" *Essays in Criticism*, x (1960), 250-74.

Weinstein, Philip M. *Henry James and the Requirements of the Imagination.* Cambridge: Harvard Univ. Press, 1971.

Wellek, René. "The Parallelism between Literature and the Arts." *English Institute Annual.* New York: Columbia Univ. Press, 1941.

Wendorf, Richard, ed. *Articulate Images: The Sister Arts from Hogarth to Tennyson.* Minneapolis: Univ. of Minnesota Press, 1983.

Winner, Viola Hopkins. *Henry James and the Visual Arts.* Charlottesville: Univ. of Virginia Press, 1970.

Woolf, Virginia. *Collected Essays.* 4 vols. New York: Harcourt, Brace, and World, 1925.

————. *Contemporary Writers.* Preface by Jean Guiguet. New York: Harcourt, Brace, and World, 1965.

————. *The Diary of Virginia Woolf.* Vol. III (1925-1930). Ed. Anne Olivier Bell, assisted by Andrew McNeillie. New York: Harcourt Brace Jovanovich, 1980.

————. *The Letters of Virginia Woolf: The Question of Things Happening.* Vol. II, 1912-1922. Ed. Nigel Nicolson and asst. ed. Joanne Trautmann. London: Hogarth Press, 1976.

————. *The Letters of Virginia Woolf: A Change of Perspective.* Vol. III, 1923-1928. Ed. Nigel Nicolson and asst. ed. Joanne Trautmann. London: Hogarth, 1977.

————. *The Letters of Virginia Woolf: A Reflection of the Other Person.* Vol. IV, 1929-1931. Eds. Nigel Nicolson and Joanne Trautmann. London: Hogarth, 1978.

————. *The Letters of Virginia Woolf: Leave the Letters till We're Dead.* Vol. VI, 1936-1941. Eds. Nigel Nicolson and Joanne Trautmann. London: Hogarth, 1980.

————. *Night and Day.* 1920; New York: Harcourt Brace Jovanovich, n.d.

————. *Roger Fry: A Biography.* New York: Harcourt, Brace, and World, 1925.

————. *To the Lighthouse.* New York: Harcourt, Brace, and World, 1927.

————. *The Years.* London: Hogarth Press, 1937.

————. *The Waves.* New York: Harcourt Brace Jovanovich, 1931.

INDEX

LIBRARY OF CONGRESS CATALOGING IN PUBLICATION DATA

Torgovnick, Marianna, 1949-
The visual arts, pictorialism, and the novel.

Bibliography: p.
Includes index.
1. English fiction—20th century—History and
criticism. 2. Art and literature—Great Britain.
3. Art in literature. 4. Ut pictura poesis
(Aesthetics). 5. James, Henry, 1843-1916—Knowledge—
Art. 6. Lawrence, D. H. (David Herbert), 1885-1930—
Knowledge—Art. 7. Woolf, Virginia, 1882-1941—
Knowledge—Art. I. Title.
PR888.A74T67   1985   823'.912'09357   84-26617
ISBN 0-691-06644-2 (alk. paper)

Marianna Torgovnick is Assistant Professor of English at Duke
University. Her previous book was *Closure in the Novel* (Princeton, 1981).